Thinking Through Film

Doing Philosophy, Watching Movies

Damian Cox
Michael P. Levine

A John Wiley & Sons, Ltd., Publication

This edition first published 2012
© 2012 Damian Cox and Michael P. Levine

Blackwell Publishing was acquired by John Wiley & Sons in February 2007. Blackwell's publishing program has been merged with Wiley's global Scientific, Technical, and Medical business to form Wiley-Blackwell.

Registered Office
John Wiley & Sons Ltd, The Atrium, Southern Gate, Chichester, West Sussex, PO19 8SQ, United Kingdom

Editorial Offices
350 Main Street, Malden, MA 02148-5020, USA
9600 Garsington Road, Oxford, OX4 2DQ, UK
The Atrium, Southern Gate, Chichester, West Sussex, PO19 8SQ, UK

For details of our global editorial offices, for customer services, and for information about how to apply for permission to reuse the copyright material in this book please see our website at www.wiley.com/wiley-blackwell.

The right of [Damian Cox and Michael P. Levine to be identified as the authors of *Thinking Through Film: Doing Philosophy, Watching Movies* has been asserted in accordance with the UK Copyright, Designs and Patents Act 1988.

Wiley also publishes its books in a variety of electronic formats. Some content that appears in print may not be available in electronic books.

Designations used by companies to distinguish their products are often claimed as trademarks. All brand names and product names used in this book are trade names, service marks, trademarks or registered trademarks of their respective owners. The publisher is not associated with any product or vendor mentioned in this book. This publication is designed to provide accurate and authoritative information in regard to the subject matter covered. It is sold on the understanding that the publisher is not engaged in rendering professional services. If professional advice or other expert assistance is required, the services of a competent professional should be sought.

Library of Congress Cataloging-in-Publication Data

Cox, Damian.
    Thinking through film : doing philosophy, watching movies / Damian Cox, Michael P. Levine.
        p. cm.
    Includes bibliographical references and index.
    ISBN 978-1-4051-9343-6 (hardcover : alk. paper) – ISBN 978-1-4051-9342-9 (pbk. : alk. paper)
    1. Motion pictures–Philosophy. I. Levine, Michael P. II. Title.
    PN1995.C682 2011
    791.4301–dc22
                                           2011012210

A catalogue record for this book is available from the British Library.

This book is published in the following electronic formats: ePDFs 9781444343816; ePub 9781444343823; mobi 9781444343830

Set in 10.5/12.5pt Galliard by Toppan Best-set Premedia Limited
Printed in Singapore by Ho Printing Singapore Pte Ltd

1 2011

THINKING THROUGH FILM

Contents

Preface

This book introduces readers to a broad range of philosophical issues though film, as well as to issues about the nature of film itself – a blend missing in most recent books on philosophy and film. Film is an extremely valuable way of exploring and discussing topics in philosophy, but it is not without its limitations and dangers. Pointing out ways in which film can obfuscate through rhetoric, by playing on the emotions, or by pandering to various desires, is an important part of any approach to thinking through film. We try to bring a critical eye to philosophical-film discussions throughout the present book.

The book has four parts. In part I, chapter 1, we discuss the possibilities of film as a philosophical medium. Why is film a good way of approaching philosophical issues and how is it possible to advance philosophical discussion through film? In the second chapter we discuss some of the philosophical issues raised by film itself. While it focuses on the power of film and its significance, other principal philosophical issues about film and film spectatorship are also raised. Further issues concerning the nature of film and film spectatorship are discussed throughout the book. Why, for example, do we like certain films? How do we get pleasure from films? How can we tell when a film is manipulating our philosophical judgment and the intuitions on which it is based? How can we make use of the confusions that abound in films for philosophical purposes? (Handling both the films and the philosophy with care, of course.)

The chapters in parts II–IV are designed to be read after viewing nominated films, and after having read part I. Part II focuses on films that raise questions about epistemology and metaphysics. These include skepticism, ontology, artificial intelligence, and time (time-travel in particular). In part III we discuss four films in relation to what may broadly be called "the human condition." Here we focus on free will, personal identity, and death and the meaning of life. We also examine the nature of film spectatorship in some depth: in chapter 9 our topic is horror, and realist horror films in particular. What, we ask, draws audiences to the experience of horror; to fear and repulsion? Part IV is concerned with ethics and values. We focus on films that address, in turn, the following: motivations for a moral life, moral luck, deontology and consequentialism, and finally virtue theory.

The book aims to give a general overview of core philosophical topics; viewed from the perspective of current work in philosophy and current work in philosophy and film. It is about both philosophy *of* film and philosophy *through* film. These two aspects of the book support one another and it is the idea of bringing these two aspects together that has structured the work. We have chosen films for content, quality, and philosophical potential; films that engage with philosophical issues – at times in circumscribed and distorted ways, but also in ways that help one appreciate the philosophical issues involved and, along with them, something of the significance of philosophy. Where we could do so, we used films to advance philosophical thought, rather than simply illustrate it.

Both classical and contemporary films are used, each chosen to highlight a particular set of philosophical questions, sometimes in unusual ways and with unlikely films. We discuss well-known and popular films, but also lesser-known films. At the end of each chapter there is a brief list of further recommended readings and a list of questions for further philosophical work.

The principle ambition of the book is to do philosophy with films and to think about films philosophically. The chapters are about the issues present in the films from a philosophical *and* filmic perspective. Films can be used to do philosophy in many ways. They can be used as illustrations of philosophical problems; as ways of testing philosophical theories; as ways of running philosophical thought experiments; as suppliers of interesting puzzles or phenomena, things in need of philosophical examination; as ways of getting clear about the significance of philosophical issues, or ways of getting clear about philosophical possibilities. Reflection on film leads to philosophy by raising questions about the nature of films themselves and film spectatorship in particular. Sometimes philosophical theories are used to interpret films; sometimes films are used to shed light on philosophical theories. All of these ways of watching movies and doing philosophy are represented in this work. There is no unique perspective that philosophy brings to film. Instead, films are themselves – often muddled, but sometimes brilliant – philosophical investigations.

Philosophy and film is still a relatively new field. What we have done in this book could not have been done without the pioneering efforts of those philosophers and film theorists who helped establish philosophy and film as a worthwhile, ongoing, and indeed burgeoning area of inquiry. Even where we disagree with them, we most certainly have learned from them.

Acknowledgments

We thank the many people that inconspicuously and often unknowingly helped us develop this text and our thoughts on the films discussed – often by just saying a few words, and sometimes by presenting more developed views about a film, character, or philosophical problem. In particular we thank our students in film and philosophy at Bond University and The University of Western Australia. We also wish to thank Marguerite La Caze, Amy Barrett-Lennard, Lorna Mehta, Bill Taylor, Ted Roberts, and Carol Mack.

Part I
Philosophy and Film

Part I has two chapters. The first chapter discusses the relationship between philosophy and film. The primary issue here is also preliminary. Is film a credible philosophical medium? Can films *do* philosophy? What should we expect from films philosophically speaking? The second chapter looks at some of the philosophical issues that are either specific to film or applicable to particular films as aesthetic objects (or works of art). What can be said, philosophically speaking, about films' ability to evoke strong emotion and to evoke and even satisfy, at least transiently, phantasies of revenge and narcissistic, even perverse, desires?

In part I objections on the part of philosophers to the philosophical possibilities of film are considered. Various ways in which film and philosophical theory are allegedly related are explained and queried. We make it clear that film can be much more than simply a test or illustration of a piece of philosophical theory. Instead of casting the philosophical possibilities of film in terms of film as servicing philosophy, we turn the tables and view film (or some film) as inherently or naturally philosophical. Various philosophical issues raised by film are discussed alongside relevant narrative and filmic techniques.

Part I constitutes both a background to and a resource for parts II–IV in which central epistemological, metaphysical, and ethical problems are analyzed in relation to specific films.

Thinking Through Film: Doing Philosophy, Watching Movies, First Edition. Damian Cox, Michael P. Levine.
© 2012 Damian Cox and Michael P. Levine. Published 2012 by Blackwell Publishing Ltd.

1

Why Film and Philosophy?

Introduction

This book examines a broad range of philosophical issues though film, as
well as issues about the nature of film itself. There are two rather distinct
parts to philosophy and film. One part seeks to examine philosophical
issues raised in films. For example, films may question a particular ethical
point of view or raise questions about skepticism or the nature of personal
identity. The other part pertains to issues raised by film understood as an
art form. What, if anything, is distinctive about film or cinematic depiction
as an art form? What is the philosophical significance of the technique and
technology film employs? What is the philosophical significance of audience responses to film? What special benefits or dangers does film harbor
given its mass appeal and ability to evoke strong emotion?

One issue that seems to relate to both aspects of film and philosophy
is the question of film as a philosophical medium. More than simply
illustrating philosophical ideas, can films actually *do* philosophy? Can films
be vehicles of philosophical investigation?[1] The present chapter addresses
this question. The second aspect of film and philosophy – philosophical
discussion of film itself – is introduced in the following chapter. Before
launching on the topic of the relation between film and philosophy, let
us briefly review some features of film that make it such an attractive basis
for philosophy.

Thinking Through Film: Doing Philosophy, Watching Movies, First Edition. Damian Cox,
Michael P. Levine.
© 2012 Damian Cox and Michael P. Levine. Published 2012 by Blackwell Publishing Ltd.

The Reach and Power of Film

Academicians sometimes refer to "the canon." This is supposedly a core body of literature ("classics") that people in successive generations refer to. The canon is supposed to transmit meaning and modes of conceptualization from one generation to another, as well as form a common body of work for those within a single generation. In theory, canonical works serve to individuate and characterize particular epochs and generations – their views on family, on love, duty to country, and ideals (or alleged ideals), for example. The canon is supposed to be a common source of reference no matter how different people within a particular culture may be. There are questions about whether there really is or ever was such a canon; what it consists in (the Bible; other scripture; Shakespeare; J. D. Salinger?) and also what its status should be. How should it be used? In what ways and for what purposes might it be authoritative?

Arguably, narrative film – and we include in this category feature films and series shown on television and available in numerous other formats – furnishes a canon, something that may even be the first real canon. If so, it is because of the popular and non-elitist status of film art. More people see and discuss films than read – certainly more people see the same films than read the same books – and films cut across socio-economic and other audience barriers in ways that the classic western canon never could do. In developed nations virtually everyone sees and talks about films on occasion. With the availability of films in inexpensive formats, many people in economically deprived circumstances also often see films. For many, films constitute a common core of reference in which values, moral issues, philosophical and other questions are examined. The way these things are presented in films is distinctive. Films are accessible, and often aesthetically engaging and entertaining in ways that make them emotionally and intellectually or ideationally powerful (see Carroll: 2004). They are generally neither obtuse nor inaccessible in the ways that philosophical texts or formal arguments often are. Films are popular, accessible, ubiquitous, and emotionally engaging.

Film frequently employs other art forms (music, visual arts, literature) and their ability to affect us is integrated into film's power. The ability of film to influence and emotionally affect us is not a straightforward sum of its component art forms, however. There is after all much music, literature, poetry, and visual art that on its own may affect us far more than when taken up in film. Nevertheless, the fact that a feature film can convey so much to so many in such a relatively short time (generally less than two hours, almost always less than three) is one of its most remarkable features. It is also something that has worried many philosophers and film theorists. Adorno and Horkheimer (1990), for example, were concerned with the possible negative influence of mass art on passive and uncritical audiences. (Why not also on active and critical audiences? Is an active and critical attitude enough to dispel the charm of film?) Alfred Hitchcock was alleged to have said "all actors are cattle." However, he didn't quite say this: "I never said all actors are cattle; what I said was all actors should be treated like cattle." One wonders what he must have thought of audiences.

On the other hand, other philosophers, for example Walter Benjamin, are optimistic about the powers of film to enhance social and political freedom and creative thought.[2] Who is more likely right on balance: pessimists such as Adorno or optimists like Benjamin? This turns out to be a very difficult question to answer. Think of a particular case: the power of political speech versus the political power of film. Is a spoken political argument more or less likely to change attitudes than a political film? Chaplin's political speech at the end of *The Great Dictator* (1940) is an interesting case in point. It has considerable power, and many people fondly remember it after watching the film. But the film's overt aim in 1940 was to turn its audience off any residual appeal that Adolf Hitler and nationalistic fascism in general might have had for them and it achieves this quite independently of the speech. Much of the real work is done when Chaplin, playing Adenoid Hynkel, Dictator of Tomania, bounces an inflated globe of the world off his rear. This is a marvelously effective way of satirizing dreams of world domination. Whether that amounts to a philosophically robust critique of fascism is another story.

By its very nature, film is an extremely valuable way of introducing and discussing topics in philosophy. But it is important to realize the dangers inherent in this. Films can obfuscate and confuse through the way they are framed and filmed, through the way they play on the emotions, or pander to various desires. Keeping track of these obfuscations is an important part of any approach to thinking through film. Many films cater to and pray on unconscious or unwelcome desires, wish-fulfillments, and prejudices. Arguably, the success of a film often depends on its success in catering to these things. (Consider revenge films such as *Harry Brown* (2009), *Death Wish* (1974), and *Once Upon a Time in the West* (1968).) Just as we often believe what we want (or would like) to believe rather that what we have good reason to believe, we often believe things because we feel a certain way. Emotions influence belief, as do desires. This is a fact that cinema often exploits, and one that largely accounts for its ability to engage an audience. This is why films so often misinform and mislead us philosophically, just as they often inform and deepen us philosophically.

As we have been at pains to point out, one of cinema's great virtues is its capacity to engage and entertain. It certainly has this virtue by comparison with most philosophical writing, which is often as dry as a desert. At the same time, the accessibility of film (and mass media generally) to audiences, its power to engage and affect, to emotionally and intellectually manipulate and "do a job" on us, is at the core of ethical concerns over mass media we mentioned earlier, for instance those raised by Adorno and Horkeheimer (1990) and others. Philosophical engagement with film is not always positive. Nonetheless, as Freud noted, art can provide the path from fantasy back to reality. Film is useful in examining a great many, albeit not all, of the areas that philosophy covers. Particular films address topics in ethics, metaphysics, religion, and aesthetics, as well as in social and political philosophy. One area perhaps stands out among all others. Like novels, films often depict and philosophically explore aspects of the multitude of human relations – especially love and friendship. This is no surprise given the extent to which we are generally absorbed most with those things which engage us emotionally.

What is the Relation between Philosophy and Film?

Philosophy and film has burgeoned into a field of its own – and it is growing. This is part of a trend of broadening the range of topics considered suitable for serious philosophical scrutiny. The broadening of philosophical subject matter has been coupled with the recognition that film and other forms of media and entertainment can be powerful vehicles for ideas. Many of these ideas are philosophically interesting and are ingrained in ordinary life – just as friendship, love, death, purpose, and meaning are. It is not exactly a new discovery that everyday life is a philosophical resource. Ancient philosophers knew it, though the twentieth-century professionalization of philosophy may have sometimes obscured such focus on the everyday. There has been a proliferation of books and journal articles not only on philosophy and film, but more generally on philosophy and culture. Some of these focus on philosophy and everyday concerns as they feature in television (a form of film) and contemporary music. Others consider more classic philosophical issues – ethical, political, epistemological, social, psychological – as they feature in mainstream movies.

Film, especially in its narrative component, provides philosophy with material (scenarios, case studies, stories, hypotheses, and arguments) to scrutinize. Films tell stories, make assertions, and state or intimate hypotheses that give people, and by extension philosophers, material to critically assess. Films can be objects of direct philosophical scrutiny. For example, Leni Riefenstahl's *Triumph of the Will* (1935), a film recording the 1934 Nuremberg congress of the Nazi Party, provides us with material for a good deal of philosophical reflection. This includes reflection on the relation between aesthetic and moral value. (Riefenstahl's film is often considered to be an aesthetic masterpiece and moral failure.) Watching *Triumph of the Will* inevitably brings out questions about artists' moral responsibility for their artistic productions. However, films don't become especially philosophical simply in virtue of their being objects of philosophical scrutiny. After all, anything and everything can be an object of philosophical scrutiny (a table, a pen, a cloud, a cathedral). Usually something becomes an object of philosophical scrutiny by representing a certain type of thing, or certain type of experience or phenomenon, that philosophically puzzles and challenges us. Films become philosophical in a more interesting and thoroughgoing sense when they do more than this. They become philosophical by engaging us philosophically as we watch them.

What is the best way to understand the relationship between film (filmmaking) and philosophy (philosophizing)? Can a film *be* a philosophical text, rather than just a resource for philosophers? Can filmmaking *be* philosophizing? Can film-watching *be* philosophizing? Perhaps it simply depends on how expansive and inclusive our conception of philosophy is.[3] One theorist of philosophy and film, Murray Smith (2006: 33), says "I take it to be relatively uncontentious that, in some broad sense, a film can be philosophical. This is hardly surprising if we regard both film (as an art form) and philosophy as extensions of the human capacity for self-consciousness, that is, of our capacity for reflection on ourselves." If we think of philosophy as simply an expression of the human capacity for reflection, then films obviously share this capacity. But there is more to the issue than this.

How should we understand the philosophical potential of film? Paisley Livingston (2008: 3) usefully frames the question in what he terms the *bold thesis*.

[Can films] make independent, innovative and significant contributions to philosophy by means unique to the cinematic medium (such as montage and sound–image relations), where such contributions are independent in the sense that they are inherent in the film and not based on verbally articulated philosophizing, such as a commentary or paraphrase? Films, it is often claimed in the large literature inspired by Gilles Deleuze's speculative writings on film, do indeed engage in creative philosophical thinking and in the formation of new philosophical concepts.

The bold thesis claims that a film's contribution to philosophy, if genuine, must be irreplaceable or irreducible to any other forms of communication. It is a strong thesis indeed. But why think that the philosophical *value* of film is determined by its philosophical *uniqueness*? Livingston himself is no fan of the bold thesis. He says (Livingston 2008:12),

> [We should] drop the bold thesis about film as philosophy and shift to more modest and viable claims. Some fiction films are made by an author who uses the medium, in conjunction with linguistic means, to express a philosophically informed perspective. Other fiction films are not so made, but can nonetheless be used to illustrate familiar but valuable views about practical wisdom, scepticism and other topics. Films of both sorts offer a vivid way into philosophical positions and arguments, and may provide worthwhile stimulus to creative philosophical thinking . . .

Livingston goes on to modify these "modest and viable" claims in a revealing way. He continues (2008: 12), ". . . as long as it [is] remembered that the introduction of sophisticated distinctions and arguments will require a verbal articulation that is not provided by the cinematic display on its own. Descriptions of the plot, no matter how subtle, are no substitute for the latter."

Livingston's suggestion seems to be that if we want to do real philosophy, the kind that requires sophisticated distinctions and arguments, we will need to knuckle down and explicitly – that is verbally – articulate an argument. There is no question that certain kinds of philosophical argumentation require this. We know that film is no substitute for certain useful ways of doing philosophy. Why would anyone claim that it is? Why would they want it to be? But Livingston's claim is more deflationary than this. He implies that film is, in some sense, philosophy's handmaiden. Film is (on occasion) an impetus to philosophizing; it is not a way of philosophizing. In contrast to the bold thesis, let us call this suggestion the *null thesis*. According to the null thesis, film has no role at all to play in philosophizing as such. Its only role is to provide an impetus to, or material for, philosophical work that is done wholly linguistically in written and verbal texts. Films don't themselves make philosophical points (except where they have characters make philosophical points verbally). To make philosophical points films must be paraphrased, interpreted, and then integrated into philosophical argument that carries on much as usual. This is the null thesis. The null thesis is a rather unadventurous and disappointing conclusion to draw. Are there more ambitious options for those who are wary of the bold thesis?

Stephen Mulhall is one prominent figure who rejects what we have called the null thesis. Mulhall (2002: 2) says

> I do not look to these films as handy or popular illustrations of views and arguments properly developed by philosophers; I see them rather as themselves reflecting on and evaluating such views and arguments, as thinking seriously and systematically about them in just the same ways that philosophers do. Such films are not philosophy's raw material, are not a source for its ornamentation; they are philosophical exercises, philosophy in action – film as philosophizing.

At first glance, there is something a little puzzling in this passage. What does Mulhall mean by "just the same ways?" Films can be philosophy in action and just as philosophical as texts (sometimes more so) without being so in "just the same ways." If taken too literally, Mulhall's insistence on equivalence would mean that, methodologically speaking, there is really no distinct category of philosophy in film after all. There would simply be philosophy done in the same way in one medium as in another. It would then, paradoxically, imply that there is no particular value in film "doing" philosophy. Of course, Mulhall can be interpreted more charitably than this. The essential claim in the passage is that philosophy done verbally and philosophy done cinematically are both ways of thinking seriously and systematically about views and arguments. Let's call this the *modest thesis*. Whereas the bold thesis claims that the cinematic performance of philosophy is unique and irreducible to other forms of doing philosophy and the null thesis claims that, strictly speaking, there is no such thing as a cinematic performance of philosophy, the modest thesis claims that there is such a thing as the cinematic performance of philosophy and it really is a performance of philosophy. However, the modest thesis denies the uniqueness of film-philosophy. A cinematic performance of philosophy is not untranslatable into verbal philosophical forms; the philosophy can be re-expressed verbally without loss, at least in principle. Philosophy done cinematically need not be done in the same way that philosophy is done verbally (usually it isn't); but it needn't follow from this that doing philosophy cinematically grants us access to philosophical truths and insights that are inaccessible to philosophers working non-cinematically. (This last condition is a way of restating the bold thesis.) The modest thesis lies somewhere between the bold thesis and the null thesis.

The bold thesis might turn out to be false without making the question of the relation between film and philosophy otiose or uninteresting. And for many, the bold thesis is too bold. The modest thesis, on the other hand, seems too modest. It could be right without there being anything particularly interesting to say about the relation between film and philosophy. Is there anything especially philosophically valuable about philosophy done cinematically? Irving Singer suggests that this has something to do with the artistic qualities of films *per se*. He writes (2007: 3) "Apart from any unfortunate efforts to duplicate what trained philosophers do, films we consider great are philosophical insofar as the meaningfulness they embody, and the techniques that convey their type of meaningfulness, exploit at a significantly deep level the visual, literary, and sonic dimensions of this art form."[4] Is Singer right about any of this? Why can't a film be considered "great," embody meaning, employ techniques to convey that meaning, and "exploit at a significantly deep level the visual, literary, and sonic dimensions of this art form" and yet not be particularly philosophical? (Consider great musicals like *Meet Me in St Louis* (1944) and *42nd Street* (1933).) Furthermore, what is it that Singer thinks "trained philosophers" do? Among the things that trained philosophers do is to examine many of the very same sorts of ethical, political, social, and personal issues sometimes examined in film. They assemble reminders of persistent and persistently overlooked features of human experience; they reflect on the phenomenology of human experience as well as the coherence and evidential soundness of philosophical theories. And there are some films that undoubtedly do a far better (i.e. insightful, accurate, intellectually convincing) job doing at least some of this work than many trained philosophers do.

Perhaps, then, we should adopt a moderate thesis: certain philosophical things are better done in film than in written texts. Perhaps films sometimes deepen philosophical perspectives in ways that written texts struggle to. This would not require film to have unique access to its own mode of philosophizing or its own branch of philosophical insight. It would not require that films be capable of performing philosophical activities that *can't* be managed at all in written or verbal philosophical performances. So it isn't the bold thesis. On the other hand, the moderate thesis requires that films can sometimes do some things better than written texts can. So they aren't simply resources for philosophizing and they aren't *merely* ways of reflecting systematically on fundamental beliefs. They are ways of doing philosophy *especially well.* The moderate thesis is enough to vouchsafe the deep philosophical significance of film.

The key idea behind the moderate thesis is that films can sometimes be better at presenting certain kinds of philosophical material than standard philosophical genres are. This is not just because film can be more emotionally engaging and entertaining. Films are, mostly, more engaging than standard philosophical writing. After all, philosophers like Kant, Hegel, Hume, Rawls, Dummett – none are real page-turners. If film can be a superior philosophical medium at times, this is partly because film can present a kind of nuance and perspective that is not often found in professional philosophy and is hard to reproduce within the genres of professional philosophy. And this, in turn, is partly because professional philosophy has been too bound by its own specialized genres: the journal article and the monograph.

Underlying some conservative views on whether or not film can do philosophy lies a precious, overly-fastidious, and territorial notion of what philosophy is. It might be that some philosophers simply do not wish to entertain the possibility, let alone the simple truth, that poets, novelists, filmmakers, and others with less lofty professions, may often succeed where they fail and sometimes be better at doing philosophy than professional philosophers are. Concerning a "precious" notion of philosophy, the alleged supposition is that film has something to live up to, standards it must achieve, if it is to be considered as doing, or contributing to, philosophy. It is worth considering, however, whether philosophers have not misconstrued the proper order of the relation between philosophy and film. A more fertile avenue might be to ask the question "What does philosophy have to do, what standards should it strive for, to become more like, or contribute to, (certain) films?"

Some philosophers think that contemporary philosophical practice distorts many philosophical issues. In particular, some philosophers (for example, Iris Murdoch (1970) and Martha Nussbaum (1990)) think that philosophy, at least sometimes and in domains such as ethics, is more at home – more intelligible and more finely tuned – in literature and the arts than it is among the philosophers. The aesthetics and techniques of film, such as montage, deep focus, close-up, and the tracking shot are all suited to focusing and enhancing the attention and due consideration that Murdoch and Nussbaum think good fiction embodies. Film however has an even larger bag of tricks than novels. The camera takes us precisely to where the director wishes to take us, and a point of view can be further emphasized with sound or music. And films show us faces; they give full rein to our capacity to read faces and grasp the significance of gesture. A novelist has to say or hint at things a filmmaker can simply show. This is not to say that films are, on Murdoch and Nussbaum's terms, always better at morally and critically engaging the viewer than novels. (Films generally lack the obvious authoritative voice of some novels – though this is by no means always a bad thing.) Even with the extra dimensions or devices in film, many novels (virtually all the great ones) are better at drawing the viewer in, at morally focusing the viewer, aiding their discernment of relevant particulars (sometimes by obscuring certain things), than films tend to be. Nevertheless, the variety of techniques available in film may well make possible a degree of moral and emotional engagement that in many cases literary fiction is unable to muster. The argument can be expanded beyond ethics and beyond the novel. Film is capable of presenting some philosophical views and perspectives better, for example with greater clarity, than they can be presented in any written form. This view, of course, is what we have been calling the moderate thesis about the relation between film and philosophy.

In this book, we will be examining many films, some of them will illustrate philosophical ideas; some will represent phenomena that call for philosophical scrutiny; some will themselves *be* objects of philosophical scrutiny. Alongside this, however, are films we interpret as evoking philosophical thought experiments, and others as realizing nuanced investigations of philosophical topics by assembling powerful reminders about various aspects of our experience of life and drawing conclusions from them. In this second category of cases we will be assuming the moderate thesis. We think that thought experiments are sometimes (not always) better run in cinematic form than in the deliberately thin and context-free form typical of philosophical writing. We think that film can sometimes offer nuanced investigation of fundamental features of our experience, well beyond the ordinary achievements of written philosophical texts, and in doing so robustly refute hollow and simplistic ways of understanding life.

Cinematic Philosophy and Authorial Intention

If films do philosophy, then *who* is doing the philosophizing? In *Thinking on Screen: Film as Philosophy* (2007) Thomas Wartenberg argues that Michel Gondry's *Eternal Sunshine of the Spotless Mind* (2004) presents a cogent criticism of utilitarianism. This is offered as part of Wartenberg's attempt to defend the claim that films actually *do* philosophy – in this case, by offering a strong counterexample by means of a thought experiment. In the process of developing his case, Wartenberg assumes that the source or home of utilitarianism as a normative ethical view is nineteenth-century England – and its progenitors are John Stuart Mill and Jeremy Bentham. His view is that the film's creators intend to argue against utilitarianism by means of a counterexample. The film portrays such a counterexample through narrative in particular, but also sound, acting, camera-work, etc. Wartenberg's particular concern is to show that this philosophical objection is not some philosopher's (his) imposition or projection of a philosophical view onto the film, but is inherent in the film as part of its creators' intention. Furthermore, whether or not the filmmakers actually know that their target is a standard philosophical theory of normative ethics called utilitarianism is, on Wartenberg's account, largely irrelevant. It is enough that they had some conception of the relevant idea and a good grasp of where it might be going wrong. (*Eternal Sunshine of the Spotless Mind* is the story of two people who have the memories of their relationship artificially removed from their consciousness after a particularly painful breakup. The film usually has the effect of gaining assent from the audience that this is a very bad idea; that there are more important things in life than minimizing pain.[5])

The relation between filmmakers' intentions and the philosophical scrutiny of film raises a number of questions. An interesting aspect of film, like other forms of narrative art (such as novels), is that it often lets us see and surmise a great deal more than its creators intended. A philosophical view may be embedded in a film without its being the director's or writer's intention that the view be apparent and sometimes without them even being aware that it is a view they hold or one implied by other views they hold. Apart from the explicit endorsement of a view by the director or writer (and even with such an endorsement) care must be shown in attributing such views to them. Do the creators of vigilante movies – say Michael Winner, director of *Death Wish* (1974), or Don Siegel, director of *Dirty Harry* (1971), endorse the views about justice portrayed by actors in those movies – even when the audiences overwhelmingly do? The films operate as (very bad) arguments for vigilante justice irrespective of the answer to this question.

The philosophical views presented in films, or thought to be presented in films, can be assessed independently of authorial intention. Of course not every view attributed to a film, whether as intentionally or unintentionally present in the film, is correctly attributed, and since some films may be ambiguous, unclear, or confused about the views they present, it will not always be possible to discern whether a position is being presented or argued for. This is the case with philosophical arguments in texts as well, and there is no reason to suppose that film has a natural advantage in terms of unambiguously or clearly presenting philosophical views or arguments.

Determining just what the creators' intention is may or may not help the process of extracting a philosophical response to the film. Without a good deal of corroborating evidence it may well be impossible to determine authorial intent, or to justify the attribution of authorial intention, even in cases where one is right. In any case, authorial intention is not always, perhaps not even very often, particularly important – unless one is specifically interested in an individual filmmaker's views. For example, it seems important to understand the intentions of very deliberate and provocative filmmakers such as Michael Haneke. But Haneke's underlying intentions in films such as *Benny's Video* (1992), *Funny Games* (1997; 2007), and *The White Ribbon* (2009) do not determine or limit the philosophical potentiality of these films. What should be of philosophical interest in the vigilante movies noted above is not whether the filmmakers believed in the conception of justice they portray, but whether the films do anything to substantially bolster the case for them. Indeed, if we conclude that they do not, then the more interesting question for philosophy and film becomes a question about the reception of films. How do audiences relate cognitively to a massaging of their instincts for vengeance? Why do they get so much satisfaction (of some kind – of what kind?) from such movies?

Livingston (2008: 4) remarks that "Wartenberg wisely concedes that saying that a film 'does philosophy' is only a 'shorthand expression for stating that the film's makers are the ones who are actually doing philosophy in/on/through film." If agency is required to do anything at all and a film is not an agent then of course film can no more "do philosophy" than tie its shoelaces. Livingston's point may seem obviously correct, but in fact it is not at all obvious. There is a natural sense which films, much like works of fiction, can have a sense of agency attributed to them. Films can do things because they can have meaningful effects well beyond the intentions of their creators. Much like character development in fiction, though possibly to an even greater extent, film can present nuanced perspectives and unintended consequences that may further a philosophical argument or make a point whether or not the filmmakers intend or foresee them. Part of the task of a film editor is to extract or highlight narrative, plot development, and meaning that is present or nascent in the film. But the film may be greater or lesser than the sum of its parts in terms of its overall aesthetic value and meaning – intended or not. It is often possible to distinguish authorial intention from what is revealed in film narrative, visual effect, or performance.

Like novels, films have lives and meanings of their own which will vary over time and are relative to a degree to particular audiences. These kinds of considerations suggest that to say that films "do philosophy" is more than a *façon de parler*. Good films often outdistance even the combined creative intentions of those who create them. Consider too that it is common in film theory to query the notion of the auteur. Films do (or may) express the personal ideas of the director, as Truffaut (1954) claims with his coining the phrase *la politique des auteurs*. But film theorists point out that, unlike a novel, a film is a collaborative project and the product of many more people than just the writer/director. Insofar as a film embodies collaborative agency, it should also be seen as something greater than the sum of its parts; where the results, including meanings, can be wholly attributed neither to the director nor to the writer, nor even to the sum of all those involved with the production of the film.[6]

Conclusion

Let's return to Wartenberg's account of Gondry's *Eternal Sunshine of the Spotless Mind*. We want to take up an earlier suggestion that in order to appreciate and understand the relation between film and philosophy one must see films' philosophical preeminence. At least to some extent and in some ways, philosophy should look towards film rather than vice versa.

Wartenberg (2007: 91) calls attention to the "distinction between creator-oriented and audience-oriented interpretations of works of art."

[C]reator-oriented ones . . . present interpretations that a work's creator could have intended it to have. But . . . this did not mean that the creator had to have direct acquaintance with the philosophical position that the creator-oriented interpretation . . . [presents] as the focus of the work, only that it had to be plausible that he might be responding to the positions or ideas contained in that work. Although philosophical texts are the origins of many ideas, theories, and positions, they acquire a life of their own within a culture and all that is necessary for a creator-oriented interpretation to be acceptable in this regard is that the creator might have been acquainted with the philosophical ideas, etc., because of, for example, their general circulation within a culture. Utilitarianism is a philosophical theory that has gained wide-ranging recognition within American culture in general. The slogan "the greatest good for the greatest number" is known by many more people than have read the texts from which it springs. It therefore seems plausible to me that a contemporary film might target such a view.

For further confirmation of his view Wartenberg (2007: 92) points to "the film's explicit invocation of Nietzsche" along with the fact that "one of the targets of Nietzsche's philosophical critique is utilitarianism."

One need not reject Wartenberg's account of this film as doing philosophy to suggest that the form the defense of film as philosophy takes has a curious presupposition. Unless we see what this presupposition is, we are likely to misunderstand how and why film and philosophy are often intimately connected. Wartenberg successfully argues that films can and often do present, illustrate, or argue philosophical positions and raise philosophical questions; we suggest – in what we have called the moderate thesis – that films are often quite better at doing this than written or verbal philosophical texts. Perhaps the key question here is not whether or how films could do these things but how could they not? Wartenberg (2007: 93) says "We have seen that one film *Eternal Sunshine of the Spotless Mind* presents a counterexample to utilitarianism and thus actually *does* philosophy . . . [C]ounter-intuitive as it might seem to film scholars and philosophers alike, fiction films can present arguments through their narratives because they screen thought experiments that play a crucial role in providing counterexamples to philosophical theses." This is an expression of what we are calling the modest thesis. It seems to us that such a tame position is likely to strike us as counterintuitive only if we are knee-deep in some implausible ideology concerning film, philosophy, or both. The point here is not necessarily directed at Wartenberg so much as the philosophical objectors he has in view. They have in mind, it seems, a remarkably shallow conception of philosophy and the origin of philosophizing.

Wartenberg presupposes two things in his discussion of this matter. First, he presupposes the primacy of philosophy. If a film screens a thought experiment in philosophy, it does so by lining up against a well-known philosophical position. The philosophical position comes first and the film does philosophy by reacting to it in some way. (This is very often the case, but is it always the case? *Need* it be the case?) Second, he appears to overemphasize the intellectual content of filmic arguments rather than the way the argument is packaged and delivered in a film. An important part of the way film does philosophy is that it is able to capture argument in affective ways, i.e. in ways that have emotional as well as intellectual resonance for us. The emotion generated by a film can focus attention and enables one to "see" or consider or appreciate aspects of an argument that might otherwise go by the wayside. Except in the cases of empirical facts (i.e. "I see the cat is on the mat") belief is more often than not a function of desire and emotion as well as reason and evidence. Sometimes philosophical thought should take notice of this affective component of good philosophy.

Consider the sorts of philosophies Wartenberg thinks are at issue in *Eternal Sunshine of the Spotless Mind.* With the exception of staunch utilitarians and deontologists, the one fact that seems to have made the debate between these two normative ethical theories (or supreme normative principles) intractable is that neither theory alone seems to do justice to or satisfy ordinary intuitions regarding what is right for all moral cases.[7] Imagine Mill and Bentham, together with Kant, taking in an afternoon matinee at the movies. *Eternal Sunshine of the Spotless Mind* is Mill's and Bentham's choice of film. Kant is headed towards cinema 2 to see a re-run of *The Diary of Anne Frank.* They meet in the lobby after the movies are over. Kant says "Well, I had that business about lying all wrong. Those protecting Anne and her family did the right thing in lying when asked about their whereabouts. I must rewrite my *Grundlegung zur Metaphysik der Sitten* and *Kritik der praktischen Vernunft.*" Mill and Bentham respond, "No, no, actually we think you were onto something. It's utilitarianism that needs to be seriously modified." On Wartenberg's account of how films generate philosophical argument, it is hard to imagine anyone – let alone Kant, Mill, or Bentham – changing their mind as the result of intellectually registering a filmic counterexample. The counterexamples will be finessed in the context of prior intellectual commitments. However, some films, for some people at some times, are able to generate the kind of attentiveness and emotional insight that may undermine prior commitments and suppositions even when they had been thought to be intellectually and rationally grounded. Films can *force* counterexamples on us in ways that allow us to better understand and appreciate their power and value as counterexamples, which is not to deny that they may still be rejected or that they sometimes ought still to be rejected.

Wartenberg's presupposition of the primacy of philosophy over film might be grounded in a mistaken view about the genesis of philosophical problems. He says (2007: 91) "Although philosophical texts are the origins of many ideas, theories, and positions, they acquire a life of their own within a culture." However, it is not always, or even very often, philosophical texts that are the origin of ideas, but culture. It is in philosophical texts rather than culture that "many ideas, theories, and positions" acquire a life of their own. Outside some of professional philosophy's narrow scope, philosophy does not constitute its own source. Philosophical inquiry is generated by a sustained and focused sense of wonder, engagement, and bewilderment with life as lived – one's own as well as everybody else's.

The ethical questions that utilitarianism raises, the answers that it gives, are not, in the first instance, found in Mill and Bentham – nor were they invented *ex nihilo* by them. They are ethical issues that arise in ordinary life. It is only after the fact that ethicists and the philosophically minded get hold of the relevant issues and, in this case, that utilitarianism endeavors to organize and systematize responses to them. The belief, as *Star Trek*'s Spock puts it, that "the needs of the many outweigh the needs of the few" (or those of the individual) predates nineteenth-century formulations of utilitarianism. Philosophical problems that are not highly specialized are not found first and foremost in philosophical articles and tracts, but are ingredients in life. As such, and with varying degrees of success, they are often depicted and analyzed in literature and film, as well as in art forms such as music and painting that have less explicit narrative content, or perhaps no narrative component at all.

Philosophers do not, at least not ordinarily, invent the broad philosophical problems that are ingredients in life. These are neither philosophy's invention, nor its exclusive property. Thus, to understand the fundamental connection between film and philosophy and to understand film as philosophy, one should not look only to film's capacity to illustrate pre-set philosophical ideas or make philosophical arguments about pre-set philosophical positions. The more basic connection is to be found in a common source of philosophical engagement, life as it is lived, and particularly in film's engagement with the stories we tell ourselves by way of seeking to understand, explain, justify, excuse, and guide ourselves. Film's capacity as a philosophical resource is not exhausted by its ability to deal with standard philosophical issues in various ways. Its capacity in this regard is formidable but not the sole feature of film's relation to philosophy. Much like literature, film is a medium employing various techniques, not all of them wholly its own, that portrays philosophical issues as they arise, or could arise, in life and in the imagination. It is film's capacity to depict life as real and imagined, and life is always imaginary to a degree, that constitutes the fundamental connection between philosophy and film.

The chapters in the second part of this work suppose that film and philosophy are often intertwined in ways that mutually illuminate them. Combining in-depth critical discussion with the experience of viewing a film can be an engaging way into philosophy as well as into film. There is no unique perspective that philosophy brings to film and no singular connection between the two. Instead, films are themselves (often muddled) philosophical investigations, just as such investigations by philosophers are often muddled.

Questions

Can film change, or has film changed, the way philosophy is done?

Can philosophy change, or has philosophy changed, the nature of film?

Can philosophy do film? What are the strongest objections to the claim that it can?

The bold thesis claims that a film's contribution to philosophy, if genuine, must be irreplaceable by or irreducible to any other forms of communication. What is the significance and plausibility of the thesis?

Many films people like are "escapist fluff." Are such films suitable for philosophical inquiry? If so, how; if not, why not?

"Emotions influence belief, as do desires. This is a fact that cinema often exploits, and one that largely accounts for its ability to engage an audience. This is why films so often misinform and mislead us philosophically, just as they often inform and deepen us philosophically." Is this true? How?

In what ways, if any, do some films resemble life? Does this resemblance play a role in film's ability to do philosophy?

Are films better suited for dealing with certain topics philosophically than fiction or the visual arts? Can they be better than philosophy books and journal articles?

Notes

1 Smith and Wartenberg (2006a) focus on this question and sees it as perhaps the dominant or "very prominent" (1) question in philosophy and film.
2 See Laura D'Olimpio (2008). *The Moral Possibilities of Mass Art*, unpublished dissertation, The University of Western Australia. See Carroll (2004) for a discussion of "The Power of Movies."
3 See Smith and Wartenberg (2006a), "Introduction," 1–4; Smith (2006: 33–42).
4 This passage is also quoted by Livingston (2008:11).
5 You might wonder, then, just how successful Wartenberg's interpretation of the film is. Perhaps the real target, when translated in standard philosophical terminology, is negative hedonism. Negative hedonism is the view that we ought to do what it takes to remove pain from our lives. (The most famous negative hedonist in the history of philosophy is not a utilitarian, but the Hellenistic philosopher Epicurus.) The characters in the film both try to escape

from pain merely to find themselves in a desolate place where important aspects of their identity are missing in action. This is only tangentially related to the classical utilitarianism of Bentham and Mill (neither of whom were negative hedonists). If utilitarianism is the issue of the film, it might be that version of utilitarianism that contemporary philosophers call preference utilitarianism. According to preference utilitarianism, the best state of affairs is obtained when people have their preferences realized. The characters in the movie get what they want; but that's far from the best state of affairs.

6 See Livingston's (2008:4–7) discussion of authors and intention.

7 See note 5 above where we question Wartenberg's interpretation of the film. We investigate the relation between utilitarianism and deontology with the help of *The Dark Knight* (2008) in chapter 13.

Further Reading

Adorno, T. W. (1982). "Transparencies on Film." *New German Critique* 24/25. Special Double Issue on New German Cinema (Autumn 1981–Winter 1982), 201–2.

Adorno, T. W., & M. Horkheimer (1990). "The Culture Industry: Enlightenment as Mass Deception." In T. W. Adorno & M. Horkheimer, *Dialectic of Enlightenment*. New York: Continuum.

Benjamin, Walter (1969). "The Work of Art in the Age of Mechanical Reproduction," trans. H. Zorn. In H. Arendt, ed., *Illuminations*. New York: Schocken Books.

Blessing, Kimberly Ann, & Paul J. Tudico, eds. (2005). *Movies and the Meaning of Life: Philosophers Take on Hollywood*. Peru, IL: Open Court.

Carlshamre, Staffan, & Anders Pettersson, eds. (2003). *Types of Interpretation in the Aesthetic Disciplines*. Montreal: McGill-Queen's Press.

Carroll, Noël (1988). *Philosophical Problems of Classical Film Theory*. Princeton: Princeton University Press.

Carroll, Noël (2004). "The Power of Movies." In Peter Lamarque & Stein Haugom Olsen, eds., *Aesthetics and the Philosophy of Art: The Analytic Tradition*. Oxford: Blackwell.

Carroll, Noël (2006). "Introduction: Film and Knowledge." In Noël Carroll & Jinhee Choi, eds., *Philosophy of Film and Motion Pictures*. Malden, MA: Blackwell, 381–6.

Carroll, Noël (2008). *The Philosophy of Motion Pictures*. Malden, MA: Blackwell.

Carroll, Noël, & Jinhee Choi (2006). *Philosophy of Film and Motion Pictures: An Anthology*. Malden, MA: Blackwell.

Cavell, Stanley (1981). *Pursuits of Happiness: The Hollywood Comedy of Remarriage*. Cambridge, MA: Harvard University Press.

Choi, Jinhee (2006). "Apperception on Display: Structural Films and Philosophy." In Noël Carroll & Jinhee Choi, eds., *Philosophy of Film and Motion Pictures*. Malden, MA: Blackwell, 165–72.

Colman, Felicity (2009). *Film, Theory and Philosophy: The Key Thinkers.* Durham: Acumen.

Deleuze, Gilles (1983). *L'image-mouvement.* Paris: Minuit.

Deleuze, Gilles (1985). *L'image-temps.* Paris: Minuit.

Devereaux, Mary, (1998). "Beauty and Evil: The Case of Leni Riefenstahl's *Triumph of the Will.*" In J. Levinson, ed., *Aesthetics and Ethics: Essays at the Intersection.* New York: Cambridge University Press.

Falzon, Christopher (2007). *Philosophy Goes to the Movies: An Introduction to Philosophy.* 2nd edn. New York: Routledge.

Flaxman, Gregory, ed. (2000). *The Brain is the Screen: Deleuze and the Philosophy of Cinema.* Minneapolis: University of Minnesota Press.

Frampton, Daniel (2006). *Filmosophy.* London: Wallflower.

Freeland, Cynthia, & Thomas E. Wartenberg, eds. (1995). *Philosophy and Film.* London and New York: Routledge.

Gilmore, Richard A. (2005). *Doing Philosophy at the Movies.* Albany, NY: State University of New York Press.

Grau, Christopher, ed. (2005). *Philosophers Explore The Matrix.* New York: Oxford University Press.

Irwin, William, ed. (2002). *The Matrix and Philosophy: Welcome to the Desert of the Real.* Chicago: Open Court.

Isaacs, Bruce (2008). *Toward a New Film Aesthetic.* New York and London: Continuum.

Kania, Andrew, ed. (2009). *Memento: Philosophers on Film.* London: Routledge.

Kupfer, Joseph (1999). *Visions of Virtue in Popular Film.* Boulder, CO: Westview Press.

Light, Andrew (2003). *Reel Arguments: Film, Philosophy, and Social Criticism.* Boulder, CO: Westview Press.

Litch, Mary (2002). *Philosophy through Film.* New York: Routledge.

Livingston, Paisley (2005). *Art and Intention: A Philosophical Study.* Oxford: Clarendon Press.

Livingston, Paisley (2006). "Theses on Cinema as Philosophy." In Murray Smith & Thomas E. Wartenberg, eds. (2006a), 11–18.

Livingston, Paisley (2008). "Recent Work on Cinema as Philosophy." *Philosophy Compass* 3, 1–12.

Livingston, Paisley, & Carl Plantinga, eds. (2008). *The Routledge Companion to Philosophy and Film.* London: Routledge.

Mullhall, Stephen (2002). *On Film.* London: Routledge.

Murdoch, Iris (1970). *The Sovereignty of Good.* Boston: Routledge & Kegan Paul.

Nussbaum, Martha (1990). *Love's Knowledge.* Oxford: Oxford University Press.

Pataki, Tamas (2004). "It's (Not Only) Entertainment." Review of Christopher Falzon (2002), *Philosophy Goes to the Movies: An Introduction to Philosophy* (London: Routledge). *Australian Book Review* 242, June/July, 50–51.

Plantinga, Carl, & Greg M. Smith (1999). *Passionate Views: Film, Cognition and Emotion.* Baltimore and London: Johns Hopkins University Press.

Read, Rupert, & Jerry Goodenough, eds. (2005). *Film as Philosophy: Essays on Cinema After Wittgenstein and Cavell*. Basingstoke: Palgrave Macmillan.

Rowland, Mark (2005). *The Philosopher at the End of the Universe*. London: Ebury Press.

Russell, Bruce (2006). "The Philosophical Limits of Film." In Noël Carroll & Jinhee Choi, eds., *Philosophy of Film and Motion Pictures*. Malden, MA: Blackwell, 387–90.

Scruton, Roger (1998) [Methuen, 1983]. "Photography and Representation." In *The Aesthetic Understanding: Essays in the Philosophy of Art and Culture*. South Bend Indiana: St Augustine's Press.

Singer, Irving (2007). *Ingmar Bergman, Cinematic Philosopher: Reflections on his Creativity*. Cambridge, MA: MIT Press.

Smith, Murray (1995). *Engaging Characters: Fiction, Emotion and the Cinema*. Oxford: Oxford University Press.

Smith, Murray (2006). "Film Art, Argument, and Ambiguity." In Murray Smith & Thomas E. Wartenberg (eds.). Malden, MA: Blackwell, 33–42.

Smith, Murray, & Thomas E. Wartenberg, eds. (2006a). *Thinking through Cinema: Film as Philosophy*. Malden, MA: Blackwell.

Smith, Murray, & Thomas E. Wartenberg (2006b). "Introduction." In *Thinking through Cinema: Films as Philosophy*. Malden, MA: Blackwell, 1–9.

Stoehr, Kevin L., ed. (2002). *Film and Knowledge: Essays on the Integration of Images and Ideas*. Jefferson, NC: McFarland.

Stone, Alan A. (2007). *Movies and the Moral Adventure of Life*. Cambridge, MA: MIT Press.

Truffaut, François (1954). "A Certain Tendency in French Cinema." In *Cahiers du cinema*.

Wartenberg, Thomas E. (2007). *Thinking on Screen: Film as Philosophy*. Basingstoke: Palgrave Macmillan.

Wartenberg, Thomas E. (2009). "Film as Philosophy." In Paisley Livingston & Carl Plantinga, eds., *The Routledge Companion to Philosophy and Film*. London: Routledge, 549–59.

Yeats, W. B. (1956). *The Collected Poems of W. B. Yeats*. New York: Macmillan, 240.

2

Philosophy and Film Spectatorship

Introduction

In the previous chapter we asked whether films can do philosophy. Can films be vehicles of philosophical investigation? The answer was decidedly "yes." In this chapter we introduce philosophical questions about the nature of film. What are some of the philosophical issues raised about film itself? Here is a sampling of a broad range of overlapping issues, most of which have been widely discussed.

- Why is film such a powerful medium – affecting so many, and at times intensely?
- What, if anything, is distinctive about film or cinematic depiction as an art form?
- What is the philosophical significance of the technique and technology film employs?
- What is the philosophical significance of audience responses to film?
- What special benefits and dangers can film harbor given its mass appeal and (what may be the same thing) its ability to evoke strong emotion?
- What is filmic representation? Films are, in part, visual representations, but how should this be understood and what is its significance?
- If film is an art form, what makes a film excellent? How are films to be judged?
- The "paradox of horror" (or "negative emotion"): If people do not like to be frightened, then why do they see horror films? If they do

Thinking Through Film: Doing Philosophy, Watching Movies, First Edition. Damian Cox, Michael P. Levine.
© 2012 Damian Cox and Michael P. Levine. Published 2012 by Blackwell Publishing Ltd.

like to be frightened, then why do they like such negative emotions? What does this tell us about spectatorship?

- The "paradox of fiction": How is the fact that we relate emotionally to characters and situations that we know to be fictional best explained? Unless the so-called paradox of fiction can be satisfactorily resolved, it is unlikely that the power of movies could ever be explained.
- What is character identification, and how significant is identification and imagination in relation to spectator response?
- Ideology, politics, ethics, and film: What is the relationship between the ethics and aesthetics of film? What is the moral and political responsibility of the artist?
- Representation of women in film (gender and "gaze"): How are women represented in film, and what is the philosophical significance of such representation? What does it tell us about film and what does it say about spectatorship?
- How significant is psychoanalytic theory and other specialized approaches to film, such as semiotics, to understanding the relation between cinema and spectator?
- How significant is the author's (or director's) intention in understanding the cinema–spectator relation, and for interpreting the film itself?
- Many films people like are "escapist" "fluff." Are such films suitable for philosophical inquiry? If so, how? If not, why not?
- What is the philosophical significance of so-called children's films for understanding audience response and spectatorship?
- To a considerable extent, economic forces control the nature of cinema by controlling the kinds of films being made. This directly and indirectly affects the cinema–spectator relation. What is the significance of this?
- How do movie theatres and other features of the viewing environment (big screen vs home DVD) affect spectatorship?

This is a long list; and also a partial one. We can't cover them all, of course. The first of the questions – the power of movies – will occupy us in this chapter initially. It is an issue related in different ways and varying degrees to just about all philosophical issues about film. It also underwrites the significance of these issues. If our conceptions of love and relations, of justice and value, and of the ways we choose to live and seek meaning are affected by film, then it is little wonder that philosophers and film theorists have turned their attention to philosophical issues raised *about* film. The question of how to account for the power of movies is at the center of a constellation of philosophical problems associated with film and relates indirectly to many others.

Not only is it possible to discuss philosophical issues raised in films without considering philosophical issues raised *about* film; many, if not most film and philosophy texts do just that. Nevertheless, there is good reason to insist that this second aspect of film and philosophy – issues raised about film, be addressed as well. Awareness of central questions about the nature of film and how they have been addressed can enhance discussion of philosophical issues raised in film. Philosophical questions about the apparent attractiveness of horror and violence in cinema, for instance, are better understood if film's ability to evoke horror is also addressed. The nature of audience response to horror, although contested among film theorists and philosophers, is also relevant. (We revisit the question of horror and film spectatorship in chapter 9.)

Equally significant is the way in which an appreciation of some of the issues raised *about* film can enhance the cinematic experience – much like knowing something about the nature of music or contemporary art can help hone our critical skills and attentiveness in these areas. In addition to enhancing cinematic experience, a critical acquaintance with philosophical controversies about film, as with other arts, can sometimes alter the way we watch and think about films. It can change viewing habits and, for better or worse (not necessarily for better), new perspectives and modes of enjoyment may ensue.

Some of the central philosophical issues raised about film are also raised about other art forms – like fiction-writing, theater, still photography, art, and music – all of which are employed in film. The so-called "paradoxes" of fiction and horror, neither of which are genuine paradoxes as we shall see, are equally present in other art forms (e.g., fiction and theater). This makes none of the issues less important, but it does serve to remind us that while film is a unique art form and more than the sum of its component and contributing art forms, it is, as noted in the previous chapter, also made up of many distinctive arts. In arguing that film can do philosophy, we claimed that there is no reason to insist that the philosophical work be done by something intrinsic to the nature of film itself, something not found in any other art form. So too, there is no reason to insist that the philosophical issues that are raised by and about film all relate to the intrinsic and unique nature of film.

Nothing in these first two chapters should be taken as prescribing ways of analyzing film. Nor should the philosophical content of the films discussed in later chapters be taken as the last word on them, either from a philosophical point of view or from the point of view of film criticism in general. Many films can be discussed in terms of rather independent sets of philosophical issues. *The Lives of Others* forcefully illustrates the problem of "moral luck." But it can also be used in discussions of liberty, corruption, political power, deprivation, fear, and torture – and the human condition. It has been discussed, for example, in terms of how the architecture we see in the film, the cityscape, plays a philosophically significant role.

The idea that some films should be interpreted in a variety of ways – pluralistically if you like – and on their own terms, sits well with the contention in chapter 1 that much philosophical inquiry is generated by a sustained and focused engagement with life as lived. Good films should be capable at times of generating new insights, new interest and excitement, along with various and even disparate philosophical approaches to their content. Films do this partly by their ability to illustrate the multifaceted and contextual nature of various problems, and also by the fact that they are frequently emotively thought provoking and can generate enough entertainment and emotive response to hold our attention.

Let's now turn to a close consideration of some prominent philosophical issues that have arisen about the nature of film. These are certainly not the only questions of philosophical interest and they may not even be on everyone's list of the most important. They are however among the most widely discussed in the philosophical literature.

The Power of Film

Talk about "the power of film" is ambiguous between, on the one hand, the way particular films may strongly affect individual spectators and, on the other, the influence that particular films or film in general may assert on wider audiences, socially and politically, and also in terms of personal beliefs and values. Those like Adorno and Horkheimer (1990), who were rightly concerned (even if their concerns were not always right) with the possible negative influence of mass art on passive and uncritical audiences, were bothered with the power of film in the second sense. Nevertheless, it is clear that apart from a film's ability to strongly affect individuals, there would be little need to even raise the kinds of issues that Adorno and Horkheimer worry about. We are going to examine the question of film's power to move individual spectators by critically examining one of the most prominent accounts of it: that of Noël Carroll.

Carroll (2004a: 486–7) says that "The power of movies comprises two factors: widespread engagement and intense engagement. . . . [He seeks to] explain the former in terms of those features of movies that make them highly accessible to broad audiences." This may seem a little odd. Why think that the explanation of film's power lies in its accessibility to broad audiences, rather than in its ability to intensely engage audiences? Widespread accessibility is a necessary condition for widespread engagement – people are rarely engaged by stories they don't understand – but why think that a film's accessibility to an audience adequately explains the intensity of the audience's engagement with it? Carroll's strategy becomes even more open to question when he tries to explain "the intensity of movies by examining those features that enable movies to depict a very high degree of clarity. . . . [T]he power of movies resides in their easily graspable clarity for mass audiences." Clarity – and Carroll means here narrative clarity, the capacity to portray the elements of a story with unforced precision and obviousness – seems like the wrong sort of property to account for emotional impact. And emotional impact is central to the power of film. Many movies, books, plays, and other narrative art forms portray crystal clear and easily graspable narratives without being particularly engaging or moving.

There would be no reason to be concerned about the effects of mass art, like film, if it were powerless. And unless film can, in the first instance, strongly affect people on a personal level, the cinematic medium must remain relatively inert and impotent on a social and political level. The first question regarding the power of film is, therefore, how is it able to exert such an effect on individual spectators? Why do we leave the cinema in tears, or disappointed, elated, satisfied, frightened and worried? In most cases the effects, whatever they may be, are temporary. But why, after watching some films, are we resolute in efforts to "change our ways," our loyalties, the ways in which we interact with others, and even at times our lives?

The power of film to affect us need not reside wholly or even primarily in factors unique to film. Consider explanations grounded in the nature of narrative itself: the ability of film, for reasons not too different from fiction (why should it be?), to generate strong emotion. There are also possible explanations provided by psychoanalysis, such as film's ability to temporarily satisfy wishful thinking and desires.[1] Isn't this what an audience's desire for a "happy ending" (the "magic" of movies) is grounded in? Then too, on some accounts, there is film's ability to transiently invoke and satisfy spectators' voyeuristic, narcissistic, sadistic, masochistic, misogynistic, and otherwise perverse (though not necessarily problematic or even immoral) desires at times.

We saw in the first chapter that a response to the question of whether film can do philosophy need not be in terms of properties unique to film, but may better be answered in terms of properties that while ingredient in film are found elsewhere as well. So too might film's power be explained in terms of a variety of filmic properties (e.g. narrative, music, acting), rather than as some irreducible and essential element or set of properties uniquely constitutive of film. Nonetheless, much discussion of the power of film seeks to explain its power in terms of something unique to the cinema. Perhaps films have a powerful hold over us because they are realistic in a way that other art forms are not. A painting is artificial no matter how realistic a representation it offers, because it is still; it represents a frozen moment, but we don't experience the world as a succession of frozen moments. It is not possible for a painting not to be artificial in this way. A film, however, depicts a world in what seems like a fundamentally more realistic mode. The idea that the uniqueness and power of film resides somehow in its realism can be traced back to the film theorist Andre Bazin. Noël Carroll is an important critic of this view.

Carroll rejects the idea that film's power is to be accounted for in terms of Andre Bazin's view that "the film image was an objective representation of the past, a veritable slice of reality." Carroll writes (2004a: 485):

> Contemporary film theorists . . . deny there is any literal sense to be made of the idea that film is some kind of natural mirror onto reality. Yet [they] . . . do hold onto a portion of the realist approach, notably its psychological presuppositions . . . [W]hile rejecting the notion that film is a slice of reality, [they] nevertheless agree that in its standard uses, film imparts a *realistic effect* to its viewers. This effect, a psychological effect, is described by various formulas, including the notions that film gives the impression of reality narrating itself; film causes an illusion of reality; or film appears natural.

Carrol (2004a: 485) goes on to claim that

> these variations on the realistic effect are suspect because they attribute to spectators states of belief that would preclude our characteristic forms of response to, and appreciation of, cinema. For, were we spectators ever to mistake the representations before us for the referents those images portray, we could not sit by comfortably, inactively, and appreciatively while buffaloes stampede toward us, while lovers reveal their deepest longings to each other, and while children are tortured.

Is someone who thinks that "film imparts a realistic effect to its viewers" committed to any of the views Carroll claims they are? Is the realist approach to film theory, either as an ontological thesis or in its more contemporary, psychologized variations, a "dead end" as Carroll claims?

Can the psychologized variation of Bazin's thesis be saved? Can one literally maintain the "realistic effect" of the stampede one is viewing without dropping one's popcorn and running towards an exit?

Carroll (2004a: 486) offers another criticism of the realist thesis – or some psychological version of it.

> The reference to reality here won't give us much help . . . because in large measure we conceive of the intensity of movies exactly in contrast to our more diffuse responses to quotidian life . . . [S]ince our response to reality is so often lackluster, claiming that a film appears to be a slice of reality promises no explanation of our extraordinarily intense response to films. So another explanation, one not reliant upon realism, must be found to account for the power of movies.

Isn't Carroll missing something here – equivocating on the notion of "reality" in play, or else assuming a far too constricted notion of what "reality" pertains to? Of course movies do not generally reflect quotidian life in Carroll's sense. (Not even Andy Warhol's 1964 silent film *Empire* – one continuous, eight-hour shot in black-and-white of the Empire State Building at night – does that.) But this does not entail that the "realistic" effect films impart is not necessary in accounting for their ability to engage spectators (at times emotionally and powerfully). If real life was much more on a par with movies in terms of the narrative and action contained, then real life would indeed engage us in more emotionally powerful ways – no doubt to an even greater extent than film.

In short, while Bazin's view, depending on how it is interpreted, may be extravagant and mistaken, the idea that the power of movies depends in part on its ability to "impart a *realistic effect* to its viewers" seems not only unproblematic but true. Carroll's own account of pictorial representation in film emphasizes features accounting for the "clarity" and easy accessibility of film, rather than its realism.

Summing up his account of the power of films, Carroll (2004a: 189) writes:

> [C]ontemporary film theorists hold that the typical film image imparts the illusion of reality, transparency, or naturalness. This paper, though, has not invoked any of these realist psychological effects, nor anything like them. It has instead claimed that the untutored spectator recognizes what the film image represents without reference to a code; it has *not* claimed that the spectator takes the pictorial representation to be, in any sense, its referent.

But perhaps it should have, in one sense. When we see horses galloping in a film, we do, in some sense, take the "representation for its referent."

There are two main ways of interpreting this claim about a "psychologically realist" response to the cinematic image. First – a maximal interpretation – an audience is taken to assume that that the image of horses galloping represents an historical event. Horses really had to be galloping in the world before a camera which then "captured" their galloping in a manner that enabled it to be transmitted to a projector that "replays" it for us. Second – a minimal interpretation – the audience assumes that the cinematic image of horses galloping is a representation of particular horses in the fictional world of the film; and what they are represented as doing – galloping – is just what they are doing in that world. And, as a general rule, the more like horses they look, the more realistic the portrayal, the more powerfully and engagingly the picture will evoke a world of galloping horses for us. Of course, we tend not to confuse the fictional world created by the film with the real world. Film theorists use the term "diegetic" to refer to elements of a film that are contained within the fictional world of the film. A normal viewer does not confuse obvious diegetic aspects of a film with non-diegetic aspects of it. For instance, if background music is playing in a film of galloping horses, we don't assume that the horses can hear the music. (Background music is non-diegetic.) It would take an extra representational element to introduce the music as a diegetic element of the film. (For example, we might see in the film loudspeakers blaring out the music.) The capacity of film to *realistically* portray a fictional world is an obvious aspect of its power, even if it is not a sufficient explanation of any particular film's power. Carroll does not overlook the pictorial character of filmic representation, but he plays no special heed to the realistic character of this representation in his explanation of film's power to move an audience. We think this is a mistake. Carroll is right to object to what we call the maximal interpretation of the realist psychological effects, but he overlooks the central importance of the minimal version of realism.

But what are the details of Carroll's own theory? We have noted that he emphasizes the clarity of film art, as opposed to other art forms, in an attempt to explain the great scope of film's power to move audience. It's time to take a look at some of the details of his account.

Carroll's (2004a: 487) explanation "of our extraordinarily intense response to films" comes in parts. First, there is pictorial representation. "Whatever features or cues we come to employ in object recognition, we also mobilize to recognize what pictures depict . . . The rapid development of this picture recognition capacity contrasts strongly with the acquisition of a symbol system such as language." People's facility with pictorial representation is one of the "features that make it [film] generally accessible to mass, untutored audiences . . . Movies became a worldwide phenomenon . . . because in their exploitation of pictorial recognition – as opposed to symbol systems that require mastery of processes such as reading . . . in order to be understood – they rely on a biological capability that is nurtured in humans as they learn to identify the objects and events in their environment."

Thus far Carroll has tried to explain why movies are generally easier to follow and more accessible than novels. "[R]ecognition of movie images is more analogous to a reflex than it is to a process like reading" (Carroll 2004a: 489). However, he has not yet explained why "the typical movie is, all things being equal, easier to follow than the typical play" (2004a: 490), since in theatre (and some other art forms) "recognition of what the representations refer to is, like movies, typically not mediated by learned processes of decoding, reading, or inference" (2004a: 489).

This brings us to the second part of Carroll's explanation for "our extraordinarily intense response to films."

> the filmmaker in the movie genre has far more potential control over the spectator's attention [for example, due to variable framing – techniques like camera positioning by which the filmmaker is able to focus the attention of the spectator] than does the theatrical director. The consequence of this is that the movie spectator is always looking where he or she should be looking, always attending to the right details and thereby comprehending, nearly effortlessly, the ongoing action precisely in the way it is meant to be understood . . . movies are more perspicuous cognitively. The element of cognitive clarity afforded by movies may well account, too, for the widespread intensity of engagement that movies elicit. (2004a: 490)

There is something to this. However, cognitive clarity, afforded to film by means of specific devices that focus the attention of viewers, seems hardly likely to fully account for the intensity of movies as compared to plays even if it is true that movies generally affect us more intensely than plays do. Again, more obvious explanations shouldn't be overlooked. Perhaps the subject matter of most plays, as compared to movies, is – while no less clear – less appealing in other ways. Perhaps theatre does not pander to the emotions to the extent that films do. Perhaps Carroll is confusing the idea that movies "affect us more intensely" with the idea that movies "affect more of us more intensely." The latter is hardly a surprise since the audience for movies dwarfs that for plays. A night at the theatre is generally pretty expensive. Movies are relatively cheap (even if popcorn isn't) and can often be watched for free. Lastly, we ought not to be too quick to accept the claim that movies can engage us more deeply than theatre as a fundamental truth about the two art forms. Powerful theatre affects us deeply indeed. Perhaps it is harder to achieve powerful effects in theatre than in film, in part for the reasons Carroll identifies – filmmakers have an easier time directing an audience's attention than theatre directors do – but this is not yet a good explanation of why films move us when they do. It helps explain why film has the widespread appeal it does (it is cheap compared to theatre and mediocre films are more engaging than mediocre plays); but there are deeper and more complete explanations of the power of film to be found. And they may share elements with the power of other narrative (and indeed non-narrative) art forms.

The second aspect Carroll cites for the power of movies – directed focusing of the viewer's attention – even in conjunction with pictorial representation seems insufficient to fully explain the power of film. What they may in fact do is aid in engaging and affecting the audience emotionally. They may help generate the emotional effect movies have on spectators, without actually constituting the direct means of producing this effect. There may be many other things that contribute to our emotional engagement with film – or prevent it – in far greater ways than the elements Carroll cites.

The third element in Carroll's account has to do with the way in which the narrative aspect of film aids its accessibility and hence power. Narrative explains action and audiences are naturally interested in explanations of action. He says (2004a: 493) "Insofar as movie narratives depict the human actions of characters in forms that are reflective of the logic of practical inference, the movies will be widely accessible, since practical inference is a generic form of human decision-making." Building on this theme of accessibility, another rather independent aspect of narrative is raised. Films create suspense by creating situations, or raising questions, through narrative that we wait in suspense to have resolved or answered. Carroll (2004a: 494) sees this question-and-answer model (which he calls the erotetic model) as "the most characteristic narrative approach in movies." Few would deny that an engaging – better yet, gripping – narrative is a necessary element in explaining the power of film.

But again Carroll seems to overlook the erotetic model's role in evoking emotion in favor of its cognitive role and the way it moves plot forward by posing problems and then addressing them, thus satisfying our curiosity. While the intrigue associated with a good plot does function to hold an audience's attention and may contribute to a strong emotional response, the fact that it raises questions it then answers is often rather independent of those elements in the narrative that produce strong emotional responses. Remember that Carroll sets out to answer twin questions: Why are films powerful and why is their power so widespread? Narrative clarity may be part – though only part – of the explanation of film's widespread appeal; it is ill-suited to explain film's power as such. It helps explain the narrative appeal of films – how they grip an audience – but it is hardly likely to explain why an audience can come to care so much about the fictional question-and-answer session they witness. The power of films often lies in an emotional engagement that is not explained by the cognitive grip of a narrative.

Film technique, plot, and the nature of filmic representation are all important elements in an explanation of the power of movies, but they are by no means the only elements, and quite possibly not even the most crucial. They are only important insofar as they can help to explain the impact that *some* films have on *some* spectators *some* of the time. The three elements that Carroll focuses on are important insofar as they serve character identification, phantasy, wish-fulfillment, imagination, desire (for revenge and other things), prejudices of various kinds, and voyeuristic and other tendencies transiently invoked. When Harry Callahan (a. k. a. "Dirty Harry") in the 1983 film *Sudden Impact*, looks down the barrel of his giant .44 Magnum at the bad guy and says "Go ahead, make my day," he says it for us all – and we are grateful; we are satisfied. In that moment justice reigns supreme; not just *a propos* of Harry's situation but so too for the wrongs – perhaps for all the wrongs – (real and imagined) that we have all suffered and have yet to suffer.

It is Carroll's focus on the cognitive rather than the affective that is the source of the problem and that (arguably) keeps him at hand's length from giving a plausible account for the power of movies. Carroll (2004a: 496) disagrees.

> [I]n this attempt to account for the power of movies, we have restricted our purview to features in movies which address the *cognitive* faculties of the audience. This is absolutely central to the argument. For only by focusing on cognitive capacities, especially ones as deeply embedded as pictorial representation, practical reason, and the drive to get answers to our questions, will we be in the best position to find the features of movies that account for their phenomenally *widespread* effectiveness; since cognitive capacities, at the level discussed, seem the most plausible candidate for what mass-movie audiences have *in common*.

In effect, Carroll's focus has been misdirected. The cognitive faculties of an audience are virtually always in the service of spectators' affective natures and their incessant demands.

The Paradox of Fiction

If Carroll is mistaken in seeing film's power as a function of its cognitive rather than affective aspects, then it is cinema's ability to evoke such emotion that needs to be accounted for. The "tricks of the trade," so to speak, are in the filmmakers' ability, technical skills, and talents – along with those of the writers, actors, cinematographers, set designers, costumers, etc. – to employ their crafts so as to at times evoke such emotion.[2]

In attempting to evoke emotion in film a substantial barrier must be overcome. Generally speaking, the events portrayed in a film have not happened and an audience knows that they have not happened. How, then, does an audience come to care so much about them? What kind of emotional response is this? Questions of this kind have been widely written about and are enshrined in something called the paradox of fiction. Despite disagreement as to how the paradox is to be resolved, virtually no one thinks that is a genuine paradox.[3] The paradox of fiction is better, though less dramatically, posed as a question about the relationship between belief and emotion in film spectatorship; or, more generally, about the nature of emotional response to fiction as such. Like the question about the power of movies, the paradox of fiction is also linked to the question of the nature of cinematic representation.

Consider the fact that we sometimes emotionally respond to fictions as if they were real, while we know that they are not. Emotion is ordinarily connected to belief such that only if we believe something is the case, for example that a person's pain is real, will we feel some corresponding emotion such as sympathy for them. If we came to believe that the person was not feeling pain but only faking, we would, ordinarily at least, stop feeling sorry for them. Emotion, in such cases appears to require the belief that the object of the emotion is real or genuine. How are we moved by fictional events even though we are aware that what we are watching or reading is not really happening or has not really happened?

The paradox of fiction can be formulated as follows.

1 Emotion requires belief in the reality of its object.
2 When watching a film or reading a book we are aware that the characters do not really exist (except as fictions) and the situations are not really occurring.

3   Nevertheless, we feel emotion, often strong emotion, when reading a
    book or watching a movie.

Murray Smith (1995a: 56) says:

> The problem, as Radford (1975; 1977) sees it, "is that people *can* be moved
> by fictional suffering given their brute behaviour in other contexts where
> belief in the reality of the suffering described or witnessed is necessary for
> the response" (Radford 1975: 72). Proffering several possible solutions to
> this paradox, he concludes that none are satisfactory and declares that emo-
> tional responses to fiction are not merely inconsistent with our emotional
> responses to actual events, but absurd, "unintelligible," and "unmanly"
> (Radford 1975: 69–70). A further feature of Radford's argument, then, is
> an implicit privileging of emotional responses to real events over emotional
> responses to fictional events. That we respond emotionally to real events is,
> to use Radford's phrase, a "brute fact" of human existence; that we can also
> respond emotionally to fictional events is merely "inconsistent" with this
> "brute fact."

A moment's introspection is all that it really takes to defeat the alleged
paradox. As Smith (1995a: 56) says "Radford never explains why
emotional responses to fictional events should not also have the status of
'brute fact.' . . . Why should we accept this [link to real events] as a condition of all emotional response, when our experience of fiction tells us
otherwise?"

But Smith's response is also misleading since it isn't just fictional art
that generates emotional response in the absence of corresponding belief.
Everyday emotional experience can have a similar structure. You are upset
at someone – a parent or friend – and you imagine yourself at your own
funeral. The people you are upset with are all there, dressed in black,
miserable, and saying wonderful things about you. You are aware you are
not dead, that no one is really mourning you and the things you imagine
being said are not being said; yet tears well up in your eyes. Or consider
the case of what Amelie Rorty (1980) calls "anomalous emotion" or
inappropriate emotion, where an emotion is present and the usual corresponding belief is not. Suppose you think your cat was run over, but
lo and behold she runs into your arms. There she is – alive and purring.
Nevertheless, you continue to cry and be upset while scratching "Sushi"
behind her ears. Or consider a case in which you are angry with your
boss and yet recognize there is no reason to be. In fact the boss has been
particularly good to you and you believe that, nevertheless the anger
remains. No one is reading a novel here – the beliefs that often do

accompany or correspond to the emotions in question are absent, and yet the emotions are present.

Thus, emotion is not necessarily linked to real events and we do not need fiction to tell us this. In Rorty's (1980) terms, if anomalous and seemingly irrational emotions are to be accounted for, as in situations in which emotions occur seemingly independent of beliefs that would rationalize and perhaps explain them, then the immediate cause (or trigger) of an emotion needs to be distinguished from the significant cause of the emotion. The "significant cause" of the emotion may be in the distant past and have to do not only with some significant past events but also with an individual's dispositions to perceive certain things as salient and be affected in certain ways.[4]

Note too that this suggests that one does not have to suppose any intrinsic connection between a realist conception of cinematic representation and film's emotional effect on spectators. A recognition that what one is watching is not "really" happening should be no barrier whatsoever to an audience's emotional response – even if it is supposed that the response is not identical to what we would emotionally experience if we were to believe those events real – and even if we do not act (for example, run from the theater) as we would in the "real" case.

Rorty's account of anomalous emotion, along with a psychoanalytic account of emotions as grounded in infantile phantasy (Gardner: 1992) suggest a further more radical thesis regarding both the nature of emotion and also of spectatorship.[5] It is one that turns Radford's thesis and the so-called paradox of fiction on its head. These accounts of emotion as originating in and causally connected to events in our distant past (in early infancy on the psychoanalytic account), suggest that the emotions we experience in connection with fiction and film are not secondary to emotions attached to beliefs about "reality," but are instead primary. Indeed, such accounts liken *all* instances of emotion to those we experience in fiction.

On this account, emotions are virtually never what we take them to be about – and can never be adequately explained in terms of their immediate causes (Levine: 2000). What a startlingly different view of the nature of spectatorship is intimated by such an account of emotion! If such an account is more or less correct, then many of the philosophical problems raised about film would need to be rethought. More than this of course, it is not just the nature of spectatorship that would need to be reassessed but human nature itself. We need to be seen as beings significantly detached from ourselves and hamstrung to a degree in our efforts at self-understanding – a view of human beings that is at the core of psychoanalysis and confirmed in ordinary life.

Feminist Critiques of Film and the "Paradox of the Depraved Spectator"

The discussion of emotion and the paradox of fiction gives us an opportunity to introduce one further issue – the representation of women in film. Suppose some of the following character features are singly or in combination essential to understanding cinematic spectatorship, and especially to enjoying movies: voyeurism, fetishism, masochism, sadism, and various other perversions – along with other psychoanalytic categories like phantasy, projection, introjection, denial, defense, repression, etc. (the list is long). Laura Mulvey (1975), for example, has argued that contemporary cinematic spectatorship must be understood in such terms. The claim by Mulvey, and some others who offer feminist critiques of film, is that spectators' emotional responses and pleasures are a function, not of their beliefs (or at any rate not of conscious beliefs), but instead of film's ability to invoke and temporarily satisfy voyeuristic and misogynistic desires, as well as wishes associated with other perversions or perverse tendencies.

Berys Gaut (1994: 12) gives the following account of Mulvey's position.

> For Mulvey, the mainstream, illusionistic, narrative film is structured around an active, scopophilic male gaze. Within the fiction, men look actively at passive women, seen as erotic objects, controlled by the male gaze. The men drive the story forward; the women are there as mere erotic spectacle . . . The mainstream film is constructed so as to imply a male spectator . . . his look locking with that of the male protagonist, with whom he identifies. Should the protagonist come to possess the woman, his triumph is vicariously enjoyed by the viewer. But the woman, impotent as object of the male gaze, still has a capacity to unsettle it; for as woman she evokes castration anxiety, causing male unpleasure. The threat must be mastered. And mastered it is, either by voyeuristic investigation of the female body and sadistic punishment for its bodily challenge, or by fetishistic scopophilia, converting her body or a bodily part into a fetish for the missing phallus . . . Both responses restore the woman to her impotence, reinscribing her in the film in her "to-be-looked-at-ness," and male hegemony is restored. The feminist response is clear: theory must unmask and destroy the corrupt pleasures of illusionistic narrative film; practice must create an alternative, a reflexive cinema which exposes the male gaze in its misogynistic dominance.

Whether or not Mulvey's account is correct, or the extent to which it is correct, depends heavily on whether a psychoanalytic account of spectatorship is correct – which in turn depends on the extent to which psychoanalysis is correct. Leaving the important issue of the truth of Mulvey's account aside, we want to explore the implications of such an account not merely for the nature of spectatorship but for the future of cinema as well. If Mulvey's account of cinematic pleasure is right, then is it even possible to make films that are not subject to her feminist critique? If Mulvey is right, then there is reason to believe it will be impossible either to "destroy the corrupt pleasures of illusionistic narrative film" or to create an alternative, since these features would be regarded as (more or less) intrinsic to cinematic pleasure and spectatorship.

Mulvey's critique may be partly based on the misconception that all forms of voyeurism, sadism, masochism, and fetishism are undesirable. Some forms are, but not all. It depends on whether or not they are harmful to oneself or others; whether, for example, they dominate one's psyche in ways that undermine relationships – as pornography is sometimes alleged to do. The so-called corrupt pleasures of illusionistic narrative film that Mulvey calls attention to may be every bit as necessary to any alternative cinema as it is to the current. This is not to deny that misogynistic and exploitative features of cinema should be exposed, and that some new cinema can and should try to do away with these. But if the nature of spectatorship is dominated by such pleasures, then how can they be gotten rid of without at the same time doing away with the attraction of film? Let's call this conundrum "the paradox of the depraved spectator."

Nothing in the paradox of fiction is exclusive to film as opposed to literature; the same is true of the paradox of the depraved spectator. Much the same psychoanalytic account is required to explain why some novels are difficult to read and others are page-turners. Stephen King dominates popular horror literature to an extent that no maker of horror movies has ever come close to. He too exploits and relies upon the "depravity" of his readers.

The paradox of the depraved spectator can be formulated as follows.

1   Cinematic pleasure is reliant on some combination of the following: voyeurism, fetishism, narcissism, feeding prejudices, and various perversions (including sadism and masochism).
2   It is possible to construct a new kind of cinema, cinematic language, and spectatorship that is not reliant on exploiting features like voyeurism, violence against women, sex, etc. – a cinema in which such pleasure-making features are (relatively) absent.

3 This new kind of cinema will have an audience that *will be* or *can be* generally entertained and get pleasure from the cinema.

If one assumes that people will not *generally* go the cinema unless they are entertained, then (3) can more simply be stated as follows:

3a This new kind of cinema will have an audience.

These three propositions appear to be mutually incompatible.

The paradox of the depraved spectator is no more a real paradox than the paradox of fiction. If cinematic pleasure requires the kinds of things Mulvey claims it does, then this is an important general feature of what is required for a person to be entertained by a movie, or by certain genres of cinema and literature – or perhaps to be entertained at all. And if having an audience depends upon entertaining that audience, then films that fail to provide such pleasures will have no audience. There is a great deal to say about such a state of affairs, but nothing about it is paradoxical.

Mulvey talks about a new language of cinema – free of the objectionable elements she claims dominate contemporary mainstream cinema. However, for a new language you need new speakers and a new audience. How is this possible? If voyeurism, etc., is essential to cinematic pleasure, then this must severely restrict the new kind of non-sexist cinema that Mulvey hopes for. If entertainment depends upon the negative features Mulvey points to, then her new cinema will not entertain people.

Mulvey (1993 [1975]: 123) says

> cinematic codes create a gaze, a world and an object, thereby producing an illusion cut to the measure of desire. It is these cinematic codes and their relationship to formative external structures that must be broken down before mainstream film and the pleasure it provides can be challenged. To begin with (as an ending), the voyeuristic-scopophilic look that is a crucial part of traditional filmic pleasure can itself be broken down.

Even aside from the psychoanalytic, there are good grounds (such as views about human nature and psychology) for challenging Mulvey's view that the cinematic codes she refers to can be broken down.[6] But suppose they can be? If cinema is to provide pleasure, then it must find a substitute for the pleasures rooted in, for example, the voyeuristic-scopophilic look. But why assume such substitutive pleasures can be found?

Mulvey does not appear to address this issue. She writes (1993 [1975]: 123):

> The first blow against the monolithic accumulation of traditional film con-
> ventions (already undertaken by radical film-makers) is to free the look of
> the camera into its materiality in time and space and the look of the audi-
> ence into dialectics and passionate detachment. There is no doubt that this
> destroys the satisfaction, pleasure and privilege of the "invisible guest," and
> highlights the way film has depended on voyeuristic active/passive mecha-
> nisms. Women, whose image has continually been stolen and used for this
> end, cannot view the decline of the traditional film form with anything
> much more than sentimental regret.

Thus, while acknowledging and celebrating the fact that the techniques
of radical filmmakers may destroy the "satisfaction, pleasure and privilege
of the 'invisible guest,'" she does not explain what the new sources of
cinematic attraction might be – nor is a clear account of how they are to
be gotten explained above. And as anyone who goes to the movies to be
entertained will tell you, without some such source, there will be no more
moviegoers.

Only with consciousness raising can a new cinema find a new audience.
But it is far from clear that even consciousness raising can suffice to create
an audience whose pleasures are qualitatively different from those of previous audiences. What is needed, or so it seems, is not consciousness raising
but *unconsciousness* raising. Psychoanalysis holds that aspects of the unconscious (or preconscious) can be intimated, brought to consciousness, and
dealt with in ways that enable people to overcome certain neurotic tendencies. However, there seems little ground in psychoanalysis, at least
Freudian psychoanalysis, for supposing that the human psyche can be
changed in the ways Mulvey thinks necessary for the coming-to-age of a
new, enlightened cinematic audience – one capable of experiencing alternative cinematic pleasures. On certain readings of psychoanalysis, perverse
pleasures are constitutive of human beings, constitutive of pleasure itself.
While certain forms of overt sexism and some prejudices might be gotten
rid of, there is little hope that voyeurism and masochism (and the pleasures
thereof) can, or *should*, be done away with. That is what our pleasure in
the cinema, and of course in much of life, depends on.

All is not lost, however, since not all forms of voyeurism, fetishism,
masochism, sadism, etc., are harmful. Fetishism is only harmful if, for
example, one in the end opts more or less completely for the shoe rather
than for the person. For example, look at what Freud (1993 [1927]: 27)
says about fetishism:

> In the last few years I have had an opportunity of studying analytically a
> number of men whose object-choice was dominated by a fetish. There is

no need to expect that these people came to analysis on account of their fetish. For though no doubt a fetish is recognized by its adherents as an abnormality, it is seldom felt by them as the symptom of an ailment accompanied by suffering. Usually they are quite satisfied with it, or even praise the way in which it eases their erotic life. As a rule, therefore, the fetish made its appearance in analysis as a subsidiary finding.

Masochism may well be part of ordinary grief, and sadism (certain forms of it) may serve a protective, even moral purpose. We take up these issues again in chapter 9, where we discuss a particularly extreme form of reliance on what appear to be the sadistic desires of the spectator: horror films, and in particular realist horror films (i.e. films that elicit a horror response without a supernatural prop).

This chapter is introduces only a small selection of philosophical problems about film. We chose problems that are interrelated and that seem to lead into (implicate) one another. They are all related in some way to the relationship between cinema and spectator. You will have to judge for yourselves, however, as to whether we are right in claiming that an awareness of issues about the nature of film can not only enhance discussion of philosophical issues raised in film, but may also enhance one's night out (or in) at the movies.

Questions

What makes a film ethical or unethical?

Is there anything significant to be gleaned from the fact that we do not all like the same films; that films which some of us find deeply moving (or funny, or frightening, or insightful) leave others unimpressed and unmoved?

How do movie theatres and other features of the viewing environment (big screen vs home DVD) affect spectatorship?

Why are films (some films) powerful? Have we given an adequate account of this? Have we suggested a plausible replacement for the theory we criticize (Carroll's)?

We argued that it is Carroll's focus on the cognitive rather than the affective that keeps him from giving a plausible account of the power of movies. Did the argument work? Clearly cognitive qualities of films influence their power to affect audiences; how could you show that cognitive qualities aren't enough to fully explain this power?

We emphasized the emotional and desire-based aspects of film's capacity to deeply affect us. What are some of the philosophical concerns and worries about this capacity?

Can an appreciation of philosophical issues raised about film enhance the cinematic experience? Does it undermine the affective power of film? Does it enhance the exercise of critical capacities in film spectatorship? Is it largely epiphenomenal to the critical appreciation of films?

Is there a way of reworking Andre Bazin's view that "the film image was an objective representation of the past, a veritable slice of reality," that withstands Noël Carroll's criticisms? It clearly isn't literally true, or true of all moving images, or all narratives of moving images, but is there still something to the idea?

Just how plausible is the paradox of the depraved spectator? Is film spectatorship based on psychological processes that are problematic, processes we would like to be able to do without? Does it matter if absorption into a film requires that the spectator undergo a problematic psychological process?

What makes a movie star? Would understanding this better help us understand spectatorship (the relation between audience and film)?

Notes

1   Except for films that self-consciously employ psychoanalysis, or ways in which psychoanalysis has become part of western cultural thought with notions like repression, projection etc., Carroll (2004b) largely rejects the significance of psychoanalysis for understanding film and philosophical problems associated with film.

2   Carl Plantinga (1997) addresses the question (a variant of Adorno & Horkheimer's) of whether the emotional manipulation that goes on in film – that clearly goes on – can be grounds for ideological and ethical critiques of cinema. This in turn is connected to philosophical problems of film associated with aesthetics and ethics, as well as the moral responsibility of the artist (filmmaker).

3   A genuine paradox resists easy resolution and calls for a deep philosophical reconceptualization. The liar paradox is an example of a genuine paradox. The liar paradox is generated by sentences such as "This sentence is false." If the sentence is true, then it is false. And if it is false, then it is true. But can anything be both true and false? Attempts to resist the paradox by declaring the sentence neither true nor false lead straight to something known as the

"strengthened liar." Consider the sentence: "This sentence is not true." If the sentence is neither true nor false, then it is not true. But that would make it true. There is no easy way out of the liar paradox; it requires a substantial reworking of our ordinary concept of truth.

4   Rorty (1980: 106) "The significant cause of an emotion is the set of events – the entire casual history – that explains the efficacy of the immediate or precipitating cause. Often the significant cause is not in the immediate past; it may be an event, or a series of events, long forgotten, that formed a set of dispositions that are triggered by the immediate cause."

5   The psychoanalytic view rejects what Sebastian Gardner (1992: 36) calls the "rationalistic account" which "holds that emotions are direct and sufficient outcomes of complexes of belief . . . beliefs which identify the emotion's kind, cause, and object and reflect its normative framework." See Gardner (1992: 35) for a critique of the rationalistic account of emotion in favour of the psychoanalytic theory that sees emotion as "a kind of mental state which cannot be understood apart from – for the reason that it is derived from – the kind of mental state that psychoanalytic theory refers to as phantasy."

6   See Doane (1993) for a discussion of the problematic nature of female spec-tatorship and related difficulties in altering aspects of it. Her essay, however, presupposes and is so steeped in the language, concepts, and arguments of Lacanian psychoanalysis and related feminist film theory that anyone not well acquainted with the genre may find it unclear. She says that

> the formal resistances to the elaboration of female subjectivity produce perturbations and contradictions within the narrative economy. The analyses in this study emphasize the symptoms of ideological stress which accompany the concerted effort to engage female subjectivity within conventional narrative forms. These stress points and perturba-tions can then, hopefully, be activated as a kind of lever to facilitate the production of a desiring subjectivity for the woman – in another cine-matic practice." (Doane 1993: 175)

Further Reading

Adorno, T. W., & M. Horkheimer (1990). "The Culture Industry: Enlightenment as Mass Deception." In T. W. Adorno & M. Horkheimer, *Dialectic of Enlightenment*. New York: Continuum.

Allen, P., & M. Smith, eds. (1997). *Film Theory and Philosophy*. Oxford: Clarendon Press.

Allen, R. T. (1986). "The Reality of Responses to Fiction." *British Journal of Aesthetics* 26.1, 64–8.

Bazin, Andre (1971). *What is Cinema?* Berkeley: University of California Press.

Carroll, Noël (1988). Philosophical Problems of Classical Film Theory. Princeton: Princeton University Press.

Carroll, Noël (2004a). "The Power of Movies." In Peter Lamarque & Stein Olsen, eds., *Aesthetics and the Philosophy of Art: The Analytic Tradition.* Oxford: Blackwell, 485–97.

Carroll, Noël (2004b). "Afterword: Psychoanalysis and the Horror Film." In Steven Schneider, ed., *The Horror Film and Psychoanalysis: Freud's Worst Nightmares.* Cambridge: Cambridge University Press, 257–70.

Carroll, Noël (2008). *The Philosophy of Motion Pictures.* Malden, MA: Blackwell.

Carroll, Noël, & Jinhee Choi (2006). *Philosophy of Film and Motion Pictures: An Anthology.* Malden, MA: Blackwell.

Colman, Felicity (2009). *Film, Theory and Philosophy: The Key Thinkers.* Durham: Acumen.

Currie, Gregory (1990a). *The Nature of Fiction.* Cambridge: Cambridge University Press.

Currie, Gregory (1990b). "Emotion and the Response to Fiction." In *The Nature of Fiction.* Cambridge: Cambridge University Press, 182–216.

Currie, Gregory (1997). "The Paradox of Caring: Fiction and the Philosophy of Mind." In Mette Hjort & Sue Laver, eds., *Emotion and the Arts,* 63–77.

Doane, Mary Ann (1993). "Subjectivity and Desire: An(other) Way of Looking." In Anthony Easthope, ed., *Contemporary Film Theory.* London: Longman, 161–78.

Easthope, Anthony, ed. (1993). *Contemporary Film Theory.* Longman: London.

Elsaesser, Thomas, & Malte Hagener (2010). *Film Theory: An Introduction through the Senses.* New York and London: Routledge.

Feagin, Susan, L. (1997). "Imagining Emotions and Appreciating Fiction." In Mette Hjort & Sue Laver, eds., *Emotion and the Arts,* 50–62.

Freeland, Cynthia, & Thomas Wartenberg, eds. (1995). *Philosophy and Film.* New York and London: Routledge.

Freud, Sigmund (1993 [1927]). "Fetishism." Reprinted in Anthony Easthope, ed., *Contemporary Film Theory.* London: Longman, 27–32.

Gardner, Sebastian (1992). "The Nature and Source of Emotion." In Jim Hopkins & Anthony Savile, eds., *Psychoanalysis, Mind and Art: Perspectives on Richard Wollheim.* Oxford: Blackwell, 35–54.

Gaut, Berys (1994). "On Cinema and Perversion." *Film and Philosophy* 1, 3–17.

Hanfling, Oswald (1996). "Fact, Fiction, and Feeling." *British Journal for Aesthetics* 36, 356–66.

Hartz, G. (1999). "How We Can Be Moved by Anna Karenina, Green Slime, and a Red Pony." *Philosophy* 74, 557–78.

Heinämaa, Sara (1995). "On Thoughts and Emotions: The Problem of Artificial Persons." *Acta Philosophica Fennica* 58, 269–86.

Joyce, R. (2000). "Rational Fear of Monsters." *British Journal of Aesthetics* 40.2, 209–24.

Lamarque, Peter (1981). "How Can We Fear and Pity Fictions?" *British Journal of Aesthetics* 21.4, 291–304.

Levine, Michael (2000). "Lucky in Love: Love and Emotion." In *The Analytic Freud: Philosophy and Psychoanalysis*. London and New York, Routledge, 231–58.

Livingston, Paisley, & Carl Plantinga, eds. (2008). *The Routledge Companion to Philosophy and Film*. London: Routledge.

Matravers, Derek (1997). "The Paradox of Fiction: The Report versus the Perceptual Model." In Mette Hjort & Sue Laver, eds., *Emotion and the Arts*, 78–92.

Miller, Toby, & Robert Stam, eds., (2003). *A Companion to Film Theory*. Blackwell Reference Online. www.blackwellreference.com

Moran, R. (1994). "The Expression of Feeling in Imagination." *Philosophical Review* 103.1, 75–106.

Mulvey, Laura (1993 [1975]). "Visual Pleasure and Narrative Cinema." *Screen* 10.3, 6–18. Reprinted in Anthony Easthope, ed., *Contemporary Film Theory*. London: Longman, 111–24.

Neil, Alex (1991). "Fear, Fiction and Make Believe." *Journal of Aesthetics and Art Criticism* 49, 48–56.

Novitz, D. (1987). *Knowledge, Fiction and Imagination*. Philadelphia: Temple University Press.

Plantinga, Carl (1997). "Notes on Spectator Emotion and Ideological Film Criticism." In P. Allen & M. Smith, eds., *Film Theory and Philosophy*, 372–93.

Radford, C. (1975). "How Can We Be Moved by the Fate of Anna Karenina?" *Proceedings of the Aristotelian Society*, Supplemental Vol. 49, 67–80.

Radford, C. (1977). "Tears and Fiction." *Philosophy* 52, 208–213.

Rorty, A. O. (1980). "Explaining Emotions." In. A. O. Rorty, ed., *Explaining Emotions* Berkeley: University of California Press, 103–26.

Säätelä, S. (1994). "Fiction, Make-Believe and Quasi Emotions." *British Journal of Aesthetics* 34, 25–34.

Schaper, E. (1978). "Fiction and the Suspension of Disbelief." *British Journal of Aesthetics* 18, 31–44.

Smith, Murray (1995a). *Engaging Characters: Fiction, Emotion, and the Cinema*. Oxford: Clarendon Press, 40–69.

Smith, Murray (1995b). "Film Spectatorship and the Institution of Fiction." *Journal of Aesthetics and Art Criticism* 53, 1–13.

Turvey, M. (1997). "Seeing Theory: On Perception and Emotional Response in Current Film Theory." In R. Allen & M. Smith, eds., *Film Theory and Philosophy*. Oxford: Oxford University Press, 431–57.

Walton, Kendall (1978). "Fearing Fictions." *Journal of Philosophy* 75, 5–27.

Walton, Kendall (1997). "Spelunking, Simulation, and Slime: On Being Moved by Fiction." In Mette Hjort & Sue Laver, eds., *Emotion and the Arts*, 37–49.

Part II

Epistemology and Metaphysics

In part II we explore some of the central topics in epistemology (the philosophical study of knowledge) and metaphysics (roughly, the philosophical study of the fundamental nature of reality).

Chapter 3 explores epistemology, looked at through the lens of skepticism. (Skepticism is a philosophical rejection of the possibility of knowledge of various kinds.) Our film is the 1990 Arnold Schwarzenegger vehicle, *Total Recall*; perhaps not the most high-minded of the films we study, but a brilliant exploration of skepticism nonetheless.

Chapter 4 starts our journey through metaphysics. We start with the obvious question: what exists? What are the fundamental constituents of the world? This is the study of ontology, and our guide is the film that, in many ways, kicked off recent interest in studying philosophy through film: *The Matrix* (1999). *The Matrix* is often studied in terms of skepticism; but, in our view, it is rather inferior in this respect to *Total Recall*. *The Matrix* has the singular virtue of framing the issue of ontology in an especially perspicuous way.

Chapter 5 looks at the metaphysics of mind, not directly, but through the lens of artificial minds. One reason to do this is that artificial minds have a long and distinguished history in cinema. Another is that philosophical issues about the nature of mind come into especially sharp focus when we ask the question: What would it take to create an artificial mind? (Could we ever do it, even in principle?) Our guide here is the 2001 Steven Spielberg film *AI: Artificial Intelligence*. Spielberg's film is not universally regarded as a great film (it would be fair to say), but in the central character of David he has given us an exemplary illustration of

Thinking Through Film: Doing Philosophy, Watching Movies, First Edition. Damian Cox, Michael P. Levine.
© 2012 Damian Cox and Michael P. Levine. Published 2012 by Blackwell Publishing Ltd.

what is required for something to possess an artificial mind (a human-like one).

Chapter 6 examines the nature of time. Time is at once the most familiar and the most mysterious of things. Again, we don't take the issue head on, but examine the topic by concentrating on something that cinema has been particularly keen on representing in one form or another: time travel. To philosophically confront the possibility of time travel, one has to understand at least something of the nature of time. We explore it all with a discussion of a short, extraordinary film from 1960, made by the French auteur, Chris Marker. The film is *La Jetée* and it is a particularly elegant example of the time travel narrative. We use it to show how time travel is at least logically possible; and also how many time travel films (maybe most) are quite incoherent.

3

Knowing What's What
in *Total Recall*

Introduction

Epistemology is the study of knowledge and related concepts like doubt, certainty, justification, evidence, and warrant. Three questions dominate the field. What is knowledge? What can be known? How do we know what we know (if we do know anything at all)? These may seem to be somewhat dull, if worthy and important, questions, but things are spiced up by the presence of the skeptic. The skeptic is someone who denies knowledge. They can deny that we know what we think we know; or they can deny that one or more of our methods of acquiring knowledge are actually capable of yielding knowledge. A skeptic about other minds, for example, denies that we know anything about other people's minds, or even whether other people have minds. The religious skeptic denies that we know anything about God, including whether she exists or doesn't exist. Perhaps the most ambitious of all skeptics was conjured by the great seventeenth-century French philosopher René Descartes. This is a hyperbolic skeptic: someone who claims that we know nothing at all except that we exist. (I know I exist because I can't coherently doubt that I exist. When I ponder the question "Do I exist or not?" something must be doing the pondering, and that's me. As Descartes sums it up: *cogito ergo sum* (I think, therefore I am).)

One of the most interesting kinds of skeptic is the skeptic about sensory knowledge. This kind of skeptic denies that we know anything at all based on our observation of the world. They deny that our senses are a source

Thinking Through Film: Doing Philosophy, Watching Movies, First Edition. Damian Cox, Michael P. Levine.
© 2012 Damian Cox and Michael P. Levine. Published 2012 by Blackwell Publishing Ltd.

of knowledge: our senses, they maintain, are neither secure nor certain enough to provide us with knowledge of the world. All sciences – except mathematics – are based on information gleaned from our senses, so if the senses don't produce knowledge, science doesn't produce knowledge either. Some skeptics about sensory knowledge deduce that we can't even know that an external world exists! So skepticism about sensory knowledge reaches a long way. To keep things simple, we'll call this kind of skeptic: the skeptic. Keep in mind, however, that we are only talking about one member of a bewilderingly diverse group of skeptics.

Much of the best work in contemporary epistemology is done by trying to refute the skeptic about sensory knowledge. This is worth doing, not just because this skeptic is a splendidly annoying figure, but because in refuting the skeptic we shed important light on the nature of knowledge. Knowledge, it turns out, is a complicated and controversial thing. Our guide through contemporary epistemology's battle with the skeptic will be the 1990 Arnold Schwarzenegger vehicle, *Total Recall*. Many wonderful films evoke and explore skepticism in one way or another, but *Total Recall* is special, at least from a contemporary epistemologist's point of view.[1] We will soon see why.

In *Total Recall*, in the year 2048, on Earth, Douglas Quaid dreams of Mars. Quaid desperately wants to travel to Mars, to visit the Mars Colony, but his wife Lori will have nothing to do with it. Instead of traveling to Mars, Quaid agrees to take a virtual Martian holiday, courtesy of a rather suspect outfit calling themselves ReKall. ReKall promise to implant memories of a holiday to Mars. The memories are to replace an actual holiday, which would, after all, be long, arduous, and contain many boring bits. (The assumption seems to be that actual holidays are no more than inconvenient ways of storing up happy memories, which is plain silly. But let that pass.) Quaid agrees to take more than a run of the mill holiday; he signs up for a premium Martian adventure called "Blue Sky on Mars" in which he is to be a secret agent having the ride of his life before finally getting the girl of his dreams (literally as it turns out) and saving Mars. During the memory implant procedure, however, things go horribly wrong.

Quaid interrupts the memory implantation procedure yelling something about having his cover blown. He is subdued, drugged, and dumped in a taxi (as you would expect). Then his wife – who it turns out isn't his wife – tries to kill him; then others try to kill him; then he gets hold of a mysterious package, escapes to Mars, and meets up with Melina (a rebel fighting the tyranny of Mars's Administrator, Cohaagen). Quaid and Melina have a series of riotous adventures, culminating in terraformation of the Martian atmosphere.[2] (Thanks to ancient alien technology, the complete transformation of Mars' atmosphere takes approximately 1 minute 45 seconds – which turns out to be very handy indeed.) OK; this summary misses out on nearly all the twists and turns of what is a remarkable (i.e. remarkably silly and remarkably entertaining) plot. In particular, it misses all the convolutions to do with Quaid's identity crisis and his unwitting role in a plot to destroy the Martian rebel leadership.[3] But there is one crucial scene we need to examine.

In this scene (starting at 0:58), Quaid, relaxing in his hotel room (the Mars Hilton, no less), gets a visit from Dr Edgemar of ReKall. They have this conversation at the point of Quaid's gun:

EDGEMAR: I'm afraid this is going to be very difficult for you to accept Mr Quaid, but you're not really standing here right now.

QUAID: You know Doc, you could have fooled me.

EDGEMAR: I'm quite serious. You're not here and neither am I.

QUAID: [laughing; patting Edgemar down] That's amazing. Where are we?

EDGEMAR: We're at ReKall. You are strapped into an implant chair and I'm monitoring you from the psycho-probe console.

QUAID: Oh, I get it. I'm dreaming and this is all part of the delightful vacation your company has sold me.

EDGEMAR: Not exactly. What your experiencing is a free-form delusion based on our memory tapes, but you are inventing it yourself as you go along.

QUAID: Well if it's my delusion, who the hell invited you?

EDGEMAR: I've been artificially implanted as an emergency measure. I'm sorry to tell you this Mr Quaid, but you've suffered a schizoid-embolism. We can't snap you out of your fantasy. I've been sent in to try to talk you down.

QUAID: How much is Cohaagen paying you for this?

EDGEMAR: Think about it. Your dream started in the middle of the implant procedure. Everything after that: the chases, the trip to Mars, the suite at the Hilton are all elements of your ReKall holiday and ego-trip. You paid to be a secret agent.

QUAID: Bullshit. It's coincidence.

A moment later (after Lori has been introduced into the picture in one last-ditch attempt to convince Quaid of the dream hypothesis) Edgemar sums up the case beautifully.

EDGEMAR: What's bullshit Mr Quaid? That you're having a paranoid episode, triggered by acute neuro-chemical trauma, or that

> you're really an invincible secret agent from Mars who's the
> victim of an inter-planetary conspiracy to make him think he
> is a lowly construction worker?

It seems as if Quaid *should* be convinced by Edgemar's arguments. Quaid
finally sees through the plot when he spies a bead of sweat rolling down
Edgemar's face. If Edgemar really were no more than a virtual presence,
the gun pointed at him would not be real and he would under no real
threat. So why is he so nervous? Without further epistemological dis-
course, Quaid shoots Edgemar in the centre of his forehead, and narrative
momentum is saved.

Of course, Quaid's *bead of sweat* deduction is rather fragile. There are
many reasons why Edgemar might be nervous. Edgemar's job might be
on the line, and his nervousness at the psycho-probe monitoring console
might affect his virtual body-image in Quaid's free-form delusion. At least
this seems to be a possibility Quaid ought to be able to rule out if he is
to have justified confidence in his *bead of sweat* deduction. (In Quaid's
defense, shooting a virtual Edgemar would not seriously harm anybody
except Quaid himself, while shooting a lying Edgemar might be deemed
an act of self-defense.)

What evidence could Quaid produce that would enable him to rule
out Edgemar's delusion hypothesis? It seems that he has no decisive evidence. If a schizoid-embolism, supported by ReKall memory tapes, is
capable of sustaining a sufficiently robust delusion – one which is thoroughly plausible and consistent (events follow each other in rational order,
people and things don't shape-shift arbitrarily, and so on) and one which
is so rich in detail as to be indistinguishable from the quality of waking
experience – then Quaid is in no position to rule out the possibility that
he is in a delusional state. On the other hand, we – the audience – know
perfectly well that Quaid isn't delusional. This is because much of the film
is told from a third-person perspective. Sometimes we follow the action
from Quaid's point of view. At other times we witness events Quaid is in
no position to witness. (If these events are part of a dream, then whose
dream is it? It can't be Quaid's. He doesn't know about them.) In the
fictional world of *Total Recall*, Quaid really is a secret agent, and he really
is about to save Mars.[4] In this fictional world, Quaid's basic presumptions
are all true. But does he know they are true? There is more to having
knowledge than having a true belief.

At the very end of the film (at 1:44), as Quaid and Melina stare out
in wonder at the newly minted Martian sky (blue of course), Quaid is
epistemologically discomfited once more.

MELINA: I can't believe it. It's like a dream. . . . What's wrong?
QUAID: I just had a terrible thought. What if this is a dream?
MELINA: Well then kiss me quick before you wake up.

Quaid seems to be in a skeptical pickle. Even though his beliefs are, as it happens, true (i.e. true in the fictional world of *Total Recall*), it seems that he can't really *know* that they are true. For all he knows, he is strapped into a memory implant machine and suffering the effects of a schizoid-embolism. (Great term this: it doesn't really mean anything, but that won't stop us using it as much as possible.) Certainly, the skeptic interprets Quaid's plight like this. And the skeptic insists that we are all in essentially the same epistemological situation as Quaid. We gain nearly all our beliefs about the world through our senses, and the skeptic holds that *even if all these beliefs are true* (and the skeptic isn't saying that they are true), *but even if they are true, they don't count as knowledge*. On what basis can the skeptic make this claim? Quaid, after all, is the hero of a very outlandish story. We can see how he might be in a skeptical pickle. But what about us?

The Skeptical Argument

The skeptic argues like this. If our senses are telling us the truth, then we aren't suffering a schizoid-embolism (which would cause us to have delusional experiences and delusional beliefs). But we don't know whether we are having a schizoid-embolism or not. So we don't know if our senses are telling us the truth. The skeptic thinks this argument applies to all of us, all the time (and not merely on the basis of a possible schizoid-embolism: that is just a prop; any equivalent skeptical predicament will do as well.) It might seem obvious that Quaid can't know whether the schizoid-embolism hypothesis is true or not. He encounters plenty of evidence that it is true. Even if *we* know that this evidence is misleading, *he* doesn't. And Quaid's attempted refutation of the hypothesis (the *bead of sweat* deduction) fails miserably on close inspection. So Quaid is stuck. But can we rule out the same sort of hypothesis for ourselves?[5] Quaid remembers going to ReKall; he is a victim of his own curiosity and trusting nature. We haven't done anything so foolish, at least as far as we can remember. OK, perhaps we have had a ReKall-like adventure, but have had all memory of it wiped from us. If this *had* happened we couldn't tell that it had. Therefore, the argument goes, if it *hasn't* happened to us, we can't tell that it *hasn't*. Whether it has or has not happened to us – we cannot know either way. This is the general character of skeptical hypotheses. We can't show once and for all that they are false, because all the information we might use to show that they are false is information that could be fed us as part of the hypothesis. Skeptical hypotheses are the ultimate conspiracy theories.

So this is the line of reasoning we get from the skeptic: we can't know that skeptical hypotheses are false because we can't access information that would show that they are false, and since we know that they have to be false in order for our senses to work properly, we can't ever know that our senses work properly. In other words, we gain no knowledge through our senses (at all).

How to respond to an argument like this? First we should set it out a bit more precisely, separating out the various premises and the conclusion. Let us stick with a schizoid-embolism-induced delusion as our skeptical hypothesis, though others would do as well. (We will summarize the hypothesis as the claim: I am delusional.)

1 I do not know that I am not delusional. (I don't know that I am delusional either, but that's another matter.)
2 I know that if my senses tell me the truth, then I am not delusional.
3 So, I do not know if my senses tell me the truth.

OK; maybe the logical force of this argument isn't completely obvious, so let us fill it in a bit.

1 I do not know that I am not delusional. (This is our first premise.)
2 I know that if my senses tell me the truth, then I am not delusional. (This is our second premise.)
3 Just suppose that I *do* know that my senses tell me the truth. (This isn't a new premise, it is just a supposition. We are setting it up for a fall.)
4 Then I would know that I am not delusional. (We deduce this from (2) and (3).)
5 But, we already agreed at (1) that I do not know this, so my supposition at (3) must have been wrong.
6 Therefore I do not know that my senses tell me the truth.

Arguments like this work by introducing a hypothetical supposition (in this case (3)) and using it, in combination with other premises, to deduce a contradiction. Whenever we manage to deduce a contradiction, something has gone wrong. Either the hypothetical supposition is wrong or one or more premises of the argument are wrong. The skeptic thinks that the hypothetical supposition is the obvious villain of our argument and that all the other premises can't be sensibly denied.[6] The argument only works, however, if all the deductions performed in it are in fact logically valid. Are they?

Relevant Alternatives and the Closure Principle

Is the argument logically valid? That is to say, does the conclusion of the argument follow from the premises by logic alone? The answer is no. The argument is what logicians call an enthymeme. This is to say that it relies on a missing premise, a premise that isn't true by logic alone. The missing premise is known as the *closure principle for knowledge* (or the *closure principle* for short). In the longer version of the argument, we use a combination of (2) and (3) in order to deduce (4). I know that my senses tell me the truth (3), and I know that if my senses tell me the truth, then I'm not delusional (2). From this we conclude that I know I am not delusional (4). (And since (4) is wrong, (3) is wrong.) It sounds very reasonable. But it does rely on a principle about how the concept of knowledge works. It relies on the idea that knowledge is transmitted through entailment. Here is a bald statement of the principle, using the symbols p and q to stand for any propositions.

> *Closure principle for knowledge*
> If a person knows p and also knows that p entails q, then that person knows q.

Without this principle, the skeptical argument is just not going to work. You may be wondering what the big deal is, because the closure principle looks to be obviously correct. If you know something, and you know that this something entails something else, then how can you *not* know this something else? It seems hard to argue with the closure principle. But argue with it we will. (This is just one tactic for responding to the skeptic. There are plenty of others, but in this chapter we are going to explore attempts to refute the skeptical argument by denying closure.)

Fred Dretske first fully developed this line of attack against the skeptic's reasoning. It is commonly called the *relevant alternatives* reply to the skeptic. (We will soon see why.) Dretske argues that the closure principle doesn't always hold. To illustrate the idea, let us go back to the movie.

At the very end of the film, Quaid wonders whether he has dreamed his adventure. He hasn't, but isn't so sure about it. Now think about Melina. She isn't confused like Quaid. Nor is she a figment of Quaid's imagination.[7] She is real, and she knows it. She is on Mars, and she knows it (she has been there all her life). She knows that Cohaagen is a tyrant (she's had dealings with him). And so on. Does she know that she isn't dreaming it all? Does she know that she hasn't been captured by Cohaagen, implanted with false memories, and put on a fake Mars movie set with an actor who looks a lot like Arnold Schwarzenegger? Perhaps she doesn't know this, even though she knows plenty of other things about her life. How can this be?

To get clear on this, we have to think about the nature of knowledge. (It's about time, you might be thinking.) What do we mean when we attribute knowledge to a person? The kind of knowledge we are talking about is propositional knowledge: i.e. knowledge that some proposition is true. To have this kind of knowledge we have to believe a proposition and that proposition has to be true. But that's not enough to give us *knowledge* that it is true. What else do we need? Dretske's answer is that we need to have come by our belief reliably. If our true belief is to count as knowledge, we can't believe it by accident, or because we just guessed it, or because we were indoctrinated to believe it. Dretske proposes this test: If the proposition had been false, would we still have believed it? If the answer to that is yes, then our belief does not track the truth well enough to count as knowledge. If the answer is no, then our true belief counts as knowledge.

Dretske's test for knowledge
Would I believe this proposition if it were false?

The big competitor for Dretske's account of knowledge (and many variations of it) is the *justified true belief* model of knowledge. According to the justified true belief model, a true belief counts as knowledge if and only if you are justified in holding it. The justified true belief model looks very sensible, and has been popular in philosophy for a long time. But there is a problem with it. Consider the following case. Suppose you look at the clock on your bedroom wall and it says it is 10 o'clock. Suppose, furthermore, that it is 10 o'clock and you quite justifiably believe the clock is working properly (it's worked well since you've owned it, say, and you replaced the battery only two weeks ago). Seeing the clock would be justification for believing that it is 10, and if it is 10 then you would have a justified true belief that it is 10. But do you know it is 10? Suppose that, unknown to you, the clock actually stopped three days ago at exactly 10. In this case we would say that although you have a justified belief that it is 10, and it is indeed true that it is 10 o'clock, you nevertheless do not know it is 10 o'clock. You only got hold of your justified true belief by accident. And that seems to rule out the knowledge claim. (Counterexamples like this are called "Gettier counterexamples" because they first came to prominence in a famous paper by Edmund Gettier (1963).) Dretske has a ready answer to Gettier counterexamples. You don't know that it is 10 o'clock because it turns out that you haven't acquired your belief that it is 10 o'clock through reliable means. If it weren't 10 o'clock, would you still believe that it was? Yes you would. The clock would still say 10 o'clock. But this time it would be wrong. So the case doesn't pass Dretske's test for knowledge. You don't, in the example, know the time after all. This seems intuitively the right answer.

Let's look at Dretske's test more closely. Does Melina know that she is on Mars? She believes truly that she is, but does she pass the test? The test looks simple enough. Melina's belief that she is on Mars is true. But if it were false, would she still believe it? How do we judge a question like this? It is asking us to judge the truth of a special kind of assertion called a counterfactual conditional. Counterfactual conditionals pose a purely hypothetical scenario (one we think is false: counter to the facts) and then advance a claim about what would happen in this hypothetical scenario. Consider a different example of a counterfactual conditional: *If the USA had not bombed Hiroshima and Nagasaki, they would still have won the Second World War.* Is this true or not? How are we supposed to work it out? The counterfactual conditional is making a claim about what would have happened if the bombings hadn't happened, *everything else being equal.* It's no good responding to the conditional by imagining bizarre possibilities. (The USA spares Hiroshima. Next day aliens from Jupiter land in Hiroshima and present the Japanese military with a super-weapon. They go on to win the war and found a thousand-year dynasty.) Bizarre possibilities are irrelevant. The counterfactual is making a claim about what would have happened if one thing changed (the bombings never took place) and everything else stayed the same apart from those produced by the change. Philosophers would call this possible situation the closest possible world in which the bombings of Hiroshima and Nagasaki did not happen. It is a possible world in which the course of the war up until the attack on Hiroshima and Nagasaki remains the same. All the factors leading to a Japanese defeat would remain in play. Japan's military were in a perilous position just prior to the bombings, without any likely path to victory, and so in due course, Japan would have been defeated. This is to say: Japan is defeated in the closest possible world in which the attacks on Hiroshima and Nagasaki did not take place. If this is right, then our counterfactual is true. If it is not right, then the counterfactual is false.

Let's see how this plays out in Melina's case. Melina believes, truly as it turns out, that she is on Mars. Would she still have believed she was on Mars when she wasn't? What is the closest possible world in which Melina isn't on Mars? Is it the world in which she is on Earth, having traveled there in a commuter shuttle? Is it the world in which she has been kidnapped by Cohaagen's henchmen, strapped into a memory-implant machine and then force-fed a delusion that she is on Mars? Which do you think is the closer possible world? That is, which scenario departs least from the actual world (remember, this is the world in which Melina really is on Mars and the film is recording events pretty much as they happen.) It is obvious (isn't it?) that the boring commuter shuttle story departs from the actual world much less dramatically than the skeptical scenario story. And in this case Melina could easily spot that she's on Earth and not on Mars (it's not that hard to spot the difference). So, we have an answer. Melina *wouldn't* believe she was on Mars if she weren't. She passes Dretske's test. She knows she's on Mars.

So far so good. But what about the closure principle? How does Dretske's account of knowledge lead us to reject closure and thus reject the skeptic's argument? Melina knows that she is on Mars. Does she know she is not being deluded by Cohaagen and his cohorts into thinking she is on Mars when she is not? That's a different question. She might believe that she isn't being deluded, and she might be right about that. But does she know she isn't being deluded? Let's apply Dretske's test a second time, this time to Melina's belief *I am not being deluded by Cohaagen and co.* This proposition fails Dretske's test. If she were being deluded by a conspiracy into thinking she was on Mars, she would still believe she was on Mars. (That's the point of a conspiracy after all.) Of course, if she thought about the skeptical hypothesis she would probably dismiss it as false. However her dismissal, though correct, isn't robust or reliable enough to count as knowledge. The upshot of all this is that the closure principle fails in Melina's case. She knows that she is on Mars. She knows that if she is on Mars, then she isn't a victim of a Cohaagen conspiracy to delude her into thinking she is on Mars when she isn't. But still, she doesn't know that she isn't such a victim. The fact that she can't reliably rule out the skeptical hypothesis doesn't mean that she can't reliably believe a whole host of true things, including that she is on Mars, with Quaid, and they have just saved the planet. As Dretske might put it, the alternative the skeptic wants us to take seriously simply isn't relevant when it comes to assessing whether Melina's everyday beliefs count as knowledge.

Truth-Tracking and Reason-Tracking

And yet there is a problem. (Of course there is a problem: this wouldn't be philosophy if there wasn't a problem.) Dretske's analysis seems to work wonders for Melina, but it also seems to give the wrong result for Quaid. We said awhile back that Quaid was in a skeptical pickle. Not so, according to the Dretskean account of things. Apart from a few wobbles at the end of the film – and a brief interlude when Dr Edgemar had him on the ropes – Quaid believes he is on Mars. As it happens, he is right. Would he still believe it if it weren't true? Notice this isn't the question "Would he still believe it if he were back on earth suffering a schizoid-embolism?" That's an irrelevant question: we are asking whether his belief *in his actual circumstances* reliably tracks the truth. And according to the film, his actual circumstances are that he is on Mars, saving the planet. To the question – would Quaid believe he was on Mars if he were back on Earth just going about his ordinary business – the answer is: no, he would not. Put Quaid back on Earth and he would have no trouble spotting the difference; the difference isn't subtle, after all. So, according the Dretskean theorist, Quaid knows perfectly well that he is on Mars. His doubts are misplaced. But of course, he doubts are anything but foolish. *Total Recall* is brilliantly set up to illustrate just how someone can be a reliable truth-tracker and yet be beset by entirely legitimate doubts. It seems that Quaid *ought* to doubt that he is on Mars given his experiences over the last few days, and not just doubt it in the abstruse way skeptics doubt just about everything, but *seriously* doubt it. (Indeed this is exactly what he does at various points in the film; had he been a bit smarter he would have doubted it more regularly.) It seems rather odd to say of a person that they know something, but ought to seriously doubt whether it is true. *I know that p, but I ought to seriously doubt whether it is true.* This sounds rather paradoxical.

So what has gone wrong? Here is one diagnosis. Dretske's test works very well a lot of the time. However, it is too much of a *one size fits all* solution. And it is insufficiently sensitive to the way believers don't just track the truth (like the heads of sunflowers track the sun), but also track reasons. Two people can track truths as reliably as one another and yet differ completely in what they have reason to believe. One person may have reason to doubt the veracity of their experience (Quaid). Another person may have no such reason (Melina). Attributions of knowledge should keep track of the reasons people have to doubt or not doubt their beliefs. It shouldn't just keep track of the external status of their performance as epistemic agents.

We don't want to throw the baby out with the bathwater. Is there any way of modifying Dretske's test so that it gets the right result both with cases like Melina's and with cases like Quaid's? Here is a stab at one. It consists of two questions which must both be answered in the negative in order for any true belief to count as knowledge.

> Truth-tracking: Would I still believe p, if it were false?
> Reason-responding: Do I have a good reason to think that not p?

A true belief that effectively tracks the truth and effectively responds to reasons in the way this test specifies counts as knowledge.[8] Of course, this doesn't get us very far without an account of what a "good reason" is. But this is something we can't investigate here. Intuitively, Quaid has good reason to think he is not on Mars (all the coincidences that have dogged him in his adventure; the mere fact that he paid for an adventure entitled "Blue Sky on Mars" and here he is looking at a blue sky on Mars; and so on.) Melina, on the other hand, doesn't have a good reason to think she isn't on Mars. I don't have a good reason to think that the hand I see before me (imagine one of the authors waving his hand in front of his face) isn't really there.[9] The key point in the battle with skepticism is that skeptical possibilities don't, in the normal run of things, give us good reasons to doubt ordinary beliefs. It's just that Quaid's run has been anything but normal.

Questions

Cogito ergo sum (I think therefore I am) is Descartes' Archimedean point. Archimedes claimed (rightly) that if you could supply a fixed point (one that never moved) and a perfectly rigid lever of sufficient length (it would have to be long), then a person could move the Earth with their own strength. Was Descartes able to move the skeptic out of the way from his own Archimedean point, using his own powers of reason and nothing else? What does absolutely certain knowledge of your own existence yield apart from absolutely certain knowledge of your own existence? If all you know is that you exist, how do you know you are a "thinking thing"? What made Descartes confident of this? What else could he be confident of?

Were we right to claim that Quaid really is on Mars (in the movie)? Is there support for a more ambiguous interpretation of the film? We claimed that the film was constructed in the third person because there are many scenes in which we see what happens quite independently of Quaid's viewpoint. If it is all a delusion, what parts of the delusion are these third-person bits? Can you have a delusion in the third person? Would it still be a successful delusion?

Most skeptical films (i.e. films that play with skeptical themes) work by putting the audience in a skeptical predicament (i.e. the audience, identifying with a protagonist in the film, doesn't know what is real any more than the protagonist does). *Total Recall* works in the opposite way. It shows a protagonist who doesn't know what is real – who should be beset with doubts and who should reject his beliefs about what is real or at least accept that he doesn't know – all the while showing the audience what is in fact real (in the movie). We claimed that this is a much more interesting scenario for the study of knowledge and skepticism than the usual run of skeptical films. Are we right? Why?

We concentrated on one skeptical argument and claimed that it presupposes the closure principle. If we can knock out the closure principle, we can dismiss the skeptic's argument. Is Dretske successful in refuting the closure principle? He gives an account of knowledge in which the closure principle no longer applies universally. But is this a satisfactory account of knowledge? We criticized Dretske's account of knowledge in the chapter. (Indeed the great value of the film is that it puts pressure on Dretske's account.) Does this mean that the skeptic's argument is now back in play? (Maybe not. It depends upon what aspect of Dretske's theory survives our criticism; or indeed upon whether our criticism works at all).

At the end of the chapter we proposed a hybrid account of knowledge: knowledge requires both truth-tracking and reason-responding. The account was concocted to deal with the *Total Recall* example, whilst keeping as many of the merits of Dretske's account as possible. The reason-responding element of the account is very minimal. It requires only that one not have sufficient reason to reject the belief in question. Should this be made stronger? Should we have a positive reason to believe in a proposition in order for our belief to count as knowledge? What would be the strengths and drawbacks of such a revision?

There are many different accounts of knowledge in contemporary philosophy. We have discussed only two accounts (Dretske's theory and our hybrid modification of it). Certain other philosophical accounts of knowledge rest on the idea that a belief's counting as knowledge is something that varies from context to context. If you are asked by a friend if you know where your car is parked, you might be able to say, correctly, that you do. (You remember parking it.) If asked by a skeptical philosopher, all bets are off. This kind of theory of knowledge is called "contextualism." There are numerous varieties of it. Do you think that knowledge-claims vary from context to context like this? What might be done with the theories we have discussed to make them compatible with contextualism?

Notes

1   Other films with interesting skeptical themes include *The Usual Suspects* (1995), *Open Your Eyes* (1997) and its US remake *Vanilla Sky* (2001), *The Truman Show* (1998), *Dark City* (1998), *The Matrix* (1999), *The Thirteenth Floor* (1999), and *Inception* (2010). (As you can see from our list, the late 1990s were a high-water mark for films about skepticism.)

2   Terraformation is a process of transforming the atmosphere, climate, and surface of a planet so that it becomes habitable by humans. The terratransformation of Mars has been suggested quite seriously. See Fogg (1995).

3   Mark Rowland exploits this crisis to argue, rather persuasively, for the psychological continuity theory of personal identity. (See our discussion of personal identity in chapter 8.)

4   The filmmakers themselves appear rather confused on this issue. In the audio commentary to the 2005 Universal DVD release of the film, both the film's director, Paul Verhoeven, and its star, Arnold Schwarzenegger, insist that the film is completely open to two interpretations: a dream interpretation and a realist interpretation. They appear not to appreciate the full significance of their film's third-person perspective.

5   Perhaps the most famous skeptical argument of this kind is Descartes' dreaming argument, introduced in his *Meditations on First Philosophy*. Descartes asks us whether there are any certain marks by which we can tell that we are awake rather than dreaming. Any criterion we might try to use (we pinch ourselves; we try turning on a light-switch) could be one we are dreaming, so it can't be used to definitively mark out dreaming from waking experience. Eventually (in Meditation Six), Descartes tries to show that there are criteria for distinguishing waking from dreaming that we can be completely certain about, but when he first introduces the argument (Meditation One) there seems to be no grounds at all for such optimism.

6   Some philosophers have attempted to reject premise (1). (1) says that we don't know that we are not the victim of a skeptical scenario. We don't know that

we aren't having a schizoid-embolism. Or we don't know that we are not now dreaming. Or we don't know that we are not what philosophers call "a brain in a vat" being fed signals from a computer (as depicted in *The Matrix* (1999)). Putnam (1981) argues that we can prove we aren't a brain in a vat. Using philosophy!

7 In spite of the fact that her last line in the film makes her sound like a dream-figment. She says (at 1:44) "Then kiss me before you wake up." She should have said, "Then kiss me before I wake up." Apart from being an exercise in sexism, Melina's dialogue is an attempt by the filmmakers to press the schizoid-embolism interpretation. As we have seen, however, they completely undermine all such attempts by shooting much of the film from a non-Quaid perspective.

8 Philosophers distinguish between internalist and externalist accounts of knowledge. Internalists tie knowledge to some condition accessible to the believer (for example, justification). Externalists don't do this. They tie knowledge to some condition that need not be accessible to the believer (e.g. reliability of belief-forming processes). This account is internalist because whether or not one has a good reason to believe something looks like a condition we should potentially be aware of.

9 This example is based on G. E. Moore's famous proof that an external world exists. See Moore (1959, chapter 7).

Further Reading

Descartes, René (1996). *Meditations on First Philosophy*, trans. John Cottingham. Cambridge: Cambridge University Press.

Dretske, Fred (1970). "Epistemic Operators." *Journal of Philosophy* 67, 1007–23.

Dretske, Fred (1971). "Conclusive Reasons." *Australasian Journal of Philosophy* 49, 1–22.

Dretske, Fred (1981). "The Pragmatic Dimension of Knowledge." *Philosophical Studies* 40, 363–78.

Fogg, Martyn J. (1995). *Terraforming: Engineering Planetary Environments.* Warrendale, PA: Society of Automotive Engineers.

Gettier, Edmund L. (1963). "Is Justified True Belief Knowledge?" *Analysis* 23, 121–3.

Klein, Peter (1981). *Certainty: A Refutation of Skepticism.* Minneapolis: University of Minnesota Press.

Kornblith, H., ed. (2001). *Epistemology: Internalism and Externalism.* Oxford: Blackwell.

Moore, G. E. (1959). *Philosophical Papers.* New York: Macmillan.

Nagel, Thomas (1986). *The View from Nowhere.* Oxford: Oxford University Press.

Nozick, Robert (1981). *Philosophical Explanations.* Oxford: Oxford University Press.

Putnam, Hilary (1981). *Reason, Truth and History*. New York: Cambridge University Press.

Steup, Matthias (1996). *An Introduction to Contemporary Epistemology*. Upper Saddle River, NJ: Prentice Hall.

Steup, Matthias, & Ernest Sosa, eds. (2005). *Contemporary Debates in Epistemology*. Malden, MA: Blackwell.

Unger, P. (1975). *Ignorance: A Case for Scepticism*. Oxford: Clarendon Press.

4

Ontology and *The Matrix*

Studying Ontology

Neo takes a pill and wakes up. He learns that he has a second body, one which lies naked and hairless, immersed in a kind of gel, in a pod. All his life, this second body has lain in its pod, connected to a giant computer through a spike in the back of its head. The computer stimulates the pod-body's sensory system. In doing this, it embeds Neo in a virtual world, one shared with millions of other people. This is the matrix.[1] Neo has been using the brain of the pod-body – his pod-brain – to think, to make decisions, to be conscious, to love and hate and fear all the things he has loved and hated and feared. He has been using the computer for everything else. It supplies the environment in which he lives; it provides the conduit through which he is able to communicate with other pod-brains. It provides his matrix body image (which, curiously, resembles his pod-body in everything except hair). The computer does all this by storing, updating, and controlling a flow of information. Neo has been what philosophers like to call a brain in a vat.

The Matrix (1999) depicts Neo's discovery of life outside the matrix and the war that rages still between un-podded humanity and the machines that created and control the matrix. But what should we think about life inside the matrix: the virtual world Neo has been living in all his life? How are we to understand the relation between the two worlds? Is one world real, while the other is mere appearance or even illusion? Is Neo outside the matrix more in touch with reality than Neo inside the matrix (before

Thinking Through Film: Doing Philosophy, Watching Movies, First Edition. Damian Cox, Michael P. Levine.
© 2012 Damian Cox and Michael P. Levine. Published 2012 by Blackwell Publishing Ltd.

he took the pill and before he became adept at moving back and forwards between worlds)? When we ask such heavy-duty questions about the nature of reality we are raising a basic issue in metaphysics: the issue of ontology. Ontology is branch of metaphysics that seeks to answer "What exists?" and "What is real?" It is concerned with questions about the kinds of things that exist and their natures.

We will introduce the philosophical study of ontology by way of an example. Do minds exist? Perhaps it seems obvious that they do, so let us ask a slightly different question. If we were to make a list of all the things that exist but left out any mention of minds and states of mind like intention, belief, hope, love, fear, and joy, would the list be incomplete? The list might include brains, all that goes on inside them, and all they interact with. It just wouldn't include any special mention of minds. Say that you see two people in the street arguing. Our list might include the people and the noises they make, and the immediate causes of these noises in neural pathways that send instructions to the vocal cords, and so on. It wouldn't include mention of the fact that the first person has forgotten an appointment with the second person and the second person thinks this a clear sign that the first person does not love them, or does not love them enough. If you think that this kind of commonsense psychological talk could in principle be replaced by more precise or scientifically respect-able talk – not for practical purposes but for explanatory purposes – then you reject the idea that minds are ontologically fundamental. You might think that the world consists of particles in space–time and that everything that happens in the world could be explained – in principle – in terms of what happens to these particles. If so, then you might be a reductionist about minds or you might be an eliminativist about minds. These are philosophical terms of art; let us introduce them informally.

The reductionist about minds thinks that when we talk about minds and mental states, our language really picks out facts about something else. It might pick out facts about brains and their activities. Perhaps it picks out facts about brains and their interactions with their environment (which includes their body and its surroundings, other bodies, and other brains). Perhaps it picks out other kinds of facts. If reductionists are right, talk of minds can be replaced for explanatory purposes by talk about other things. This means that we aren't ontologically committed to the existence of minds as a special category. Minds are not, in the reductionist's view, ontologically fundamental. Because mind-talk is reducible to talk of other things, minds exist only as an aspect of the way other things are.

On the other hand, eliminativists about minds think that when we talk about minds, we are advancing a fundamentally false theory of the world.

Eliminativists think that we should replace talk of minds with more sci-entifically respectable talk, say about activation of neural pathways. If eliminativists are right, talk of minds and their special properties no more refers to real things than talk of witches and *their* special properties refers to real witches and real magic. Nothing in the world has the core properties we ascribe to witches, so witches don't exist. According to eliminativists about the mind, nothing in the world has the core prop-erties we ascribe to minds, so minds don't exist. Reductionists believe in minds, but don't think they are ontologically fundamental. Eliminativists don't believe that there is any such thing as minds (as we conceive of them) at all.

Philosophers who think minds are ontologically fundamental are tra-ditionally called dualists.[2] They have a fundamental ontology that consists of at least two kinds of things: minds and material objects.[3] As you might expect, matters of ontology get rather complicated, rather quickly. Minds and their place in our ontology are only some of the things we have to worry about. We also have to worry about material objects (trees, clouds, mountains, motorbikes, and so on), and about mathematical objects (numbers, sets, geometrical shapes – things that appear to be neither material nor mental). There are further kinds or categories of things whose ontological status is unclear and disputed. These are things like possible worlds, space, time, gods, and so on. You will also find philosophers arguing over fundamental metaphysical categories. Do universals exist? (These are properties, like "having a mass of exactly one gram," which are said to inhere in objects, to be wholly present in the objects they inhere in, and thus to exist, in full, in many places at the same time.) Do unin-stantiated universals exist? (These are universals out of luck, not managing to inhere in any object in the actual world.) Does the fundamental ontol-ogy of the world include objects? Or does it only include states of affairs or events? Or is it made up of something else entirely? (Objects are just what you would expect them to be; states of affairs are ways that things are; and events are happenings. A car is an object. A car's being a red car is a state of affairs. A car's now absorbing all visible light frequencies except red is an event.)

Philosophers have a busy time trying to understand the fundamental ontology of the world. How can the *Matrix Trilogy* enlighten us about this branch of philosophy? It provides us with a kind of ontological laboratory: a fictional test case in which we can examine the business of settling on the most reasonable ontology and asking questions about the nature of reality and the relation between thought and reality. We are going to proceed by setting out three different interpretations of the matrix scenario: a *Cartesian interpretation*, a *realist interpretation* and a *Platonic interpretation*.

The Cartesian Interpretation

You might think that Neo has every right to be angry at the machines. After all, it seems they have been fooling him all the while: making him think that he is living in a nice, clean, safe city in 1999, with a job in software development. In fact he isn't living in 1999, the real world isn't nice and isn't clean, and he doesn't have a job as a software developer. He has a job as a battery. It looks like Neo has been living an illusion. This is primarily a skeptical interpretation of *The Matrix* – see our discussion of skepticism in chapter 3 – but it has important consequences for ontology. We will call it the Cartesian interpretation of the matrix scenario.

We call it the Cartesian Interpretation in honor of the seventeenth-century French philosopher René Descartes. In his *Meditations on First Philosophy*, Descartes imagined a predicament scarily reminiscent of the matrix scenario. Descartes was searching for an absolutely secure foundation for our knowledge of the world. Is it possible to find a set of beliefs so clearly and obviously true that they cannot be doubted by any rational and sane person? And could we use this set of beliefs as the foundation of our best scientific understanding of the world? Descartes thought we could find such a set of beliefs, and he had a method for finding it. He called it "the method of doubt." It works likes this. If it is at all possible that a belief is false, then it can't serve as an absolutely secure foundation for knowledge (because it isn't absolutely secure). So we examine our beliefs as systematically as we can and reject any belief that could be false. As long as it is barely possible that a belief is false, we will do without it. We then see if it is possible to do philosophy with what remains.

There's no point going through all our beliefs one at a time (that would take forever), so Descartes used some shortcuts. His most powerful shortcut is called the *evil demon hypothesis*. This is how Descartes (1996, Meditation One) describes the hypothesis:

> I will suppose . . . some malicious demon of the utmost power and cunning has employed all his energies in order to deceive me. I shall think that the sky, the air, the earth, colours, shapes, sounds and all external things are merely delusions of dreams which he has devised to ensnare my judgement. I shall consider myself as not having hands or eyes, or flesh, or blood or senses, but as falsely believing that I have all these things.

The evil demon hypothesis allows us to exclude any belief that could have been instilled in us by a deceiving demon. That's a lot of beliefs. In a first run through, the only belief that I wouldn't be able to exclude is my belief that I exist. If I think that I exist, then I do. Something must be doing the thinking. And that is me. I am a thinking thing. So my belief that I exist and that I think survives the method of doubt (so long as I continue thinking of course; if I stop thinking, all bets are off). This is Descartes' absolutely certain foundation for our knowledge of the world. Descartes hoped to do much more than prove that he exists, of course. He hoped eventually to disprove the evil demon hypothesis itself. And he thought he could do this by proving the existence of a good and non-deceiving God, one that would certainly not leave us to the mercy of an evil demon. (To find out how Descartes got from *I think therefore I am* to the existence of God, we recommend that you read through the *Meditations*.)

The matrix scenario looks like an updated version of Descartes' evil demon hypothesis. As the character called Morpheus puts it, the matrix is "the world that has been pulled over your eyes to blind you from the truth" (28:17). Instead of an evil demon, *The Matrix* depicts evil machines and the shadowy figure of the Architect as the creators of the matrix. Whereas Descartes offers no explanation of how the evil demon instills false thoughts in us, *The Matrix* tells us how the Architect works. He works by programming a computer. According to the Cartesian interpretation of the matrix scenario, the end result is the same. The matrix is a world of illusion, instilling false beliefs in its victims. If the Cartesian interpretation is correct, then the right stance to take towards objects of matrix experience is an eliminativist one. Inside the matrix people might think that they work in a skyscraper. They think they can see it. But the skyscraper doesn't exist. In reality there is nothing made of concrete and steel and towering eighty floors. Belief that there is such a thing is simply false. And this generalizes to most of the beliefs people inside the matrix have about their environment. Their beliefs are radically false. What they say exists, simply doesn't. A true ontological reckoning would eliminate all talk of skyscrapers and the like. (Their philosophical problem, of course, is that they have no way of arriving at a true ontological reckoning; not until they leave the matrix and enter the desert of the real.)

The Realist Interpretation

Is the Cartesian interpretation right? The filmmakers flirt with the Cartesian interpretation at various points in the film. At 1:08 Neo says "I have these memories of my life [he means his life in the matrix]. None of them happened." However, the film itself can't settle the question we are asking.

We are looking for a philosophical interpretation of what the film portrays; not an interpretation of what the filmmakers intended it to portray. So let us consider Neo's experience and beliefs in a more philosophical light. Before he took the red pill and left the matrix, what ordinary beliefs did Neo get wrong? Pre-pill Neo thinks he is in trouble with his boss. He *is* in trouble with his boss. He is in matrix-trouble with his matrix-boss. That's trouble enough. If he gets fired and goes hungry it won't much matter that he is only matrix-fired and is only matrix-hungry. Matrix-hungry is hungry enough. The key to understanding thought within the matrix is to reflect on the contents of beliefs. What are a person's beliefs *about*? How do beliefs acquire the content they do? Where does this content come from? The most plausible answer to this last question is that beliefs get their content from the environment believers interact with. If pre-pill Neo says in all good faith "here is a spoon," he is talking about the spoons he has interacted with in his environment. He is not trying to talk about spoons outside the matrix, like the crude devices you might encounter in Zion.[4] Zion-spoons are fundamentally different from matrix-spoons. Matrix-spoons are products of the information-processing of the machines; they are made of matrix-code. Zion-spoons are not; they are made of metal or wood. Pre-pill Neo has never interacted with a Zion-spoon. He has never seen or handled one, or talked to anybody who has. (At least he hasn't talked to them about spoons.) The spoons of Zion aren't part of his environment, so they aren't what his claims about spoons refer to. When pre-pill Neo talked about spoons (which we suppose wasn't all that often) he was talking about what he interacts with and these are matrix-spoons. And what he says about them is mostly quite true.[5]

Most beliefs inside the matrix are vindicated by this strategy. The strategy involves interpreting thought and speech inside the matrix in terms of the elements of the matrix-environment itself. Once we get our matrix-semantics right, matrix-beliefs turn out to be true by and large. Thus the Cartesian interpretation is wrong. The world of the matrix is not an illusion. That is, it does not make its denizens think that they are seeing something that isn't there or make them ascribe a property to an object that isn't a property of that object. The objects of matrix-thought are there: they are there in the matrix. And, generally speaking, they have the properties ascribed to them. If pre-pill Neo says that a spoon is stainless steel, chances are it is stainless steel: it is matrix-stainless matrix-steel. (What else was it supposed to be?) The matrix is a virtual world with its own spatiotemporal order and its own ontology of objects and properties, events and processes. We shouldn't be eliminativist about matrix-beliefs. We should be reductionist about them. Let's see why.

Inside the matrix, Neo refers to a spoon. So Neo is committed to the existence of spoons (or at least one spoon). But what *is* this thing he is committed to? To a first approximation, a matrix-spoon is a structured array of information stored in the machines' computer together with certain operations performed on this information. Matrix-spoons are bundles of information, for short. This goes for all material objects in the matrix. They are not ontologically fundamental. They exist, but only as aspects of something more fundamental: bundles of information. We should take the same approach to space in the matrix. Material objects in the matrix exist in a three-dimensional matrix-space, but matrix-space isn't ontologically fundamental. It exists as an informational structure, something that coordinates the way bundles of information interact with each other. Matrix-space is real, but it is just another aspect of the operation of the machines' computer.

Now you might be tempted to object that matrix-space isn't really *space*. For one thing, it doesn't take up room – it's not extended – so shouldn't we be eliminativist about objects supposedly existing in matrix-space? Our reply goes like this. It might be true that matrix-space isn't space-like in certain ways. It has certain formal characteristics of space without being fully space-like. Indeed. But matrix-space is still real; the informational structure is real. And claims about matrix-objects in matrix-space are still mostly true. This is why we should be reductionists about objects in matrix-space rather than eliminativists about them.

What about people? They seem to exist in the matrix. Are they reducible to information and its processing in the machines' computer? The answer is no. In the matrix, people consist of bodies and minds. Their bodies are generated by the machines, but their minds are not. Matrix-minds depend upon what happens inside pod-brains, not matrix-brains.[6] The machines can't control what people will choose, how they will act, what they will feel, what they will say, and so on.[7] Perhaps dualism about mind and body is the correct theory for matrix-people. The minds of matrix-people don't exist in the same spatial system as the bodies of matrix-people. They are ontologically distinct. And yet body and mind interact in the matrix. First, the body sends the mind signals about its environment. This is called sensation and involves signals traveling from matrix to pod-brain up the spike in the back of the pod-head. Second, the mind interprets these signals and responds to them by sending signals of its own back down the spike. It gets a signal from its body *There is a spoon in my hand* and it sends back a signal *Well then stir the coffee!* This is a rough description of the most famous version of dualism, called "Cartesian dualism" once more in honor of René Descartes, its most famous advocate. According to Cartesian dualism, a person consists of a mind and a body. Minds are distinct from bodies, but minds and bodies interact with each other in both directions. Minds affect bodies and bodies affect minds. Even if a Cartesian interpretation of the matrix – one that interprets matrix objects and matrix events as illusions – fails, it seems that at least Cartesian dualism is true for matrix-people.[8]

What we have been describing is the realist interpretation of the matrix scenario. According to this interpretation, matrix beliefs can be true and, indeed, often are true. Admittedly, they only track what is going on in the machines' computer and in the brains hooked up to it. But an awful lot is going on in there. The matrix is real. When people inside the matrix theorize about their condition and develop an account of the ontology of the world, that ontology is not radically mistaken. It is an accurate account of at least a small part of the world: the matrix world.

The Platonic Interpretation

Morpheus tells Neo that the matrix is a world pulled down over his eyes to blind him from the truth (0:28). Is he wrong? Not really. The matrix may not blind Neo to ordinary truths, but it blinds him to some pretty big ones: that he has a second body; that his world is designed by the Architect to keep people docile while machines exploit their second bodies as a source of power; that machines won a war against humans; that humans destroyed the atmosphere of Earth in order to deprive machines of access to solar power; and so on. While trapped inside the matrix, Neo didn't understand the true nature of things. But during the course of the film Neo is freed from the matrix and comes to understand deep truths.

This set of ideas has a very ancient lineage in philosophy. Much the same story is told by Plato in *The Republic*. Plato imagines a cave, in which prisoners are tied up and forced to look at a wall. (Their heads are secured so they can see nothing but the wall.) Behind the prisoners a fire burns brightly, and in front of this fire, hidden by a trench, guards walk up and down. The guards hold objects up over the trench, and these objects cast shadows on the wall. All the prisoners ever observe are shadows on the wall. The real objects are behind them, forever hidden from them. (Notice here that Plato has just invented the cinema.) Because the prisoners never experience the objects themselves, but only the shadows of objects, they take the shadows for reality. Plato then imagines one prisoner getting free. The prisoner turns around and sees the fire, sees the originals of the shadows and realizes that hitherto she has fundamentally misunderstood the nature of her world. She finds her way out of the cave into the daylight and comes across the blinding magnificence of the Sun: the source of all light. Returning to the cave, the escaped prisoner tries to tell her fellow prisoners about her adventures in the real world. But her sight is no longer adapted to the shadowy world of the cave. She can no longer keep track of the play of shadows on the wall. And she seems to speak utter nonsense. The other prisoners dismiss her as a fool.

Plato's analogy of the cave is designed to illustrate the path of the philosopher from ignorance of the true nature of things to knowledge of ultimate reality. Plato is one of the great optimists of western philosophy. He thinks that the philosophical application of reason can free us from the shackles of our ignorance and lead us to a profound understanding of what is ultimately real. Plato thought that what was ultimately real were "forms." These are perfect, changeless, ideal objects that stand as the archetypes of ordinary objects. Ordinary objects are imperfect, forever in flux, forever growing or diminishing or decaying. They are inferior copies of the real thing. The world of ordinary experience is much like the world of shadows on the cave wall. Plato doesn't deny that shadows exist; he merely observes that the shadows are mere copies of something else and one doesn't understand their nature at all until one realizes this fact. According to Plato, our everyday understanding of the world is inadequate in the same way and we fail to move beyond it until we realize that the objects of our everyday thoughts are mere copies of the forms.

The parallel with the matrix scenario is easy to spot. Inside the matrix, one is a prisoner (in a pod) observing shadows on a wall (virtual computer scenarios). Neo is the freed prisoner, who eventually comes to understand the most esoteric truths about the world of the machines. Of course, there are some differences. Unlike Plato's world of the forms, the world of the machines is not a realm of perfection. It is a dirty and depressing world. Morpheus calls it the desert of the real (0:41). Unlike the returning prisoner in Plato's story, who stumbles about in the semi-dark, Neo returns to the matrix with superpowers. And anyway he has bigger fish to fry than talking to a few pod-people about life outside the matrix. In spite of these differences, the Platonic interpretation of the matrix captures the fundamental setup of the *Matrix Trilogy* very well. The world of the matrix exists well enough, but it is merely a copy of the real thing. This is the Platonic interpretation of the matrix. It doesn't contradict the basic claim of the realist interpretation, rather it extends it. The realist interpretation asserts the existence of matrix-objects and the truth of claims about them. The temptation is to go on to equate existence with reality: the matrix-world is just as real as the world of Zion; they both exist after all and something is real if and only if it exists. The Platonic interpretation resists this temptation. It equates reality with something more than existence.

One way to express the basic point of the Platonic interpretation is this: the world outside the matrix is *more real* than the world inside the matrix. Reality comes in degrees. Reality is not the same thing as existence. Things either exist or they do not exist. By contrast, things can be more real or less real. The shadows on the wall of Plato's cave are less real that the objects that cast them. A matrix-spoon is less real than a Zion-spoon. What determines that one thing is more real than another? In both Plato's cave and the matrix scenario, the question is one of authenticity. A Zion-spoon is the more authentic article because the matrix-spoon is a copy of it. A Zion-spoon is the real deal; a matrix-spoon is a bit of a fake. Interpreting levels of reality in terms of authenticity makes sense when applied to Plato's theory of forms and it works well for the matrix scenario. But it isn't very philosophically interesting unless you subscribe to Plato's theory of forms or you think that *The Matrix* is a documentary.

Is there a more philosophically interesting way of defining degrees of reality, one that still does justice to the story of Plato's cave and of Neo's pod, but does not equate reality with authenticity? Perhaps there is. We might try defining degrees of reality like this:

> Object α is more real than object β if the theory that posits α is a more complete and accurate account of the world than the theory that posits β.

The matrix-eye view of things is not so much false as radically impoverished. And the ontology of a matrix-philosopher is not so much radically mistaken as superficial. So the elements of a matrix-philosopher's ontology will be less real than the elements of, say, the Architect's ontology. The matrix-philosopher is less in touch with reality. It's not just that he is in touch with less of the world, he is less in touch with the world.

The most important philosophical lesson to be learned from the Platonic interpretation is not necessarily Plato's, or even Neo's. Plato, as we noted, was a great optimist about the capacity of philosophical reflection to free us from the cave of ignorance and reveal ultimate reality to us. The *Matrix Trilogy* gives us pause for thought about such optimism. On what grounds can we be confident that ultimate reality is something we can know? Does even our best science give us a complete and accurate picture of the way things are, or does it yield only an inadequate and superficial picture of certain aspects of the world? (Past scientific theories have been shown wrong, why think that present theories will fare any better? Why think that *any* future theory will fare better?) Perhaps the world is much deeper and more mysterious than it seems. Perhaps the most sensible attitude to take towards knowledge of ultimate reality is a skeptical one. We wouldn't know that we had such knowledge even if we had it.

We can add to these thoughts another one. Our capacity for creating concepts, constructing theories, and observing phenomena are derived from the functionality of our brains. Our brains evolved to do some pretty basic things: keep track of who we are related to, of where the food is, of who might have sex with us, and so on. Is it reasonable to assume that a brain that evolved to deal with the problems and opportunities of social primates has the right stuff to understand the nature of ultimate reality? Why think that? There is almost no chance that we are stuck inside a matrix. Is it plausible at all to think that we are stuck within a drama whose point revolves largely around us? Yet we may well be stuck inside something or other, the nature of which we have no idea at all – the nature of which we *can* have no idea at all. Perhaps the world makes sense; it's just that it's not going to make sense to us. The great biologist J. B. S. Haldane (1930: 286) summed up this thought very nicely:

> I have no doubt that in reality the future will be vastly more surprising than anything I can imagine. Now my own suspicion is that the Universe is not only queerer than we suppose, but queerer than we *can* suppose.

Questions

Does it matter to you whether or not your experiences are real, and if so, why?

Are their alternative "realties" that might be preferable, for any number of reasons, to our own? Would it nevertheless be irrational to choose such an alternative?

We introduced the terms "eliminativism" and "reductionism" in the chapter. The Cartesian interpretation is eliminativist about matrix-objects. The Realist interpretation is reductionist about them. What is the Platonic interpretation's view of them?

We said in the chapter that "The key to understanding thought within the matrix is to reflect on the contents of beliefs. What are a person's beliefs about? How do beliefs acquire the content they do? Where does this content come from?" Why is this move so important? How does it show that ordinary beliefs of matrix-citizens are true? Does it show that they are true? What assumptions were being made in the Cartesian interpretation that led to the opposite conclusion?

Matrix-space isn't space-like. And matrix-objects aren't object-like because they don't have space-like properties and because they are not discrete existences. When matrix-citizens think that they are holding an object – a spoon, say – they wrongly conclude that it is an object. They think it exists in space (it doesn't). They think it has spatial-properties (it doesn't). They think it has weight. (It has no weight: it is an informational structure; it resides in various parts of the computer at different times; it isn't a discrete package of silicon chips, for example, and as such is weightless.) How good is this argument? Might the Cartesian interpretation of the matrix be right after all?

In the chapter we contrasted two ways in which one might say that reality comes in degrees: reality as authenticity; and reality as theory-dependent. (In the latter version, an object counts as more real than another if the theory that posits it is more complete and accurate than the other. Thus a cup is less real than an electron.) Does either of these accounts portray an intuitively plausible picture of what it might be for one thing to be more real than another? Can reality come in degrees? Or is the reality of a thing the same as its existence?

At the very end of the chapter, we hinted at an argument for skepticism about ultimate reality. How plausible is the argument? (The argument claims, roughly, that it is extremely unlikely (would indeed be miraculous) if our limited, contingently evolved cognitive capacities had the power to grasp the truth about ultimate reality.)

We only ever experience and conceive of things through our own perceptual and cognitive systems. We can never see or understand things as they are "in themselves." Thus ultimate reality is something that it is impossible to experience or think about in a completely undistorted way. How does this argument relate to the argument for skepticism about ultimate reality that we introduced in the chapter? Is it a good argument?

Notes

1   *The Matrix* (1999), written and directed by the Wachowski brothers. It is the first of a trilogy, including *The Matrix Reloaded* (2003) and *The Matrix Revolutions* (2003).

2   Dualism is the most common way of incorporating into one's philosophy the claim that minds and their properties are fundamental constituents of reality. There are other ways. Panpsychism is the view that all of reality has mental attributes. (For example, the seventeenth-century Dutch philosopher Baruch Spinoza held that everything in the world can be understood as both mental and physical at the same time. See Spinoza (1994).) Idealism is the view that all of reality *is* mental. (For example, the eighteenth-century Irish philosopher George Berkeley held that material objects are nothing more than collections of ideas. See Berkeley (1993).) We will concentrate on dualism for the purposes of our study of ontology.

3   There are two main kinds of dualists: substance dualists and property dualists. The substance dualist believes in two kinds of things: material things and mental things. Accordingly, they tend to believe that a person is made up of two fundamentally different kinds of substance (body and mind or body and soul). On the other hand, property dualists deny that a person is composed of two different substances. A person is not an amalgam of two different things. A person is a single entity with two kinds of property – physical properties and mental properties – neither of which can be reduced to the other, or eliminated from our theory of persons.

4   Zion is the city settled by those liberated from the matrix or born outside of it. The fate of Zion looms large in the second and third parts of the *Matrix Trilogy*.

5   When later on in the first *Matrix* film a spoon-bending kid advises Neo that to bend the spoon he must first realize that there is no spoon (1:12), the kid gets it wrong. How does Neo (and the spoon-bending kid) get to alter matrix-code from within the matrix? We don't know. As the trilogy of *Matrix* films proceeds, Neo comes to resemble a cross between superman and Jesus, and his miraculous powers extend further and further. By the end of the trilogy he is able to stop machines in their tracks just by thinking at them and holding up a hand. Of course, films are not required to be particularly sensible; especially when their basic premise has the world run by evil machines. Audiences tend to readily suspend disbelief and ignore peripheral inconsistencies and confusions provided that narrative logic is maintained in a convincing way.

6   Perhaps not much at all is going on inside matrix-brains. It depends upon how fully the machines have sought to copy the physical world. They could probably have gotten away without introducing code for many brain processes, at least until matrix-people invent accurate brain-imaging techniques. But even if matrix-brains are deeply structured to resemble pod-brains, and matrix-brain processes resemble pod-brain processes, it wouldn't follow that they cause matrix-thoughts. In the matrix scenario, matrix-brains would be epiphenomenal to the thoughts of matrix-people. This means that they are caused by these thoughts, but don't cause anything themselves. They are pure side-effect.

7   Agent Smith knows how to inhabit matrix-bodies and control them. Eventually he learns how to replicate himself, replacing matrix-people with replications

of himself. But, even here, Agent Smith is not controlling minds, he is destroying matrix-people, or at least making them inoperative. (Over the course of the trilogy, Agent Smith transforms into a computer virus that threatens the integrity of the matrix system. Ironically, having fought the system through two films, Neo becomes the savior of it in the third film, *Matrix Revolution,* by ridding the system of its infection. Neo is the ultimate anti-viral software.)

8   Perhaps it's not quite this simple. Matrix-minds and matrix-bodies are different things, but *how* different are they? That depends on your theory of the mind. Were you a materialist about the mind, you might think that the brain is a special kind of computer and the mind is just the software of this computer. This is a form of materialism called "computationalism." According to computationalism, human minds consist of information-processing taking place in a brain acting as computer. As we know, matrix-bodies are computer processes too, albeit ones occurring in a massive machine-built computer rather than in brains. So if you believe in computationalism, you should also think that matrix-bodies and minds are the same kind of thing. (Nonetheless, given Neo's spoon-bending, machine-stopping superpowers, the *Matrix Trilogy* doesn't seem to encourage a strictly computationalist interpretation of the mind's powers.)

Further Reading

Berkeley, George (1993). *Philosophical Works: Including the Works on Vision,* ed. Michael R. Ayers. London: Dent.

Churchland, Paul (1981). "Eliminative Materialism and the Propositional Attitudes." *Journal of Philosophy* 78, 67–90.

Descartes, René (1996). *Meditations on First Philosophy,* trans. John Cottingham. Cambridge: Cambridge University Press.

Haldane, J. B. S. (1930). *Possible Worlds and Other Papers.* London: Chatto and Windus.

Lawrence, Matt (2004). *Like a Splinter in your Mind: The Philosophy behind the Matrix Trilogy.* Malden, MA: Blackwell.

McGinn, Colin (1993). *Problems in Philosophy: The Limits of Inquiry.* Oxford: Blackwell.

Plato (2006). *The Republic,* translated and with an introduction by R. E. Allen. New Haven: Yale University Press.

Seager, William, & Sean Allen-Hermanson (2010). "Panpsychism." *Stanford Encyclopedia of Philosophy.* http://plato.stanford.edu/entries/panpsychism/

Spinoza, Baruch (1994). *The Ethics and Other Works,* ed. and trans. Edwin Curley. Princeton: Princeton University Press.

Van Inwagen, Peter, & Dean W. Zimmerman (1998). *Metaphysics: The Big Questions.* Oxford: Blackwell.

5

It's All in the Mind: *AI Artificial Intelligence* and Robot Love

Introduction

David is 11 years old. He weighs 60 pounds. He is 4 feet 6 inches tall. He has brown hair. His love is real. But he is not.

This is the tagline for Steven Spielberg's film *AI Artificial Intelligence* (2001). We are going to use the example of David as we examine the philosophy of artificial intelligence. At issue is an extraordinarily ambitious claim: that it is possible (perhaps in the distant future) to artificially create conscious intelligent beings; beings who don't just solve puzzles, but who understand what they solving, and why; who understand what are talking about, and understand who they are; who have real beliefs and real desires, feel real sensations and experience real emotions. The key philosophical question here is about possibility: is this even possible?[1] In the chapter, our chosen film won't shed much light on the issue. Instead, our philosophical discussion is designed to shed light on the film, and the possibility portrayed in the film. The primary question is whether artificially intelligent creatures can have an inner life, and the main reason films such as *AI* don't help us out much in trying to answer this question is that it is all too easy for films to cheat over the question. Science fiction films are often populated by conscious robots, but this doesn't help answer the question of whether such things are really possible. Films don't show us the inner life of characters, human or robotic; they leave us to infer this inner life, and they don't much differ from ordinary life in this respect.[2]

Thinking Through Film: Doing Philosophy, Watching Movies, First Edition. Damian Cox, Michael P. Levine.
© 2012 Damian Cox and Michael P. Levine. Published 2012 by Blackwell Publishing Ltd.

When a film presents us with something intended to function in the narrative as a conscious robot, we must infer its consciousness from the way it behaves. But there are many ways for filmmakers to ensure that we do this without advancing discussion of the question of whether the robot really is conscious.[3] We tend to attribute consciousness to a robot provided the robot's behavior appears intelligent, purposeful, and communicative, and provided the robot is treated in the film as if it is conscious (e.g. HAL in *2001 A Space Odyssey* (1968)). We are easily led to adopt what the philosopher Daniel Dennett (1989) calls "the intentional stance" towards such manifestations. Filmmakers make this process easier by giving the robot a human form (e.g. Sonny in *I Robot* (2004)). And they make it really easy by casting an actual person to play the robot (e.g. Robin Williams in *Bicentennial Man* (1999)). In *AI*, Spielberg was able to achieve his desired effect by casting a real boy, Haley Joel Osment, to play the robot boy (R2D2 be damned).

The film presents David as a fully conscious robot. It is unambiguous on this matter. As Professor Hobby announces at the beginning (0:06), David is to be a new kind of robot, one designed to have an inner life: to feel, to imagine, to long for things, to dream. Whether Hobby is right about David is a question that will occupy us throughout the chapter. David doesn't merely *appear* to be conscious. He is deeply, fully conscious. He not only seems to understand his surroundings, he struggles to satisfy his desires and he seems to feel emotions. He seems to have a boy's love for his mother (not his real mother, of course, but Monica, the person he adopts as his mother). He embarks on his quest to become a real boy (i.e. an organic boy) in order to win back Monica's love. The tagline informs us that his love is real, but how can it be? What does it take for love to be real? Before we work our way through some of the philosophy of artificial intelligence, it is worth pausing a moment to consider this question. What does it take for love to be real? It depends, of course, on what we mean by love.

A child doesn't love its parents in exactly the way that an adult might love another adult, or in exactly the way that an adult might love a child (though the similarities in both cases are worth attending to). A child's love is primarily a form of emotional dependence – an especially vivid sort of dependence, but a form of dependence nonetheless. David's love consists of a disposition to display affection – over and over again. It also consists of a kind of desperate need: a need for Monica's affection, attention, intimacy, concern, approval, and presence. David doesn't need Monica to care for him in a practical way (he is a robot and she isn't required to do maintenance on him). However, he needs her to care *about* him. David doesn't need Monica to be happy *per se*. He needs her to be happy *with him*: both pleased with him and happy in his company. In ancient Greece, philosophers distinguished between three kinds of love: *eros, agape,* and *philia*. *Eros* – typically, though not necessarily, erotic or sexual love – is based on desire and emotional need (an emotional need is a desire that may do significant emotional damage if unfulfilled). *Agape* is a kind of disinterested love: a love that invests someone with value rather than derives something of value from them. The model here is the love that God is sometimes said to have for humans and perhaps all of creation, or that of a parent for a child. *Philia*, by contrast, is a mixture of both. Paradigmatically, it is a form of pleasure taken in friendship and a concern and regard for one's friends. Viewed in the light of this three-way classification, a child's love for its parent seems to be a form of *eros* and David's love of Monica exemplifies this nicely. In this respect David's love of his mother is pretty much what you would expect of any healthy 11-year-old kid. He is affectionate, selfish, egocentric, needy, and vulnerable.

David's love for Monica may seem very much like a child's love, but does he really love her? Two things stand in the way of a positive answer to this question. The first is an issue we have already mentioned. David is a robot. He is not flesh and blood. He is "mecha," as they say in the movie. Is mecha-love an emotional experience at all? Perhaps it is a set of routine behaviors that do no more than mimic love-behavior. Perhaps it is something that looks a lot like love from the outside, but on the inside all is darkness. Maybe so. But there is a second reason to doubt the reality or authenticity of David's love of Monica. David was specifically designed to attach himself to a parental figure. Is designer love real love? Is it *authentic* love? David is designed to love – in his very own intense, childish way – the person who first imprints on him. The imprint protocol involves a person reciting a list of key words in order, while touching David's body at specific points. It's all rather cut and dried; and mechanical. Nonetheless, the imprinting scene in *AI* (starting at 21:45) is quite remarkable, thanks to Osment's subtle performance. Before imprinting, Osment plays David in a very stiff fashion, with a fixed, almost demented, smile. His face is either rigid or contorted into exaggerated expressiveness (as in the laughter scene at 19:50). On imprinting, David's features soften, his eyes focus in a more natural way, and his expression becomes more human. Imprinting transforms a robot into something much more person-like. But it is, nonetheless, a pre-installed procedure. It is not something David chooses to undertake or something that happens to him in the ordinary course of events. It is something that he is set up to undergo in a very particular way. Does this mean that his emotional attachment to Monica is artificial and inauthentic?

The concept of an *authentic* emotional experience is a tricky one, but it seems to have something to do with the cause of emotional experience. For example, were we to make a person happy by injecting them with a "happy drug," then their happiness would not seem to be authentic happiness. It hasn't been brought about in the right way, so to speak. The person isn't *really* happy, we might say; they are merely drugged up. In David's case, his love of Monica has a strange cause: a specifically designed imprinting procedure. David is designed to experience love immediately upon activation of the imprint program. Isn't this like injecting him with a "love drug"? Then again, the very idea of a child's *authentic* love for its parent may be inappropriate. Isn't David's imprint protocol in many ways an exaggerated version of the origin of any child's love? Children form emotional attachment to, and dependence on, their parents and at least part of this behavior is genetically caused. If we think that David's love is inauthentic because it is pre-installed, any child's love of its mother might also be inauthentic for much the same reason. We tend not to doubt the reality or authenticity of a child's love for its parents, so perhaps we shouldn't doubt David's love because of its designer origins.

If David's love is unreal, it isn't because it derives from a pre-installed imprinting program, but because he is a robot. David is a robotic device and perhaps robotic devices are really nothing more than complicated computational machines. Perhaps they cannot really understand anything or feel anything. There are two kinds of objection here. One imputes a sort of cognitive deficit to computational machines: they merely crunch numbers or symbols; they merely manipulate information; they cannot ever understand what they are saying and doing. The other objection imputes an emotional deficit: computational machines cannot feel anything; they might enact emotional protocols – behaving as if there they are happy or distraught – but inside the lights are out, they're not feeling anything. Just how good are the two objections? What are they based upon? We will dip into two philosophical fields in an attempt to answer them: philosophy of artificial intelligence and philosophy of mind.

Can a Robot Understand Anything?

Artificial intelligence is the science (and art) of creating machines that perform genuinely intelligent operations. Artificial intelligence systems can beat the best chess players in the world, win at *Jeopardy!*, help design a bridge so that it won't collapse if a truck crashes into one of its pylons, or compose music that is surprisingly listenable (and sometimes quite good). Artificial intelligence systems called chatterbots (also known as chatbots) can even have a conversation with you. Admittedly, the technology isn't perfect and chatterbot conversations can be pretty weird. Here is an example of a conversation between a human entity and a chatterbot. You won't have too much trouble working out which one is the human and which the artificial intelligence system.

GEORGE: Hello, my name is George and I am the human.
JOHN: Hello, I'm John.
GEORGE: Where are you from?
JOHN: I live on Martha's Vineyard.
GEORGE: I'm going to Mars and am going to smash your face with a baseball bat!
JOHN: . . . Well, let's just say that's a little rude.
GEORGE: I'm not bores.
JOHN: You're not bores? As in, an augur or something? A drill bit?
GEORGE: Just a bit.
JOHN: So, where are you from? And how old are you, etc?
GEORGE: I'm 39!
JOHN: And you reside . . . ?
GEORGE: No, I live in the Netherlands.
JOHN: Which part? Town or country? Also, do you grow flowers?
GEORGE: Lots. I'm about to plant tomatoes.
JOHN: A little late in the season for that.
GEORGE: No, a little animal.
JOHN: OK, enough for now. I'll go chat with the other entity.
GEORGE: Ok then it was nice to share your hair brush.
JOHN: What do mean by that? How have you shared my hair brush?
GEORGE: Good.
JOHN: Good?
GEORGE: Yes.
JOHN: This has become a very zen-like conversation.
GEORGE: And worse yet, I gave it to charity.

This is a transcript of a conversation held as part of the 2005 Loebner Prize competition for chatterbots.[4] George won the competition. (That's right: George is the computer program, not John.) George is a version of elegant and powerful chatterbot software called Jabberwocky.

The Loebner Prize tests conversational skill by running a version of what is known as the Turing Test. In a Turing Test, machine is pitted against person. A judge converses with both a person and a machine on any topic she likes. The aim is to discover which of her conversational partners is a person and which is a machine. If the judge can't tell the difference, the machine is said to be genuinely intelligent. The Loebner Prize competition runs a restricted version of the Turing Test (the conversations are much shorter than those in a full Turing Test). George didn't pass even this restricted Turing Test, of course. But he did better than all the other programs in competition.

The Turing Test (Turing 1950) was invented by the great mathematician and founding figure of computer science, Alan Turing (1912–1954). Turing thought that conversational competence would be a sufficient test of successful artificial intelligence. He did not claim that every intelligent machine must be able to hold a good conversation – there are many ways of being intelligent – but he did claim that any machine that could fool us into thinking that we are conversing with a human must be intelligent. Conversational intelligence is extremely demanding. It requires a very large database of background knowledge, a capacity to search this data with lightening speed, and thorough competence in a human language. It also requires a capacity to keep track of speech when topics change abruptly, to retain relevant (and only relevant) information throughout a conversation, to construct relevant and apt replies, and so on. No machine has yet come close to passing the Turing Test. However, chatterbots are improving every year.[5]

In Spielberg's film, success in the Turing Test is child's play. Even David's pet teddy could pass the Turing Test. But what exactly does the Turing Test test? It tests for conversational competence; that is, conversational *behavior*. It doesn't necessarily test for conversational *understanding*. George carries on a reasonable facsimile of a conversation (albeit with someone slightly off the planet), but he can't be said to understand what he is talking about. George is just following rules. He looks up things in a database, but he doesn't know what any entry in the database refers to. He constructs answers, but he doesn't know what they mean. Would this change if George – or one of his chatterbot descendents – got so good at constructing answers that he passed the Turing Test? That's hard to say. The American philosopher John Searle devised a very famous thought experiment aimed at settling the issue. It's called the Chinese Room (Searle 1980; 1984).

The Chinese Room

Imagine that you wake up from a drugged sleep to find yourself in a room. The room contains a very large filing cabinet, a basket full of blocks shaped like strange symbols, a table, pencils, and paper, and a folder labeled

"Master Instructions." The room also contains two slots through which things can enter or leave the room. They are labeled, ominously, "Input" and "Output." Blocks slide in through the input slot, one after the other. They appear to be shaped like symbols. In fact they are rather similar to the symbols in your basket. They look like squiggle-squaggles (Searle's term for them). Actually, they look rather like characters in Mandarin, but you can't read Mandarin (let us suppose). What are you meant to do with the symbols? You do the obvious thing – after yelling for help, to no avail – you consult the Master Instructions. The Master Instructions tell you where to start. Luckily they are written in English. Your job is to keep a record of the order in which the symbols arrive and look them up in that order in the index section of the filing cabinet. This yields further sets of instructions. The instructions are horrendously complicated, but they are set out in perfectly good English and are very precise. They tell you exactly what to do and the order in which to do it. The very last instruction tells you to choose a particular symbol from the basket provided and shove it through the output slot. You follow the instructions: day in, day out. You even get rather good at following them.

This is Searle's Chinese Room. (We've changed some minor details for ease of presentation.) He has imagined a computer from the inside. In the room, you are following a computational process of symbol manipulation. This is all computers do, says Searle. It is all they *can* do. The Chinese Room is like a super-Chatterbot program. It is expert in carrying out conversations in Chinese. The input symbols represent the interrogators' questions and comments, and the output symbols represent the Chinese Room's replies. Of course, it's all going on at a terribly slow pace. But allowing for that, competent speakers of Mandarin are very impressed by the conversational skills of the Chinese Room. They ask questions. They make remarks. You generate answers. The Chinese Room passes the Turing Test; or would if you didn't give the game away by being so damned slow. Searle doesn't think that speed is the issue at all. The important thing to notice is that, even if the Chinese Room passes the Turing Test in Mandarin, you wouldn't understand a word of its conversations. You don't know what they are about. You don't know what they mean. And yet, you perform all the operations of a computer. You recognize symbols by their shape and you follow instructions about what to do with them. But that's exactly what a computer does. If you don't understand the Chinese Room conversation, then no computer could understand a conversation. Indeed, a computer will understand even less than you do. You at least understand the instructions, since they are written in English and you follow them intentionally and thoughtfully. A computer follows its instructions blindly, mechanically, without any sort of understanding at all.

Searle devised the Chinese Room thought experiment to settle the issue of artificial intelligence once and for all. Artificial intelligence systems may be capable of *simulating* human thoughts and conversations, he concludes, but they are not capable *having* these thoughts or of *understanding* these conversations. Of course, Searle's thought experiment doesn't settle anything. Philosophers aren't persuaded that easily.[6] There are numerous replies to Searle's argument.[7] We'll have a quick look at three of them: the *robot reply*, the *systems reply*, and what we will call the *two-systems reply*. (Actually, this last one's a reply to a reply to a reply. Don't panic. You won't find it too hard to follow.)

The Robot Reply

This reply to Searle's argument is really a kind of back-handed concession. We concede that the Chinese Room doesn't understand anything, but put the blame, not on the fact that it is just running a computer program, but on the fact that it just sits there. The Chinese Room Searle imagines doesn't have the equivalent of legs and hands and eyes and ears. If someone knocks at the door, it can't get up and see who is there. It has to rely on mysterious symbols entering its input slot. These symbols might convey information about the person at the door, but the Chinese Room doesn't directly interact with the person at the door. It is disconnected from its environment. In short, the Chinese Room isn't a robot. Perhaps it would help if it was. In Spielberg's film, David's understanding and intelligence are manifested primarily in his interactions with his environment; with day to day actions as well as his carrying out of long-term plans and strategies such as his attempts to make his dream of becoming a real boy come true. David's capacity to carry on a conversation is impressive; but we are confident, it seems, that he knows what he is talking about because of the way he interacts with his environment. We are confident that David knows what the word "Teddy" means, in part, because he can call out to Teddy and then chase him and pick him up.

So, to return to Searle's story, let's imagine a Chinese Room robot. You are squeezed into its control centre performing all the computations necessary to make the robot work. Because the robot interacts with its environment, it might be able to understand thoughts about its environment. Perhaps it can know who is at the door because it can see who is at the door. The problem with Searle's thought experiment might therefore be that the original Chinese Room simply isn't equipped to be a genuine understander of things. Understanding requires thorough causal interaction with one's environment, and the Chinese Room has only verbal interaction with Mandarin speakers feeding it written conversational gambits. The Chinese Room lacks the causal interactive background needed to understand any of these gambits. This is the robot reply to Searle's argument. It has some merit. David, after all, is no Chinese Room. He might understand what is happening to him because he is a robot, not a chatterbot.

But Searle has a convincing counter to the robot reply. Say we convert the Chinese Room to a robot and squeeze you into the control centre. This Chinese Room robot is endowed with perception. It can see, hear, and touch its surroundings. But that doesn't mean that *you* can do these things. It won't do to mount a camera outside the Chinese Room robot and feed in images of the outside world to you. What would you do with these images? We don't perceive the world because there is a little person inside our heads watching TV: nor would a robot; nor would the Chinese Room robot.[8] Images enter the control centre as information and this information has to be presented in a way that allows you to follow rules telling you what to do with it. But here's the rub. If the information enters the room in this way, there is no guarantee that you will be able to decipher it. To you it might just look like more uninterpreted squiggle-squaggles. This doesn't prevent you from sorting out one kind of squiggle-squaggle from another kind of squiggle-squaggle. You have the ability to identify the unique form of each type of squiggle-squaggle and recognize it again whenever it appears, and you can do this without knowing what the squiggle-squaggles represent. This kind of information structure is called by philosophers, "syntactic structure." Searle is pointing out that information will arrive at the robot's control centre as uninterpreted syntax. You know what to do with syntactically structured information thanks to all the rules tucked away in the filing cabinet. But you don't know how to interpret the syntax. You don't know what any of it means. In this way, we can easily imagine (OK, we can imagine) a Chinese Room robot effectively doing its robot thing while you reside in the control centre facilitating it all, remaining clueless.

Searle appears to have a point. Turning the Chinese Room into the Chinese Room robot won't allow us to escape his argument. Of course, it might still help us escape it. The idea that environmental interaction is essential if an artificial intelligence system is to acquire understanding is highly plausible. The claim we are making here, on Searle's behalf, is simply that adding a robotic function to the Chinese Room will not furnish you in the control centre with an understanding of what the Chinese Room robot is up to. If the original Chinese Room argument works, a corresponding Chinese Room robot argument should work just as well.

The Systems Reply

The robot reply will not suffice, but there is a better reply to hand. You are stuck inside the Chinese Room (or in the control centre of the Chinese Room robot) and you don't understand what the system as a whole is doing. No surprise there. You aren't the Chinese Room. You are the program executor of the system. You do the hack work. You blindly follow instructions. You are like the CPU of an everyday computer. A computer is much more than a CPU. The system as a whole includes a hard drive, RAM, a cache, a video-card, an operating system, software, peripherals of all sorts, and so on. If you are like the CPU of the Chinese Room, then you aren't the Chinese Room. You aren't even the most important part of the Chinese Room. We could take you out and plug in somebody else and the system would hardly notice, provided your replacement can follow instructions as well as you can. Since you are only a small and replaceable part of the Chinese Room, it is no surprise that you fail to understand what the system as a whole is doing. If anything understands Mandarin in our thought experiment, it will be the system as a whole. And you aren't the whole system. This is the systems reply to Searle's argument.

Searle is unimpressed. How could adding furniture (a filing cabinet, a basket of squiggle-squaggles, and so on) turn something that doesn't understand (i.e. you) into something that does (i.e. the Chinese Room system)? It's tempting to respond "it just does." The filing cabinet itself can't understand: it is just inert information. You can't understand: you are just a blind instruction follower. But add the two together and we produce something that is more than the sum of its parts. We produce an active and capable information-processing system, and Searle has told us nothing that proves that such a system can't understand Mandarin.

Searle tries again. Imagine that you are in the Chinese Room for so long that you get to be very familiar with the instructions in the filing cabinet. Imagine that you have a fabulous memory and eventually commit all the instructions to memory. Now, when a squiggle-squaggle comes in through the input slot, you don't need to look up instructions in a filing cabinet in order to work out what to do with it. You simply consult your memory. In this new thought experiment, says Searle, you really are the Chinese Room system, not just the dumb CPU bit of it. And still you wouldn't know what the Chinese Room system is talking about. It's still all squiggle-squaggles to you. This shows – doesn't it? – that the Chinese Room system can't understand what it is talking about. You are the system now – you have internalized the entire system – and still you don't understand. So how could a computer ever understand?

The Two-Systems Reply

We just now examined a reply to Searle's argument (the systems reply) and Searle's counter to it. It's time for our final reply (for now): the two-systems reply. Searle asks you to imagine committing the entire list of Chinese Room instructions to memory. This is an incredible feat – but incredible things are allowed in philosophical thought experiments. Let's call the person with the incredible memory "Bubblehead." Bubblehead seems like it is simply you with a bit of added memory. But looks can be deceiving. Committing the Chinese Room program to memory might not seem to be all that different from committing other things to memory, such as the railway timetable for North America, but in fact it is very different. It is different because Bubblehead uses its memory of the Chinese Room program in a very particular way. When you use your memory of a railway timetable to catch a train, you draw on connections between the timetable and the rest of your knowledge. You know how to tell the time and how long it is till 1:00pm. You know that arriving at 2:00pm for a train scheduled to leave at 1:00pm will mean that you are probably late. And so on. When Bubblehead memorizes the Chinese Room instructions, no such integration occurs. The Chinese Room component of Bubblehead is not fully integrated into the rest of Bubblehead's cognitive system. Indeed, it's barely integrated at all.

Bubblehead seems to consist of two cognitive systems. One is your ordinary system: the system that enables you to catch trains on time. The other is the Chinese Room system: the system that allows Bubblehead to converse with Mandarin speakers. Of course you have a hard time identifying with the Chinese Room component of Bubblehead. It remains a mystery to you because it is not integrated properly with the rest of your mind. You don't understand what it is doing. But this just means that you aren't Bubblehead. Bubblehead consists of two systems and you are just one of them. The two systems are related, but in a rather strange way. Your system functions as program executor for the Chinese Room system. Without your instruction-following intervention, the Chinese Room system would sit limply in Bubblehead's memory, not achieving anything.

Now our question is this. Does Bubblehead understand Mandarin? *You* don't understand Mandarin. But then you aren't Bubblehead. Does *Bubblehead* understand Mandarin? It's hard to say. What we can't say is what Searle would have us say: that Bubblehead doesn't understand Mandarin because you don't understand Mandarin. This is an unsound argument because it assumes falsely that you and Bubblehead are the one cognitive system. You are not. The Chinese Room system in Bubblehead is like an alien invasion of your brain: it sits in your memory like a virus, exploiting your habit of following instructions.

Searle's Chinese Room argument fails. In the end, he has no satisfactory counter to the systems reply. But that doesn't mean that his conclusion is wrong. By refuting Searle's argument, we don't show that the Chinese Room *does* understand Mandarin. We only show that we can't use Searle's argument to prove that it doesn't understand Mandarin. Of course, Bubblehead is a very strange creature; and we have good reason to doubt that the Chinese Room component of it really understands anything. Because it isn't properly integrated into your cognitive system, it doesn't share your robotic proficiency. And without robotic proficiency – that is, without thorough causal immersion in its environment – it is most unlikely that it understands the content of its conversations with Mandarin speakers. We have to combine the robot reply with the systems reply in order to make the idea of an artificial intelligence system that understands what it is doing at all plausible.

This brings us back to our movie. It is no accident that science fiction portrayals of artificial intelligence systems are normally robotic. Even computers that lack the full complement of robotic skills – think HAL in *2001 A Space Odyssey* (1968) – have a rich repertoire of perceptual and executive abilities. HAL has eyes and ears everywhere. And he can open the pod-bay doors – or not open them – at will. In *AI*, David's cognitive abilities are closely tied to his robotic functionality. He learns by watching and imitating others (not too closely; things go badly when he actually tries to swallow his dinner). Perhaps he really understands in part because of this robotic functionality. Perhaps he really understands what a lock of hair is because he can cut one from Monica and talk about it afterwards. Perhaps he has some idea of what a Blue Fairy is because he can go looking for one.

Can David Feel Anything? The Qualia Objection

What is it like to be David? We can't put ourselves inside his mental world by imagining a David-like version of the Chinese Room thought experiment. As we have seen, that thought experiment misses its target. But there is another kind of reason to be suspicious of David's mental qualities. Why should we believe that he really *feels* anything? He registers experience as information flow in a cognitive system. But is he fully conscious? Is there anything that it is like to be David? Does it *hurt* when his mother abandons him in a forest? He acts like it hurts. But does it really hurt?

We can imagine David enacting convincing pain and distress responses without actually feeling pain and distress. There is something that it is like to feel a pain. And there is something that it is like to act *as if* you feel a pain, when you don't. How can we tell the difference from the outside? Philosophers call the conscious quality of an experience – the particular *painfulness* of a pain; the particular *redness* of a color perception; the particular *harshness* of a piece of discordant music – a quale. The plural of quale is qualia. So here is another objection to David's authenticity. He can't really love Monica because he is designed to act as if he has qualia-rich experiences, but he doesn't actually have them. When he seems distressed at the thought that Monica will someday die, he is just going through the motions. He doesn't actually feel distressed, though we can imagine it is absolutely impossible to tell that he does not. He lacks the distress quale. There is nothing that it is like to be David in distress. There is nothing that it is like to be David at all, any more than there is something that it is like to be a toaster. Call this the *qualia objection*.

So far, we are merely giving voice to a suspicion. Is there a philosophical argument to support it? What we need is an argument that shows that consciousness – the experience of qualia – cannot be created artificially. Since we don't really know how consciousness arises in humans – not that there is a shortage of theories – it is unlikely that we can rule out the possibility of artificial consciousness on philosophical grounds. We may feel that there is something special – perhaps something spiritual or non-mechanical – about consciousness. We may intuitively feel that only a living thing or only a thing with a soul could be fully conscious, but this intuition doesn't carry much philosophical weight all by itself.

One philosophical argument gets us close to what we are after. This is an argument purporting to show that consciousness is not really a physical phenomenon at all. If consciousness is non-physical, we may well find it impossible to replicate artificially. The argument comes courtesy of the Australian philosopher Frank Jackson (1982; 1986). It is called the *knowledge argument* and requires yet another thought experiment. (Again, we'll alter a few details to make it easier to describe.) Imagine somebody called Mary, made the subject of a cruel and prolonged psychological experiment. At birth, Mary is fitted with special ocular implants that prevent her seeing anything in color. She lives out her life seeing everything in black and white. Nonetheless – or maybe because of this – Mary becomes the world's greatest expert on color perception in humans. In fact, Mary is so good at discovering facts about color perception, she gets to know everything worth knowing about it. She knows all the physical facts about color perception: how light of various wavelengths interacts with the visual system, how the information obtained from visual transducers is processed by the brain, and so on. Mary comes to know all the physical facts about what it is to perceive a color. At the denouement of the experiment, Mary's ocular implants are removed. Now she can actually see colors, rather than just theorize about them. She wanders outside and sees a red rose. And she says to herself: *So that is what red looks like; I never knew!* There is something Mary didn't know. She didn't know the qualia facts of color perception; she didn't know what red looks like. But she knew all the physical facts. This shows that qualia facts aren't physical facts. There is more to consciousness than the physical processing of information in the brain.

Just how good is the knowledge argument?[9] Needless to say, it is highly controversial. The most well-known response to it goes like this. When Mary finally sees colors, she does not acquire new factual knowledge. We described the scene as if she does – we had her say that she never knew what red looked like – but this description is misleading. It makes it sound as if knowing what red looks like is the same kind of thing as knowing what the wavelength of red light is (about 700 nanometers). It makes qualia-knowledge seem like it is just additional factual knowledge. However, it is really a very different kind of thing. When Mary begins to see colors, she does not acquire new factual knowledge, she acquires new abilities. Now she can tell whether tomatoes are ripe just by looking at them. Before her color conversion, Mary had to measure tomatoes with a portable SpectroColorimeter (an essential fruit and vegetable shopping tool) in order to tell whether they were ripe or not. Now, she can see a color at one time and recognize the same color at another time (without measuring them both). She might even be able to imagine a color as a mental image. Perhaps she can now dream in color and remember being chased in a dream by a giant blue lobster, rather than a giant grayish lobster. The kind of knowledge Mary acquires after her color conversion is knowledge-how, not knowledge-that. She knows how to do things; she has new abilities. She doesn't identify new facts about color perception; rather, she now has the ability to identify some of the old facts in new ways. This reply to the knowledge argument is generally known as the *abilities hypothesis.*[10]

How good a reply is the abilities hypothesis?[11] That's a tough question to answer. Can we imagine somebody who has all the abilities we attribute to Mary after her color conversion, but who doesn't experience color qualia? Can qualia-knowledge be reduced to the acquisition of relevant abilities without leaving anything out? It is very hard to say. The defender of the irreducibility of qualia (Jackson calls them qualia-freaks) might respond to the abilities hypothesis by insisting that a conscious agent like Mary acquires her new abilities *because* she now knows about color qualia. How is it that Mary can now sort tomatoes into the ripe ones and the unripe ones without using her SpectroColorimeter? She now knows what ripe tomatoes look like, and that's why she can now pick them out. Perhaps the abilities hypothesis gets this the wrong way around. It assumes that in virtue of the fact that she can now pick out ripe tomatoes at a distance, Mary now knows what red looks like. Maybe this puts the cart before the horse.

Which comes first: qualia-knowledge or qualia-ability? People who hold that consciousness is reducible to physical processes occurring in the brain – they are known as physicalists – are going to want to say that the abilities come first: qualia-knowledge just is possession of qualia-abilities, and the acquisition and possession of these abilities can be explained in purely physical terms, without leaving anything out. Non-physicalists might say that qualia-abilities presuppose qualia-knowledge: to have a qualia-ability you must first know what the relevant experience is like. Alternatively, non-physicalists might claim that a person could possess all the relevant abilities – identification, discrimination, recall, imaginative production, and so on – without ever being consciously aware of qualia themselves. A creature like this is sometimes called a zombie in contemporary philosophy of mind.[12] This kind of zombie isn't a flesh-eating member of the undead, but a being in possession of all the abilities of conscious agents, without the consciousness that ordinarily goes along with it. A zombie looks like somebody's at home inside and the lights are on, but they're not and they're not.

Who wins between the physicalist about consciousness and the non-physicalist? It is hard to say. Perhaps it's a draw. Perhaps they both lose.[13] Perhaps it depends on who owns the burden of proof in the argument.

But who does own the burden of proof? Whose position is the more initially plausible: the physicalist's or the non-physicalist's? And where does this leave David? He seems to have all the abilities required of a conscious agent. Could he have these abilities without having qualia-knowledge? Could he have the full kit of perceptual and cognitive abilities without ever being conscious of the *hurtfulness* of pain, the *desperation* of distress, the *desolation* of aloneness? Could he be a zombie? Must he be a zombie? As is often the case in philosophy, we've ended up with more questions than we started with. But they are different questions. And better.

Questions

Suppose robots get much, much better; so good in fact that it is impossible to tell a robot from a person – physically or emotionally – unless you take it apart. Would a close and loving relationship with such robots be irrational, unwarranted, or even unnatural? Should person–robot marriages be legalized? Could a person and a robot be "happy" together?

In the chapter, we argued as follows. "If we think that David's love is inauthentic because it is pre-installed, any child's love of its mother might also be inauthentic for much the same reason. We tend not to doubt the reality or authenticity of a child's love for its parents, so perhaps we shouldn't doubt David's love because of its designer origins." Are we right about this? Can a (human) child's love of its parents be authentic? Could it be authentic in a way that David's love could never be? What might the authenticity of a child's love consist in? (What might the authenticity of *any* love consist in?)

John Searle's Chinese Room thought experiment was intended to refute the ambitions of the Strong AI Program. This is the belief that computers could eventually be made to possess artificial minds (with consciousness, understanding, intelligence, emotional capacity, and so on). We criticized the argument in our chapter. However, a more modest version of the Chinese Room can be directed at the Turing Test, rather than the Strong AI Program. Does it succeed in this more modest goal? (That is, does it show that something could pass the Turing Test without really possessing conversational intelligence?)

Do you need robotic capacities to understand anything? Couldn't a computer eventually come to understand things without perceiving, moving, acting, and so on? Isn't talking (i.e. outputting text-code) enough? Why not?

In the chapter we gave Searle's first response to the systems reply short shrift. Searle said it was ridiculous to think that the inert components of a system (in his Chinese Room, the filing cabinet with all its files and folders) could turn something that didn't understand into something that did. How could they; they aren't *doing* anything. Were we too swift with our rejection? Is there something in Searle's complaint? How could the addition of files of information make the difference? (Remember, the systems reply is most forceful when combined with the robot reply.)

Are you and Bubblehead the same person? That is, once in the Chinese Room, and once you have memorized all of its instructions, are you one cognitive system or two?

In the chapter, we expressed the qualia objection like this. "There is nothing that it is like to be David at all, any more than there is something that it is like to be a toaster." Could you ever tell whether an artificial mind experiences qualia? If all relevant informational and perceptual systems were functioning, could you ever tell whether the artificial mind is experiencing qualia or not? Could you ever tell that anybody apart from yourself experiences qualia? (They say they do, but of course they would, being zombies and all.) Or could you ever tell whether another person experiences the same qualia you experience when you both look at the one object? ("It looks red to me. You say it looks red to you. But how do I know that you see what I see when I say I see red?") Given this propensity towards skepticism about qualia experience, are we being too hard on David when we compare his inner life to a toaster's?

Notes

1   In chapter 6 we will pick apart this concept of possibility. For now, it will suffice to work with an intuitive notion of possibility. Is this something that could be achieved by increasing our technological powers or is there some basic and unbridgeable factor preventing our ever achieving it?

2   This characteristic of film – that, like life itself, films present us with no more than the outward signs of inner experience – paradoxically reinforces the claims of realism in films. (See our discussion of realism and Bazin in chapter 2.) By contrast, novels often exploit a convention whereby an author has magical access to the inner lives of her characters. Films manage this only through the rarely used and often intrusive devise of the voiceover.

3   We are going to discuss two famous philosophical thought experiments in this chapter: the Chinese Room and Mary in a Black and White Room. Thought experiments of this kind don't find their way into films (perhaps

because they would be too boring). But it is always a worthwhile question to ask of a philosophical thought experiment "Could this be convincingly filmed?" If not, this is an indication that something may be going wrong with the thought experiment. (See note 7 below about the Chinese Room.)

4   You can find transcripts of this and other conversations George had in the competition here: http://loebner.net/Prizef/2005_Contest/Transcripts.html. You can have a conversation yourself with George here: http://www.jabberwacky.com/chat-george.

5   The Loebner Prize competition is held every year. You can follow the progress of chatterbots throughout the competition here: http://www.loebner.net/Prizef/loebner-prize.html.

6   Cole (2009) gives a detailed account of the critical reception of Searle's argument.

7   One film-centric reply might go like this. Imagine trying to film the Chinese Room thought experiment. In order to pass the Turing Test, the action would have to be sped up to such an astonishing (really astonishing) degree that all you would ever see is a blur as Searle runs around the room doing things at impossible speeds. (Maybe faster than the speed of light; who knows how fast he would have to run around the Chinese Room). Then, the thought experiment asks us to identify very closely with this super-speeding creature and tells us what the creature knows or doesn't know. Human consciousness doesn't work at these speeds; and we know it. So we can't in all honesty make the identification. On this criticism, the thought experiment never really gets off the ground.

8   This little person is called a homunculus – and we are concerned here to avoid something called the homuncular fallacy. To appeal to a homunculus inside a robot – that's you in the control room of the Chinese Room robot – would be a cheat. Searle and his opponents all agree that we can't rescue artificial intelligence from his argument by smuggling in a homunculus who recognizes perceptual inputs into the Chinese Room.

9   Martine Nida-Rümelin (2009) gives an excellent summary of the critical reception of the argument.

10 David Lewis (1988) defends the abilities reply.

11 See Martine Nida-Rümelin (2009) for a summary of critical responses to the abilities hypothesis.

12 See Kirk (2006).

13 Another position to take on consciousness is eliminativist: claiming that consciousness is mostly an illusion. See Dennett (1991) for an argument along these lines.

Further Reading

Chalmers, David (1996). *The Conscious Mind: In Search of a Fundamental Theory.* Oxford: Oxford University Press.

Churchland, Patricia, & Paul Churchland (1990). "Could a Machine Think?" *Scientific American* 262.1, 32–7.

Cole, David (2009). "The Chinese Room Argument." *Stanford Encyclopedia of Philosophy.* http://plato.stanford.edu/entries/chinese-room/

Dennett, Daniel (1989). *The Intentional Stance.* Cambridge, MA: MIT Press.

Dennett, Daniel (1991). *Consciousness Explained.* Boston, Toronto, London: Little, Brown.

Jackson, Frank (1982). "Epiphenomenal Qualia." *Philosophical Quarterly* 32, 127–36.

Jackson, Frank (1986). "What Mary Didn't Know." *Journal of Philosophy* 83, 291–5.

Kirk, Robert (2006). "Zombies." *Stanford Encyclopedia of Philosophy.* http://plato.stanford.edu/entries/zombies/

Lewis, D. (1988). "What Experience Teaches." *Proceedings of the Russellian Society* 13, 29–57. Reprinted in Lycan (1990).

Ludlow, P., Y. Nagasawa, & D. Stoljar, eds. (2005). *There is Something about Mary: Essays on Phenomenal Consciousness and Frank Jackson's Knowledge Argument.* Cambridge, MA: MIT Press.

Lycan, W. G., ed. (1990). *Mind and Cognition.* Oxford: Blackwell.

Nagel, Thomas (1979). *Mortal Questions.* Cambridge: Cambridge University Press.

Nida-Rümelin, Martine (2009). "Qualia: The Knowledge Argument." *Stanford Encyclopedia of Philosophy.* http://plato.stanford.edu/entries/qualia-knowledge/

Oppy, Graham, & David Dowe (2011). "The Turing Test." *Stanford Encyclopedia of Philosophy.* http://plato.stanford.edu/entries/turing-test/

Preston, J., & Bishop, M., eds. (2002). *Views into the Chinese Room: New Essays on Searle and Artificial Intelligence.* New York: Oxford University Press.

Searle, John (1980). "Minds, Brains and Programs." *Behavioral and Brain Sciences* 3, 417–57.

Searle, John (1984). *Minds, Brains and Science.* Cambridge, MA: Harvard University Press.

Turing, Alan (1950). "Computing Machinery and Intelligence." *Mind* 59, 433–60.

6

La Jetée and the Promise of Time Travel

Introduction

In Chris Marker's 1963 film *La Jetée*, a young boy witnesses the shooting of a man at Orly Airport, Paris. As he grows older, the memory of this death haunts him. *La Jetée* is a film about way memories haunt us. It is also about time travel. We are going to use *La Jetée* to talk about the possibility of time travel. Along the way we are also going to examine the nature of time and also the nature of possibility.

Marker uses a series of still photographs accompanied by an expository voiceover to tell the story.[1] This was an inspired decision, given the film's theme of the power of memories to haunt. Photographs are our favorite way of trying to supplement memory, to bolster its fading claims on us, to supply the details of experiences that memory fails to preserve. Photos are complicit in the hold that images of the past have over us. *La Jetée*'s protagonist (he is never named, we'll call him the time-traveler) has no need of photographs, however. The image of the dying man is burned deeply into his memory. It turns out that this is the very thing that suits him to the difficult business of traveling through time. Time travel, it seems, requires extraordinary levels of concentration, and obsession with an image from the past furnishes this.

Here is the story. Paris is destroyed in an apocalyptic war and survivors live as prisoners underground. The world is ruined. Rescue is needed. The victors – it seems they are German – decide that rescue can only come from the future and so set about a series of time-travel experiments. Our protagonist is chosen as a test subject. He succeeds in traveling back in

Thinking Through Film: Doing Philosophy, Watching Movies, First Edition. Damian Cox, Michael P. Levine.
© 2012 Damian Cox and Michael P. Levine. Published 2012 by Blackwell Publishing Ltd.

time to Paris before the war. He visits a woman and returns to her over and over again. She calls him her ghost. They fall in love. Having mastered travel into the past, the German scientists experiment with travel into the future. This is harder than travel into the past. Something is blocking the time-traveler's progress into the future, and it turns out to be a people of the future who have mastered the science of time travel and who are reluctant to welcome a stranger from early human history. The time-traveler eventually gets to talk to them and to explain his mission. Past humanity is in peril and since it survives, the beneficiaries of its survival owe to the past the means of its survival. Apparently the people of the future accept this sophism, because they give our time-traveler a powerful energy transducer to take with him back to his own time. He does. And humanity is saved. The time-traveler having completed his mission, the German scientists plan to execute him. (They are *German* scientists after all. And this is a French film, and it is made in 1963.) People of the future come to his rescue. They offer to take him to the future, but he opts instead to return to the world of pre-war France, to the woman he loves. On his return he finds himself at Orly Airport. (This is bad.) He sees his beloved and runs to her. But he has been followed by an agent of the German scientists (they have really got the hang of time travel now) and is shot before he reaches the woman. A boy witnesses it all. As a boy the man had witnessed his own death. No wonder he was haunted by the memory of it.

This is a simple and elegant time-travel story.[2] The philosophical questions we ask are these. Could something like this actually happen? Is time the sort of thing one *could* travel through? Is time travel possible? Of course, since this is philosophy, we also have to ask: What does it mean to say that time travel is possible? What do we mean by "possible"? The modern time-travel story is an invention of H. G. Wells and Wells starts off his first time-travel story – *The Time Machine* – with a discussion of the nature of time. Time, he has his time-traveler explain, is a dimension rather like the three dimensions of space. We can travel through space. Ergo, if we knew how, we could travel through time. Just how good is this argument? To start to work this out, we have to look more closely at the metaphysics of time.

A Time Primer

Contemporary philosophical discussion of the nature of time owes a great deal to the work of the British philosopher J. M. E. McTaggart (1866–

1922). McTaggart argued that time is an illusion: we think of things existing through time, but they don't. We will have a quick look at his ingenious argument for this conclusion shortly, but first we need to set the stage. The most influential and perhaps interesting aspect of McTaggart's work is not his argument that time is an illusion, but the way he set up the problem. He distinguished between two kinds of temporal concepts – two ways of thinking of the ordering of temporal events. McTaggart called them the A-Series and the B-Series. The names stuck.

According to the A-Series, events in time are ordered according to whether they are in the past, in the present, or in the future. Time marks a process of becoming: future events become present and then become past. According to the B-Series, by contrast, events in time are ordered by the relations *earlier than, later than,* and *simultaneous with.* Take any two events you like: the execution of Charles I of England and Argentina's winning the 1978 FIFA World Cup Final. The one event either coincided with the other, or happened earlier than the other, or happened later than the other.[3] In this case, the first event happened before the second event (or the second event happened after the first event, whichever way you want to put it).

It seems that we can think of time-sequences in terms of either the A-Series or the B-Series. McTaggart, however, argued that the A-Series (the future becoming present and then past) is essential to the concept of time. Without the A-Series, there would be no time. He thought this because he thought that time presupposes change and we need the A-Series for change to be real (a controversial claim to be sure). Crucially, McTaggart thought that the A-Series is self-contradictory. It requires the one event – Argentina's winning the 1978 World Cup Final, say – to have inconsistent properties: it has the property of present and the property of being past and the property of being future. But if something is present it can't also be past. Can it? These are mutually incompatible properties. And yet the one event is supposed to have them both. How can that be? On the face of it this looks like a very bad argument. An event isn't supposed to be past and present and future *at the same time.* At one time it is future, at another it is present, and at another it is past. This seems right, but it doesn't help. For example, it doesn't help to point out that Argentina's World Cup Final winning is present on June 25, 1978, and past on June 25, 2010. If we replace the claim that the victory is past with the more precise claim that it happened on June 25, 1978, we have just replaced the A-Series with the B-Series. (Saying an event is present at a particular date simply establishes its position in the sequence of events ordered by the earlier than/later than relation. That's the B-Series.) McTaggart's claim is that the A-Series is inconsistent, not the B-Series.

We could try to be more slippery. Instead of nominating a date for the match, we could say that the match *was* present. To say that an event was present is to say that it has the property of being present in the past. (Philosophers love this kind of convoluted way of putting things. They think it adds clarity. And sometimes they are right.) Being *present in the past* does not contradict the property *is past*. So instead of saying that the one event has the property of being present and the property of being past, we could say that it has the property of being *present in the past* and the property of being *past*. We seem to avoid a contradiction now without reducing the A-Series to the B-Series. But still McTaggart thinks this doesn't help. We have replaced a first-order tense property (*present*) with a second-order tense property (*present in the past*) in order to avoid contradiction. But introducing second-order tense properties allows us to generate new contradictions. For example, Argentina's match winning has the property of being present in the past, but also the property of being present in the future. (In 1950 the victory was present in the future.) These two second-order tense properties contradict each other. It can't be true of the one event that it has the property of being present in the past and the property of being present in the future. And if we try and resolve this new contradiction by appealing to a third-order of tense-properties (e.g. in the future an event is present in the past), we run into the same problem all over again. There is no escaping the problem of the one event being ascribed contradictory tense-properties, or so McTaggart thought. This is an example of what philosophers call the problem of *vicious regress*.

Remember our topic is time travel (you might have forgotten). If there were no time, there would be no time travel; there would be nothing to move through, as it were. So what is McTaggart's argument for the unreality of time? It can be summarized like this.

1 The concept of time presupposes the A-Series.
2 Thus the reality of time requires the reality of the A-Series.
3 But the A-Series is self-contradictory and so cannot be real.
4 Thus time itself must be unreal.

Needless to say, philosophers have not let matters stand here. One way of responding to the argument is to try and save the A-Series from contradiction. As we just saw, McTaggart thought that the one event can't have both the property of being present and the property of being past.

These are contradictory properties. Perhaps we should just agree with him. How do we stop the contradiction without collapsing the A-Series into the B-Series? This might sound extreme, but maybe we could stop the contradiction by denying that events ever do have the property of being past or being future: the past does not exist; the future does not exist; only the present exists. If something is an event, then it is taking place right now. If it isn't taking place now, it is not an event. It is something else, something that doesn't exist. When we speak of "past events," we are speaking loosely. Past events aren't really events at all. Events are happenings. Past events aren't happenings. In particular, past events aren't events with the special property of being in the past. This would be equivalent to saying that they are happenings with the special property of not happening, which is absurd. So if we are clear(ish) about what we mean by events, and we are clear that past and future are never properties of events, we can ensure that the one event never has contradictory temporal properties. It can only have the property of being present. By denying that anything exists but the present, we seem to have got a way to rehabilitate the A-Series without contradicting ourselves.

The view we arrive at by evading McTaggart's contradiction in this way may seem odd, but it actually describes quite an intuitive conception of time. When we say that the past is gone, we may well have it in mind that it exists no more. Perhaps we mean that the past just does not exist, period. The present seems real – it seems *there* or rather *here* – in a way that the past and future do not. The present constantly changes, and this change constitutes the flow of time. Philosophers call this view, unsurprisingly, *presentism*. Presentism has the advantage of capturing our intuitive sense that time flows and that the present is real in a way that the future and the past are not. One way to picture the presentist's account of time and existence is to imagine the present as a point of light moving across the darkened line of the world. Darkness is the darkness of non-existence; light is the light of being. The motion of light is the flow of time. And it moves, as you might expect, at the speed of one second per second. (Presentism captures something intuitive but it is also odd in a way because the present is so fleeting. If it is only the present we live in, we might stop and wonder how it is that we ever catch our breath – time moves so fast! If we live wholly in the present, then we live, it seems, a fleeting series of momentary experiences. But life doesn't feel like that.)

Presentists confront many difficulties. First, they have difficulty explaining how we get to make true claims about the past. Are claims about the past like fictional claims? (I say Argentina won the World Cup in 1978. That's like saying that Captain Ahab tried to kill Moby Dick. In a way, he did. In another way, there is no such person as Captain Ahab and no such creature as Moby Dick.) Are claims about the past heavily disguised claims about the present? (I say Argentina won the World Cup in 1978. That's just a fancy way of talking about present FIFA records and the like.) It's hard for presentists to find a very plausible semantics for statements about the past. It is also hard for them to explain causal processes since causation appears to be a relation between events stretched over time. A past event causes a present event. But how is something that doesn't exist supposed to have the oomph to cause things? Alternatively, consider present causes of future effects: I take a pill now to kill my pain in a few minutes. How can something that doesn't exist – something future, not something *in the future* (as if the future were a warehouse storing events in waiting) – enter into causal relations with something that does?[4]

Presentism faces difficulties. We may be able to find our way through these difficulties, but they do encourage us to seek alternative views of time. The main competitor for presentism abandons the attempt to characterize time in terms of the A-Series. It does not accept the commonsense intuition that time flows, or that there is an ontological difference between the past and the present. This is the view of time H. G. Wells talks about in *The Time Machine*. Today, it is often called four-dimensionalism. Recall that McTaggart's argument for the unreality of time had two major premises. The first premise is that the A-Series is an essential characteristic of time: no A-Series, no time. The second premise is that the A-Series is self-contradictory. Presentists accept the first premise but reject the second. Four-dimensionalists go the other way: they accept the second premise but reject the first. They think we can make sense of time purely in terms of the B-Series (temporal relations between events: later than, earlier than, simultaneous with). According to the four-dimensionalist, A-Series concepts – past, present, future – don't represent ontologically significant facts. They simply indicate the temporal location of the speaker. Just say a person sees traffic lights change from red to green and utters the sentence, as they see it change, "The traffic lights are changing now." What makes this statement true? What fact does the claim pick out? That depends on the temporal location of the speaker. If the speaker utters the sentence at 9:45am November 30, 2020, the claim will be true only if the traffic light in question is changing at that time. If the speaker makes the claim at another time, it will be true only if the traffic light in question is changing at this other time. "Now" functions very much like "here." It is what philosophers call an indexical expression. And so it goes for all A-Series concepts. By four-dimensionalist lights, A-Series facts are indexical facts. An important consequence of four-dimensionalism is that time does not flow. It only seems to flow. Four-dimensionalism doesn't suffer from presentism's difficulties, though of course it has difficulties of its own. Explaining why time seems to flow is one of them; explaining why time seems to flow in the one direction only is another.

What is Time Travel?

Back to time travel. Presentists are going to find time travel incoherent. How can you travel to somewhere that doesn't exist? (It's not that the past and future exist only in the present. Presentism maintains that they do not exist at all.) Four-dimensionalists, on the other hand, have no such scruples. For them, time is a dimension and travel along a dimension is at least conceivable, even if it turns out to be physically impossible. But what exactly is time travel? In *La Jetée*, the time-traveler moves into the past and the future. This is easy to show in a film, since it only requires that the actors position themselves in an environment which the audience identifies as the future or the past. But that doesn't help us work out exactly what is going on in a time-travel scenario.

The American philosopher David Lewis suggests the following definition of time travel. Time is measured by change; the change of the hands of a clock for example. This allows us to make a distinction between personal time and external time. Personal time is measured by change in your person. (Imagine that you have a quartz clock inserted under your skin. The rate at which you age, or acquire memories, is a function of your personal time.) External time is measured by change in the environment external to you. (Imagine a clock standing 100 meters away.) You travel in time if after a relatively short interval of personal time you move to a relatively distant external time. In *La Jetée*, the time-traveler moves what must be many hundreds of years into the future. From his perspective – his personal time – the journey has taken at most a few seconds. From an external perspective, it has taken hundreds of years for him to arrive. Chris Marker, perhaps wisely, does not illustrate the transitions involved. In one scene, the time-traveler appears merely to be observing or imagining the past; in the next scene he really is in the past. We aren't told how he got there. In the 2002 film version of *The Time Machine*, we see the time-traveler actually moving through time. We see him aging barely at all (a minute or so) whilst outside his craft the world ages before our eyes (thanks to CGI time-lapse effects). When traveling into the past, the time-traveler pulls the same trick. Whilst he plods forward in time, barely aging at all (and not getting any younger either), the world outside his craft is seen running backwards at speed (thanks again to CGI time-lapse effects).

Time travel might be a continuous process like this or it might involve discrete shifts. In most time-travel films the time-traveler enters her machine at one time, presses a button, and emerges at a very different time without going through intervening periods at all. Sometimes a wormhole has something to do with it, though we are usually spared an explanation of exactly what it has to do with it. In the marvelous *Futurama* episode "All's Well that Roswell" time travel happens because Fry ignores the manufacturer's instructions whilst trying to pop corn in a microwave (just as a supernova is about to explode, in case you were wondering). In most movies, cover-stories for the ability to time travel are either entirely absent or little more than playful nonsense (a genius with bad hair, a lot of squiggling on a blackboard, a fancy, gleaming craft, or failing that a DeLorean). But the philosophical question remains. Is time travel even possible?

What is Possibility?

We are asking an ambiguous question. There is more than one kind of possibility. There are at least three kinds relevant to our inquiry: logical possibility, metaphysical possibility, and physical possibility. A sequence of events is logically possible if it can be fully described without contradiction. A sequence of events is metaphysically possible if it can be fully described without violating true metaphysical principles, whatever they happen to be. (For example, that only the present exists or that only physical things exist are metaphysical principles, though they might not be true ones.) By contrast, a sequence of events is physically possible if and only if it does not violate any laws of nature, again, whatever they happen to be.

So what question should we ask? This is a philosophy book, so we won't investigate physical possibility. It's worth noting in passing, however, that at least one kind of time travel seems not only to be physically possible, but an everyday happening. The Special Theory of Relativity predicts a form of time travel via something called the time dilation effect. Say we send a super-accurate clock up in a plane and compare it to a twin clock on the ground. It turns out that the clock on the plane will run more slowly than the clock on the ground. Air travel is a way of staying younger (though not by much). The time dilation effect increases with speed, so travel by rocket is an even more effective way of outlasting your cousins on Earth. (The downside is that you wouldn't actually live any longer measured by your personal time, which, after all, is the one that really counts.) Of course, the time dilation effect is not the only kind of time travel. Travel into the very remote future might be accomplished by some other, space–time bending, mechanism. Time dilation doesn't help with travel into the past. (As we shall see, travel into the past is the thing that causes the major philosophical problems.)

So much for physical possibility. What about metaphysical possibility? According to presentists, time travel is metaphysically impossible. Even if you seem to be able to tell logically consistent time-travel stories, they in fact contradict core metaphysical principles about the nature of time. You can't travel to a place that doesn't exist. Luckily, we have another metaphysical theory of time to ponder: four-dimensionalism. There is no metaphysical objection to time travel coming from four-dimensionalists. Still, if time travel turns out not to be logically possible, all these arguments about the metaphysics of time are beside the point. If time travel is not logically possible, then it is not possible in any flavor. And there is a famous argument that says time travel is not logically possible: the Grandfather Paradox.

The Grandfather Paradox

If travel into the past is possible, then why isn't it possible for a person to travel into the past and kill their grandfather when he was a youngster, ensuring that their mother is never born. If a person has no mother, they can't have been born themselves. And if they aren't born, they can't travel back to kill their grandfather. The possibility of traveling into the past seems to unravel before our eyes. This is known as the Grandfather Paradox. Does it show that the very idea of travel into the past is logically incoherent? Let us set out the paradox in the form of an argument against the logical possibility of time travel.

1   If time travel were logically possible, I could travel back in time and kill my grandfather, ensuring that my mother was never born.
2   If my mother was never born, then I was never born.
3   Thus I would not exist.

4   If I kill my grandfather, I do exist.
5   Therefore, in this scenario, I would both exist and not exist. This can't happen.
6   Therefore, I can't travel back in time to kill my grandfather, ensuring that my mother was never born.
7   Therefore, time travel is not logically possible.

Now this looks like a very good argument. Once you accept the first premise (1), the rest follows like a logical juggernaut. Every other step of the argument is either a logical deduction from previous steps or else makes claims so unremarkable that there isn't any plausible way to deny them. So what is the defender of time travel supposed to do? Reject the first premise, of course. But how?

Grand-patricide is only a dramatic way of pointing out something endemic to time-travel stories. It might seem that, by traveling back in time, you inevitably change the past. Your mere presence in the past looks like it constitutes a change to it. Before you time-traveled, you are absent from the past. After you time travel, you are present in it. So it seems true about the past that (a) you are absent in it and (b) you are present in it. But that's already a contradiction. There's no need to kill off your grandfather to generate logical absurdity, just hanging around in the past seems to be enough.

Things look bad for time travel, but in fact the argument of our previous paragraph is based on a grievous misunderstanding. Remember that the metaphysics of time we adopted in order to pave the way for time travel is four-dimensionalism. According to the four-dimensionalist, the past is fixed. It can't be altered. The past is not like a videotape that you can rewind and record over. If you travel into the past, you do not rewrite the past. You were already there! Just say you travel into the past and take a picture of yourself standing next to Cleopatra and then bury the photo in a hidden tomb. When you return to your own time, you search out the tomb and recover your photograph. How long has the photo been there? It has been there since you buried it about 2000 years ago. By burying the photo, you affected the past. But you didn't change it. That is, you didn't change the past from one condition (in which a tomb survives 2,000 years photo-less) to another condition (in which a tomb survives 2,000 years with a buried photo). The Grandfather Paradox assumes that it is possible to change the past. But it is not possible. So much the worse for the paradox. It's not a paradox after all. It's just a mistake. The first premise of the argument is false. Time travel is logically possible precisely because we can't rewrite the past.

These reflections should still leave us puzzled. It seems strange to say that if you had a time machine you couldn't use it to disrupt the family tree. What is to stop you? Surely you have the sheer ability to kill someone. What is to stop you exercising this ability? The laws of logic won't sweep down and ensure that consistency is maintained; they haven't got that kind of power. What does happen? Were you to go back in time and attempt the terrible deed, you would fail. You would slip on a banana skin at the last moment. Or your gun would stick. Or you would shoot the wrong person. Still, a scent of paradox hangs in the air. It seems that you have the ability to do something but, at the same time, you can't do it. So you both have an ability to kill your grandfather and don't have an ability to kill your grandfather. That sounds paradoxical.

The clearest way out is to posit an ambiguity in the concept of ability.[5] There is one sense in which you have the ability to kill your grandfather: it is an action of the *type* you could do. You could track someone down. You could point a gun and you could pull the trigger. (Not that you would.) So, in one sense, you have the required ability. But, in another sense, this particular act is not something you are able to do. It is beyond your doing. You do not have the ability to rewrite the past. Not even God has this ability. So we encounter two senses of ability: a weaker sense, in which we have the ability to do something if it is the kind of thing we could do; and a stronger sense, in which we have the ability to do something if it is possible that we do that very thing. The Grandfather Paradox argument conflates these two senses. The first premise of the Grandfather Paradox argument only seems plausible when interpreted according to the weaker sense of ability. Grand-patricide is made up of actions, each of which is the kind of thing a person could perform successfully. But the argument's premise in fact requires the stronger sense. Grand-patricide must not just consist of actions which are usually the kind of thing you could do, it must be the *very thing* that you could do. And it isn't.

Consistent and Inconsistent Time-Travel Narratives

Let's have a final look at our film. *La Jetée* tells a time-travel story in which, as a boy, a man witnesses his own death. Could the man have prevented his death? Could he have changed his mind at the last moment and headed off into the safety of the future? Could he have just run faster? Or ducked? No. He could have done none of these things because he didn't do them. The man did not know it, but he was fated to die at Orly Airport before the destruction of Paris. In fact he wasn't so much fated to die at Orly Airport; when he was puzzling over whether or not to accept refuge in the future, he had already died at Orly Airport. He had been dead for most of his life. For a short while, he was also in two places at the same time, as a boy and as a man. Can the one person exist in two places at the same time? It depends on which account of personal identity is right. The psychological continuity theory that we will discuss in chapter 8 is a four-dimensionalist theory of persons, in which persons consist of temporal parts linked together by memory. There is nothing in this theory that makes it impossible for a person to be in two places at the same time. There is nothing in the theory that makes it impossible that a person die while (at a different temporal stage) they continue to live. There is also nothing in it that prevents a person dying before they were born. Nobody suggests that time travel isn't strange. The claim is merely that it is logically, and perhaps metaphysically, possible. *La Jetée* is an example of a consistent – and therefore logically possible – time-travel narrative. The key feature of these stories is that the past is never rewritten. They may involve many weird things, but they describe a single consistent world.

Inconsistent time-travel stories are abundant. *Butterfly Effect* (2004) is a good example of one. In *Butterfly Effect*, Evan Treborn discovers that he has the ability to return to his past and construct alternative futures for himself and those connected with him. The alternative futures all go very badly (thus, supposedly, illustrating the butterfly effect).[6] The film toys with consistency (Evan's blackouts as a boy are brought about by his future self), but the filmmakers have no real interest in telling a consistent time-travel story. As the past is rewritten over and over again, you wonder what happens to all the overwritten lives. Did they ever exist? How can Evan think that by going back in time and rewriting the life of his girlfriend, Kayleigh Miller, he was ever going to improve things for her? He can't make it true that she was never abused. So what does he think he is going to achieve?

Probably the best way to think of scenarios like that of *Butterfly Effect* is not in terms of time travel, but in terms of branching worlds. When Evan returns to his past in an attempt to make a better fist of his life, he is not traveling into his past, but traveling to a parallel world, one branching off the actual world. Creating these branching worlds, or hopping onto them, doesn't undo the past. It's highly questionable whether hopping between worlds is a metaphysically coherent idea. But, in any case, world-hopping isn't a form of time travel. Were you to employ world-hopping to go back to kill your grandfather, you would still fail to kill your grandfather. You may kill somebody, but it would not be your grandfather. It would be a grandfather-duplicate living (or not living) in a different world. Back in our world, your grandfather would be hopping along just fine. The upshot of all this is that inconsistent time-travel stories tend to feature very confused protagonists. Consistent time-travel stories are the more haunting because they are stories that hang together deeply.

There is one very remarkable possibility opened up by consistent time-travel narratives. These are causal loops. In *La Jetée*, the people of the future give our hero an energy transducer (a rather unimpressive looking metal box) to take with him back to the past. Now imagine that this transducer is very successful and survives long into the future. It is still being used by the people of the future when a stranger from early human history arrives and asks for help. He is given the transducer. The past gives the transducer to the future. And the future gives it to the past. This is a causal loop. Causal loops seem to be a possible outcome of time travel. So where did the energy transducer come from? Who made it? The answers must be: it came from the past and it came from the future; and nobody made it, it just is. A miraculous causal loop to be sure, but a logically possible one. Certain kinds of time travel may be logically possible, but they are weird; sometimes very weird. That's fine. The world *is* weird; why shouldn't the cinema be weird too?

Questions

Time travel is one of the most widely used narrative devices in science fiction. Why is that? What is it about time travel that appears to interest so many? What does it have to say about regret and the wish to have lived a different life? If we can't change the past, our wish to have lived a different life is an impossible wish: there is nothing which could possibly count as the realization of the wish. Does this make it irrational?

Does the concept of time presuppose the A-Series? Is the A-Series necessary to account for change?

If you were put into a cryogenic coma for 100 years and then emerged unscathed and unchanged, feeling as if you had been asleep for only a few hours, would this count as time travel into the future? Would it satisfy the definition of time travel we used in the chapter (David Lewis's)?

Have we successfully dealt with the Grandfather Paradox in the chapter? Is there really nothing unacceptable about the solution on offer? That solution involved the claim that, were you to go back in a time machine and try to kill your grandfather (or, indeed, your earlier self), you must fail. What is to stop you succeeding?

We suggested that consistent time-travel narratives are more haunting than inconsistent time-travel stories. Is this right? Think of examples. Divide time-travel films you have seen into the consistent ones and the inconsistent ones. (You will notice that inconsistent films dominate.) Are the consistent films more powerful as narratives than the inconsistent ones? In general, does the philosophical consistency of a narrative affect its power?

World-hopping isn't time travel. Why?

"Causal loops are weird, but not impossible." What sense of possibility might be in play in this statement? What metaphysical principles might be contradicted by causal loops? Are they plausible principles?

Notes

1 You might notice that one shot isn't a still photograph.
2 A much more elaborate version of the story is told by Terry Gilliam in *Twelve Monkeys* (1995).
3 An important result of the Special Theory of Relativity is that the relations of simultaneity only exist relative to the framework of an observer. We will ignore this complication here, though we should note that Special Relativity will complicate the theories of time we are to examine.
4 Yet another problem faced by presentists is the problem of reconciling their view with Special Relativity. According to Special Relativity, simultaneity is a function of the observer's frame of reference. It is hard to see how the present can be all that exists if what counts as the present varies from one observer to another.
5 This is adapted from David Lewis (1976).
6 According to the butterfly effect, a small change to a complex system can have a large-scale effect. Pessimistically, the writers of *Butterfly Effect* appear to have taken this to mean that a small change to a complex system *must* have an unintended and very bad effect.

Further Reading

Bradbury, Ray (1952). "A Sound of Thunder." In *R is for Rocket*. New York: Doubleday.
Davies, Paul (1995). *About Time: Einstein's Unfinished Revolution*. London: Penguin.

Davies, Paul (2002). *How to Build a Time Machine*. London: Penguin.

Dowe, Phil (2000). "The Case for Time Travel." *Philosophy* 75, 441–51.

Gott, J. Richard (2001). *Time Travel in Einstein's Universe: The Physical Possibilities of Travel Through Time*. Boston: Houghton Mifflin.

Grey, William (1999). "Troubles with Time Travel." *Philosophy* 74, 55–70.

Le Poidevin, Robin (2003). *Travels in Four Dimensions: The Enigmas of Space and Time*. Oxford: Oxford University Press.

Lewis, David (1976). "The Paradoxes of Time Travel." *American Philosophical Quarterly* 13, 145–52.

Lockwood, Michael (2005). *The Labyrinth of Time: Introducing the Universe*. Oxford: Oxford University Press.

Part III

The Human Condition

Part III explores a series of topics related to basic questions of human experience, questions of our freedom, identity, pleasures, and sense of meaning.

Chapter 7 asks the question: are we the authors of our lives? Do we make our choices freely or are we the victims of fate? What is it to have a free will? Can we be responsible for our actions if we lack free will? Our guide is another Spielberg film: his 2003 film *Minority Report*. *Minority Report* is often discussed in terms of the philosophical issues around free will; and for good reason. It confronts the philosophical issue of free will directly and ambitiously. It sets up a remarkable thought experiment about the relationship between free will and moral responsibility. (This is something called the "Precrime Initiative.") At the same time, *Minority Report* is rather confused. We try to sort out the confusions while keeping the philosophical power of the film intact.

Chapter 8 asks the question: What are we? What constitutes our identity? What makes us a unique person over time and throughout change? We use Christopher Nolan's film *Memento* (2000) to put pressure on a standard philosophical account of personal identity: the psychological continuity theory. *Memento* is another film that has been much discussed in the philosophy and film literature. Understandably so, since it is a brilliant study of a person breaking all the rules: living his life without the ordinary psychological glue of memory. Our discussion of the film is focused on what we call the *Memento* Challenge. Can philosophers rise to it?

Thinking Through Film: Doing Philosophy, Watching Movies, First Edition. Damian Cox, Michael P. Levine.
© 2012 Damian Cox and Michael P. Levine. Published 2012 by Blackwell Publishing Ltd.

Chapter 9 turns attention squarely back on films themselves. We discussed a number of issues in the philosophy of film in part I. Here we take a closer look at one particular issue in philosophy and film; we do so because it promises to shed deep light on our fundamental nature. This is the issue of the spectatorship of horror. Why do people watch horror films? How do they get pleasure from being made to feel horror? The experience of horror is more than simple fear; it is fear with strings attached. It is fear with repulsion, disgust, creepiness added in. What, if anything, does it say about us that we can be made to get pleasure from the experience of horror and the witnessing of vile violence? We use a remarkable film by the Austrian filmmaker Michael Haneke to help us come to grips with these questions. Haneke's film *Funny Games* (1997 & 2007; he made it twice) is a very explicit and powerful exploration of the spectatorship of horror and violence.

In Chapter 10 we are back on less confronting ground. The issues run deep however. Our topic is death and the meaning of life and our guide is the 1952 film by the great Japanese filmmaker Akira Kurosawa: *Ikiru.* It is a complex and subtle film; but one well worth studying closely. It has much to show about post-war Japanese society, but it also deals with a simple universal theme: How to live? How to live meaningfully? The main character of the film, Watanabe, discovers an answer to the question as he struggles with terminal cancer. (It's a very sharp film, not at all maudlin; a great antidote to inferior Hollywood weepies.)

7

Fate and Choice: The Philosophy of *Minority Report*

Introduction

Imagine you travel forward in time 36 hours to visit your future self and see this future self committing a murder. You rush back determined to prevent it. Can you prevent it? Assuming that the four-dimensionalist view of time is correct (see chapter 6), and assuming that you really do travel forward in time and the person you see murdering really is your future self, then the answer is clearly no – you cannot prevent yourself committing murder. You are fated to murder. You have, it seems, no choice in the matter. If it is your fate, and you have no choice in the matter, in what sense are you really guilty of it? Are you morally responsible for actions you cannot prevent? Welcome to the challenging – and sometimes rather strange – world of the philosophy of free will.

In *Minority Report*, John Anderton (Tom Cruise) is in something like the circumstances we have just described. Anderton does not travel in time; he witnesses a pronouncement of the PreCogs. And they tell him in no uncertain terms that he will murder a man he has never heard of – Leo Crow – in 36 hours. The PreCogs are never wrong, or so we are assured. They have a gift for prophecy, but more than this, they have the capacity to actually see the future. They are witnesses to Anderton's future shooting of Crow. Can Anderton escape his fate? You might think he would try to run away, but this is Hollywood and he comes up with a different plan. He tracks down Leo Crow and confronts him. And then shoots him.

Thinking Through Film: Doing Philosophy, Watching Movies, First Edition. Damian Cox, Michael P. Levine.
© 2012 Damian Cox and Michael P. Levine. Published 2012 by Blackwell Publishing Ltd.

So far this looks like a reprise of our discussion of time travel in chapter 6. Anderton's fate is a correlate of the Grandfather Paradox. In the Grandfather Paradox it *seems* as if you can travel back in time and prevent your own birth, but of course you cannot. You have the ability to do the *sort* of thing that might be involved in your preventing your birth, but you cannot do this particular thing, this particular time. It cannot be done because it was not done. You didn't prevent your birth because you were born. In the story of Anderton and Crow, it seems as if Anderton has the ability to escape his fate (what if he stayed home and watched television for the next few days?), but he does not really have this ability. He lacks the ability to change his fate because it is his fate. It is already settled that he will shoot Crow. End of story.

But of course it isn't the end of the story. *Minority Report* is much more complicated than this – and much more puzzling. We are going to use it to pick our way through the philosophy of free will. Our key will be to ask: Just how muddled is *Minority Report*? Is the film irredeemably confused? Sometimes the best thing a film can do for us – philosophically speaking – is to challenge us to sort out its mess. In sorting out a mess we can learn a lot. Then again, perhaps *Minority Report* makes a bit more sense than it seems at first. It might even help us clarify something about the relationship between fate, free will, and moral responsibility. Let's start by examining the basic narrative setup.

If you have seen the film, you know that Anderton doesn't really murder Crow. He shoots him by accident. He has a motive to murder Crow. (He thinks Crow abducted and murdered his son.) He has an opportunity to murder Crow. But at the very last moment, under intense pressure, Anderton decides to spare Crow's life. Crow grabs the gun. There is a struggle. The gun goes off. Crow crashes out the window. The final moments are very much like those predicted by the PreCogs, but not exactly. The angles are all wrong. In the PreCog vision, Anderton shoots Crow from a distance; in the event Crow is shot at close range. In the PreCog vision, Anderton wishes Crow farewell; in the event he doesn't wish him anything. The PreCogs also get the time of the shooting wrong. The filmmakers toy with the idea that fate ensnares us, but opt instead for the possibility that we can always escape our fate, as long as we know what it is. Anderton had what is called in the film an alternate future. A person has an alternate future if there are at least two action pathways open to them – only one of which is recognized by the PreCogs – and it is not settled which one the person will take until they take it.[1] When Anderton refuses to shoot Crow he chooses his alternate future. In doing so, he exercises his free will. The way the film sets up the case, it appears that exercising free will requires the existence of an alternate future. It appears to require that the future be open; that it be possible to choose one future over another. If Anderton exercises his free will, it can't already be settled that he will do what the PreCogs have seen him do. He isn't really fated to shoot Crow. He doesn't really have a fate at all. Does this make any sense? Read on.

Precrime

Minority Report isn't just about Anderton's struggle with fate; it is about something called the "Precrime Initiative." The date is 2054. A discovery of PreCogs able to foresee murders – including visual details of a murder, the exact time of it, the names of the victims and perpetrators – is used as part of a very dubious law enforcement initiative. People identified by the PreCogs as future murderers are arrested peremptorily and haloed (a kind of suspended animation; it seems like a living death). We're told nothing of Precrime's appeals process, but since the PreCogs are considered infallible, we shouldn't hold out much hope for those arrested for precrimes. It is the discovery of the PreCogs' fallibility that finally undoes the system. Steven Spielberg – the film's director – claims in an interview that he would be in favor of a precrime initiative if only he could be absolutely sure that it was infallible.[2] Is Spielberg right?

There are two main issues at stake here. The first is about the nature of punishment. Is it ever right to punish someone for something they have not done (yet)? We might think that punishment is essentially retributive. This is to say, punishment is something meted out in response to wrongdoing. It is a reaction to wrongdoing; a way of settling accounts, as it were. This is not the only way to think about punishment, but it is a very common way. On such a view, precrime is fundamentally ill-conceived. It is a demand to settle accounts before they are drawn up. It is an attempt to react to something that hasn't happened. And this is a muddle. If we are right to think about punishment as essentially retributive, then the proper way to use the PreCogs would be in crime *prevention*, not precrime *punishment*. For example, future perpetrators might be put in short-term preventative detention rather than banished to a living death. If an act of murder had already commenced by the time precrime cops catch up with a perpetrator, then a charge of attempted murder may be fitting. If murder lies in the future, as a mere intention or as a mere future intention, then no punishment would be warranted.

The second philosophical issue raised by the Precrime Initiative concerns the relation between free will and moral responsibility. If the Precrime Initiative worked perfectly – if the PreCogs got it absolutely right – then it would be true that individuals identified by the PreCogs will murder unless they are stopped. They are fated to murder unless they are stopped. But what kind of choice do they really have? Since it is their fate, it seems that pre-criminals have no real choice about their future. If someone has no choice but to do a thing, are they really morally responsible for doing that thing? The film would have us believe that they are. The Precrime Initiative is criticized in the film, not because it is intrinsically wrong, but because it turns out that the PreCogs' predictions are sometimes incorrect. But why should we hold somebody morally responsible for choices they are fated to make, i.e. for choices they can't *not* make? Some philosophers – they are called compatibilists and we discuss them in more detail later on in the chapter – try to answer questions like this by tying responsibility to ownership of choice. Perhaps a person is responsible for their choices as long as they really are *their* choices. As long as a choice is wholly made by the person themselves, they may well be responsible for it. And they may be responsible whether or not they are fated to make the choice. People may not be responsible for actions they are compelled to take. Imagine a person being hypnotized to kill.[3] Or imagine somebody undergoing a psychotic episode in which they are not in control of their deliberative processes. When people are being compelled, they are not acting on their own will. And if they are not acting on their own will, they shouldn't be held responsible.

So this is how we might think of precrime as it is initially presented in the film. It is assumed that the PreCogs only finger individuals who are fated to murder. These future perpetrators have no alternate future; they cannot refuse their fate. Only the precrime cops can stop them killing. Nonetheless, the choice to kill is entirely their own. Nobody compels them. They are in control of their deliberative faculties. And yet, if they are not stopped, they will murder. Thus they are responsible for murder, or will be.[4] In this one respect at least, the Precrime Initiative might not be so unfair to the pre-guilty after all.

We thus arrive at two perspectives on fate and choice, both represented in *Minority Report*. In the first perspective, genuine free will requires an alternate future. To have free will it must be possible for us to escape our fate. We must have the power to choose between equally possible futures. In the second perspective, we are responsible for choices we make under our own steam. If we make a choice, and make it using the resources of our own minds, then we must own the choice. We are responsible for it. How do these two perspectives relate to each other? To get clear about this, we need to take a look at some philosophy. But first, there is a rather unsettling wrinkle in the plot of *Minority Report* that we ought to get our heads around.

What do the PreCogs see? They see murders. But how can that be when the murders are prevented? There is an attempt to deal with this problem in the film, but it is rather lame. Here is the relevant dialogue between Danny Witwer (investigating officer from the attorney general's department), Gordon Fletcher (precrime cop) and John Anderton (chief of the Precrime Initiative):

WITWER: Let's not kid ourselves. We arrest individuals who have broken no law.

FLETCHER: But they will. The commission of the crime is absolute metaphysics. The PreCogs see the future and they're never wrong.

WITWER: But it's not the future if you stop it. Isn't that a fundamental paradox?

ANDERTON: Yes it is. You're talking about predetermination which happens all the time. (Anderton rolls a ball along the desk. Witwer catches it before it falls to the floor.) Why did you catch that?

WITWER: Because it was going to fall.

ANDERTON: You're sure?

WITWER: Yeah.

ANDERTON: But it didn't fall. You caught it. The fact that you prevented it happening didn't change the fact that it was going to happen.

WITWER: Do you ever get any false positives? Someone intends to kill his boss or his wife but he never goes through with it? How do the PreCogs know the difference?

ANDERTON: The PreCogs don't see what you intend to do, only what you will do.

So the PreCogs see what you *will* do. Except you won't do it. Something will stop you: the Precrime Unit. This isn't some kind of spooky paradox. It's a flat contradiction. The PreCogs aren't seeing things that will happen. They are seeing things that *will happen unless they are stopped from happening.* They are seeing a kind of conditional future. How can we explain this kind of precognition? Here's how *not* to explain it: information from the future loops back into the present and alters the future. That sounds nice when you say it quickly, but it makes precious little sense. Rewriting the future in this way makes no more sense than rewriting the past. If the relevant information comes from the future and no murder occurs in the future, then the information received ought to reflect this. The PreCogs ought to see – not a murder – but an arrest. Given their other narrative commitments, however, *Minority Report*'s writers – Scott Frank and Jon Cohen[5] – had good reason to avoid the obvious solution of depicting

PreCog visions of an arrest. It is important for the story that the PreCogs sometimes get it wrong. They see a particular future, but people have the power to change the future. People sometimes have alternate futures; they can change their fate. John Anderton furnishes us with one example of this. At the end of the film, Lamar Burgess – the founder of the Precrime Initiative – furnishes us with an even more definitive example.

So what do the PreCogs actually see when they witness a future murder? They do not see the future. They see a possible future: the way the world would have turned out if they hadn't altered things with their prophecy. This isn't any ordinary flow of information from the future to the present. It involves access to a different kind of thing altogether: not the future of the actual world, but the future of a close possible world. The idea that a resident of one possible world can literally see into the affairs of another possible world makes no good sense on any coherent account of possible worlds. The writers' philosophical mistake was to emphasize sight. If the PreCogs were to mysteriously deduce a conditional future rather than actually see it, the story would run into less metaphysical trouble (although the idea of such a deduction is absurd enough on its own account). As it stands, however, there is no rescuing the story from its muddle.

Nonetheless, the fact that the metaphysical underpinnings of *Minority Report* are in such bad shape need not deprive the film of philosophical interest. It remains a very interesting test case for assessing our intuitions about freedom, fate, and responsibility. So let's turn to the philosophy underlying this aspect of the film.

Philosophy of Fate

Fatalism is the view that all of our actions are fated and we are powerless to alter our fate. There are three main varieties: metaphysical fatalism, theological fatalism, and causal determinism. All of them are philosophically controversial. Metaphysical fatalism (sometimes also called logical fatalism) is a conclusion some philosophers draw from the four-dimensionalist theory of time we examined in chapter 6. Recall the time-travel story we started out with in the present chapter. You travel 36 hours into the future and see yourself committing a murder. Your fate has been sealed. It is a fact about the future that you will murder. Since it will happen, there is nothing you can do to prevent it happening. A fact is a fact. According to metaphysical fatalism, every fact about the future is already settled in just this way. The only strange thing in our story is that we know our fate; but our having a fate does not depend on our knowing it. We have a fate regardless. Life is simply the business of discovering what it is. Theological fatalism adds a special twist to this story by appealing to God's omniscience and omnipotence. God decided to create the world, and She did so with full knowledge of every event that would occur in it. If God wanted us to act in a different way, God could always have chosen to create a different world. We are victims of God's choice.

Both metaphysical and theological fatalism seem to threaten our sense of ourselves as free beings. They picture us as powerless to alter our fate: as victims of future facts or as victims of God's creative choices. The third form of fatalism – causal determinism –makes us victims of the past. Causal determinism – we will often refer to it just as determinism – is the view that every state of the world is necessitated by past states of the world. When Anderton rolls the ball along his desk, the laws of physics, together with various features of the situation, conspire to ensure that the ball rolls until the end of the desk and then starts falling. The ball has no choice but to roll across the desk until it falls off. This means, roughly, that given relevant laws of physics and the ball's initial condition as it started out on its path across the desk, along with other conditions of the situation (friction between the ball and the desk surface, atmospheric pressure, the gravitational pull of the Earth, the absence of obstacles and other intervening conditions, and so on), the ball must roll. It cannot not roll. But then Witwer catches it. What happens here? Witwer sees the ball, estimates its flight path once it leaves the desk, decides to catch it, readies his muscles, gets into catching position, senses the impact of the ball on the palm of his hand, and finally closes his fingers around the ball. This is only the tip of the iceberg of course: a lot has to happen for the catch to happen. But is there any point in the chain of cause and effect that isn't simply a more complicated version of the rolling ball? Is there any point in the chain which isn't necessitated by prior states? The obvious point would be Witwer's *decision* to catch the ball. A decision is a mental action. Is it just another element of the chain of cause and effect at work in this scenario? Is Witwer's decision necessitated by prior states? Determinists say yes. They think that everything that happens in the world is necessitated by prior states of the world so Witwer's decision to catch a falling ball is necessitated by prior states of the world (probably, prior states of his brain).

Determinism represents another way in which our fate might be sealed. If determinism is correct, every decision we make is necessitated by prior states of the world and this chain of necessitation stretches back before we were even born. Every thought we have had, every choice we have made, was settled for us before we were born. We are caught in the grip of the giant machinery of the world. Determinists may not be right about this. There is good reason to think that at least some events aren't necessitated by prior states of the world. Events in very small parts of the world seem to be governed by laws that don't necessitate, but specify chances instead. For example, the laws of physics might tell us that a particular atom of plutonium has a 50 percent chance of decaying within 24,100 years (or thereabouts). If the atom suddenly decays, the decay will have been unpredictable because nothing determined it. The atom didn't *have* to decay today. It just did. If this story about radioactive decay is right, then at least some events aren't necessitated by past events. Does this help us escape determinism about human choices? That's not at all clear. It might be the case that some of the causal processes involved in our choice-making are indeterminate in the way radioactive decay is indeterminate. Then again, it might not be the case. If choices are events happening in the brain, they may be happening at a sufficiently macroscopic scale so that indeterministic laws no longer apply to them. The indeterminacy evident at a quantum level may average out at the level of brain events. If mental events are brain events, they might well be caught up in an inexorably deterministic system of cause and effect.

So we have three forms of fatalism, based on different presuppositions. They should not be confused. Theological fatalism and causal determinism each add their own extra ingredient to the metaphysical fatalist's position. Theological fatalism adds God's omniscient and omnipotent creation of the world. Causal determinism adds the necessitation of the future by the past. One can be a metaphysical fatalist without being a determinist; but not vice versa. It's not clear which form of fatalism – metaphysical fatalism or causal determinism – is being worked over in *Minority Report*. But this does not much matter because the film's philosophical interest mostly resides in the conceptual connections it draws between fatalism, free will, and moral responsibility. The film does not give us any reason to believe in fatalism or to reject it, but it does raise conceptual questions about the relationship between free will, moral responsibility, and fate.

Philosophy of Free Will and Moral Responsibility

The key philosophical questions at this point are how one or another form of fatalism affects the possibility of free will and the possibility of moral responsibility. There are two main philosophical approaches to these questions: compatibilism and incompatibilism.

According to the incompatibilist, free will is incompatible with fatalism. In order for you to act freely, your future must be open. This means either that your future is undetermined by the past (so that you escape causal determinism) or that your future is not yet factual (so that you escape metaphysical determinism). Incompatibilist theories of free will require that an agent's choices not be determined by past events (that we escape causal determinism). This may come about because choices have no cause, or because they are indeterministically caused, or because they are caused by the agent herself. The latter possibility requires something called agent-causation: a sort of causation in which an event is brought about, not via the causal powers of prior states, but via the causal powers of a substance, the agent herself. According to theories of agent causation, causation comes in two flavors. Sometimes causation involves a relation between events (as when the light comes on after you press the light switch). Sometimes causation involves a relation between a substance – namely an agent – and an event (as when God creates the world, or you make up your mind). Agent causation is often regarded as an uncongenial view of causation, but the alternative incompatibilist theories of free will have problems of their own.[6] Tracing free decisions back to an indeterministic causal event leads to the problem of luck. If a free decision is caused indeterministically, how is this different from its being a matter of sheer luck that it turns out as it does? And how is it a demonstration of our freedom to trace our actions back to a lucky or unlucky happenstance?

Compatibilists have a very different take on the relation between free will and fatalism. They think that free will is compatible with fatalism. According to the compatibilist, a person acts act freely so long as they choose under their own steam: so long as their actions are fully down to *them*. For the causal determinist and the metaphysical fatalist alike, this means that your choices are things you can be said to be the author of. Just what it takes for a choice to be authored is a matter of considerable controversy. Compatibilists want to rule out cases of compulsion (for example, when you choose at the point of a gun or under hypnosis or, perhaps, in the grip of an addiction). Often, they also want to rule out cases in which you can't be said to have properly decided to act at all. For example, you may act without consciously deliberating, in which case an action seems to befall you like an accident. Or you may act when you are not in full possession of your faculties; without being able to properly deliberate, for example, under the influence of a drug or in the midst of a psychotic episode.

Enormous amounts of philosophical ink have been used up discussing the various merits of compatibilism and incompatibilism. Mixed in with this debate is another debate about the relationship between acting freely and moral responsibility. As we have just seen, compatibilists think we can be acting freely even if our action is locked in by fate. That is, they think we can act freely even if we could not have acted otherwise. They also tend to think that we are morally responsible for our free actions, so that we can be morally responsible for an action even if we could not have done otherwise. Incompatibilists generally reject this view. They tend to insist that we can only be morally responsible for actions we have *genuine* choice about; and genuine choice requires the openness of the future. By incompatibilist lights, we do not have a genuine choice about whether we will do something if it has already been settled that we will do that thing.

It is important to notice, however, that there are two separate issues here. One is about free will. The other is about moral responsibility. Perhaps we can clarify our options if we separate them out. This is the strategy of the philosopher John Martin Fischer (1994; 1998). Fischer distinguishes between two ways in which an agent has control over her actions. He calls them guidance control and regulative control. We have guidance control of our actions if they issue from our deliberations in an appropriately reason-responding way. That is, we have guidance control of our actions if we deliberate about them, using our reason to guide our decisions. We need not use our reason very well. We might respond to very foolish reasons or we might fail to give reasons anything like their due weight. Nonetheless, as long as we use our deliberative capacities in a minimally adequate way, we can be said to have guided our actions. Working out the details of guidance control is basically the project of working out a compatibilist account of free will. Guidance control does not require the capacity to escape fate. We might have had guidance control over an action even if we were predetermined to do it. Guidance control only requires that we exercise our capacity to deliberate in an appropriate way. (Guidance control does not equate to a power to change our fate.) Regulative control, on the other hand, is the control we would have over our actions if we really could regulate their occurrence or non-occurrence. To have regulative control of our actions requires that we could really choose otherwise. It requires that the future is genuinely open to us. In this way, Fischer distinguishes between a compatibilist concept of the control of our actions (guidance control) and an incompatibilist concept of the control of our actions (regulative control). Remember, we have two different questions to address. What is required for us to possess free will? What is required for us to be morally responsible for our actions?

Fischer thinks only guidance control is necessary for moral responsibility. Regulative control might be needed if we are to gain the status of truly free beings, but only guidance control is needed for us to be morally responsible for our actions. Fischer employs an argument of another philosopher – Harry Frankfurt – to try to show that guidance control is all the control needed for moral responsibility. Frankfurt's argument is based on a thought experiment. Imagine a trained assassin set to shoot a political candidate at an election rally. The assassin has fully made up his mind to do the shooting, but his masters are not taking any chances. They install a chip inside his brain, a failsafe device. If, at the last moment, the assassin loses his courage and is about to decide against the shooting, the failsafe device will be activated and a signal dispatched to the assassin's brain, forcing him to decide to shoot. Now imagine that the assassin goes ahead with the shooting without need of the failsafe device. It seems obvious that he is morally responsible for the shooting. Nonetheless, he is fated to decide to shoot. He could not do anything other than make the decision he made. Thus it is possible to be fully morally responsible for one's actions even if one could not have decided otherwise.[7] Thus it is possible to be fully morally responsible for one's actions even if one does not have regulative control of them.

Frankfurt's argument has not convinced everybody.[8] Here is a standard argument strategy against it. The idea is to force a dilemma onto Frankfurt – the processes leading to the assassin's decision are either deterministic or they are indeterministic – and then show that the argument fails on both horns of the dilemma. Consider how the argument fares if the processes leading to the decision are indeterministic. If they are indeterministic, then the assassin's controllers will not know when to intervene. They have to be able to intervene before he makes his choice, otherwise they wouldn't be controlling his choice, but forcing him to shoot against his will. But when can they intervene? If they settle on a point and say "all the indications are that our assassin is going to decide against shooting, we must intervene now," they have left it open that the assassin could have chosen otherwise. He still had a chance to come up with a different choice, his mind being an indeterministic system and all. So the argument fails on this horn of the dilemma. Now consider the other horn. If the processes leading to the assassin's decision are deterministic, the activities of his controllers are irrelevant from a philosophical point of view. What will happen is already settled by a causal history stretching back to before the assassin was born; what the controllers would do is settled by the same causal history. So the controllers add nothing to the causal determinist's story. Therefore we can't use their presence in the story to show anything about the relation between moral responsibility and the regulative control of actions that we couldn't show by reflecting just on causal determinism and its philosophical consequences. Whether moral responsibility requires regulative control has to be sorted out on different grounds. The argument fails on this second horn of the dilemma. The argument fails on both horns of the dilemma, so the argument fails. It might be possible to rescue Frankfurt's argument from this criticism, but let's return to our movie to see if we can find alternative support for Fischer's and Frankfurt's position.[9]

The Pre-Guilt of the Pre-Criminal

When we are first introduced to the Precrime Initiative in *Minority Report*, we are told that pre-criminals will murder unless they are stopped. We are given spectacular evidence of this in the case of Howard Marks, who is moments away from killing his wife and her lover, just as the PreCogs foretold, when he is stopped by the precrime cops. Howard Marks is guilty of attempted murder. But just say that the precrime cops had got to him moments before he had made the first moves to murder. What would he be guilty of then? Carrying a pair of scissors? In his own house? The basic moral proposition of the Precrime Initiative is that the Marks who is prevented from murdering is just as guilty as a Marks who murders. There are various reasons to be unhappy with this moral proposition, but the idea that pre-criminals escape moral responsibility because they are fated to murder does not seem to be one of them. Indeed, the film illustrates the contrary argument. Precrime comes to seem morally bankrupt to Anderton only when he discovers the possibility that some pre-criminals (most notably himself) have had alternate futures. There is good reason for this, of course. If someone has an alternate future, they have regulative control of their actions. And if they have regulative control of their actions, PreCog visions are no longer reliable. A person in regulative control of his affairs might go through with murder (Anderton almost did) or he might not. If he is in regulative control, his future is not factually set and he can't be pre-guilty of anything. On the other hand, if pre-criminals only ever exercised guidance control of their actions, PreCog visions may well still be on track and the Precrime Initiative would seem to rest on sturdier foundations, at least in this respect.

Minority Report elicits intuitions supporting the idea that guidance control suffices for moral responsibility. It does this by introducing the idea of the fated killer and giving it enough narrative support to allow us to answer the question: do fated killers escape responsibility for their actions merely because they are *fated* to kill? The narrative richness of the story and its telling allows us to answer this question – negatively – in a robust way. However, *Minority Report* is a very complicated film, and it is difficult to know whether our intuitions are being distorted by its complications. Our sympathies are manipulated skillfully: from early, unreflective support for the Precrime Initiative (as we see the Precrime Unit saving innocent lives) to latter hostility to it (as we witness numerous unjust dealings, particularly with respect to the hapless Anderton). The virtues of precrime steadily recede from view as the film progresses. The precrime cops save no more lives, but spend their time chasing our protagonist, eventually capturing him and sending him, unfairly, to halo hell. The morally problematic character of precrime is not properly exposed in the film, but the historical corruption of the Precrime Initiative assumes critical importance. By the end of the film, we are thoroughly sick of the Precrime Initiative and the harm it has done, including the harm it has done the PreCogs themselves. Throughout all this noisy moral display, the one feature of precrime not problematized at all is the idea that responsibility and fate are wholly compatible; that people are responsible for their choices even if they are fated to make them.

Regulative control may not be necessary for moral responsibility, but it still seems to be something of great importance to us. *Minority Report* has a happy ending, in part, because free will is made to triumph over fatalism. At the very end of the film, Lamar Burgess chooses suicide rather than murder even though the PreCogs had pre-visioned murder. In proving the PreCogs wrong, he proves, not that he is morally responsible for his actions (that is a given in either case), but that he is able to originate his actions, not just guide them. Burgess proves that he is something more than the plaything of fate. The threat of the Precrime Initiative was twofold. First, it was unjust (either because it punished those who were not yet guilty, or because it punished the wholly innocent). Second, it denied that we have regulative control of our affairs; it portrayed us as the playthings of fate. Securing the demise of the Precrime Initiative enabled Spielberg to pull off a double happy ending (or a multiple happy ending if we count the blessings of all the surviving characters). Its demise both ends an unjust and exploitative system and reasserts something fundamentally valuable in the human condition: the possibility that we are the authors and originators of our own actions. To the extent that

Spielberg really does capture a blissfully happy outcome, the film provides evidence that regulative control is an important ingredient of what we value about free will. Of course it goes no way towards showing us that we have regulative control of our affairs, but it would be silly to expect a film to do that.

Questions

If the PreCogs were able to accurately predict attempts to murder, would the Precrime Initiative be justified? (Imagine a less extreme form of punishment than "haloing.")

Is there any way of making philosophical sense of the PreCog visions?

How do the three forms of fatalism we described in the chapter – metaphysical fatalism, theological fatalism, and causal determinism – compare with each other? Are they equally potent ways of undermining free will?

Agent causation is often regarded as philosophically suspect. Why? What are the prospects for an incompatibilist theory of free will that doesn't assume agent causation? The problem of luck haunts such theories. Is it really a problem? Can it be surmounted?

Compatibilist theories of free will face the following problem. If my decision is caused by prior events and I had no choice in those prior events (according to causal determinists, the chain of causes leading to my decision stretch back well before I was born), then I can have no choice in the decision. How can I be said to decide freely when I had no choice but to decide as I do? Is this a good argument? Is there a way around it?

Is regulative control necessary for moral responsibility? We described two arguments that say it is not necessary. One, owing to Frankfurt, involves cases in which it seems that somebody is responsible for their choices even if they couldn't have chosen otherwise. The other is an appeal to intuitions unleashed by the movie. We criticized Frankfurt's argument, but gave qualified support for the movie-based argument. Is the movie-based argument really better than the Frankfurt argument? Are the intuitions in the movie clear enough to support Frankfurt's conclusion? Are they manipulated and distorted by the narrative or the way it is filmed?

Does the film furnish intuitive support for the idea that regulative control is necessary in order to have genuine free will? How can a film manage this? What are the dangers of drawing intuitions from films in this way?

Notes

1 In the film, it seems that alternate futures are only had by those who are made aware of the PreCog's prophecy about them. The idea seems to be that choice – including free choice – requires the capacity to deliberate between alternative courses of action. If a perpetrator is unaware of the PreCog's prophecy – for example, Howard Marks at the very start of the film – then they cannot deliberate about whether to accede to the prophecy or deny it. So they are trapped into acceding to it. However, this is a mistake. Exercising free choice may require deliberation between options, but the PreCogs' prophecies don't exhaust the range of options for deliberation. For example, Howard Marks can't deliberate about whether to accede to the PreCog's prophecy that he will kill his wife and her lover because he doesn't know about that prophecy. But he can deliberate about a very similar thing: whether or not to kill his wife and her lover. We will overlook this wrinkle in the plot of *Minority Report*. (There are more wrinkles to overlook, as we shall soon see.)

2 *From Story to Screen: The Story, The Debate* on the 2003 DVD release.

3 The classic movie treatment of this scenario is *The Manchurian Candidate* (1962; remade, rather more elaborately, in 2004).

4 You might notice another flaw in the system just here. The PreCogs witness future killings. Law enforcement agents interpret these as murders and arrest the future perpetrators for precrime. But since the affair is in the future, and is prevented in any case (we're coming to the question of how *that* might be possible), its circumstances can't be investigated. So there will be cases in which the moral and legal character of the action will be unobservable. And yet those found guilty of precrime are haloed. Not such a good system, really. Anderton himself is a victim of this flaw.

5 The script is based on Philip K. Dick's story of the same name. Little remains of Dick's story in the film script, apart from the basic setup, and the prediction that John Anderton will kill.

6 See Clarke (2008) for a useful survey of the main options.

7 Frankfurt (1969) presents the argument. Note the argument doesn't require that the assassin is morally responsible no matter what he does. If the failsafe device had to be deployed, then the assassin escapes responsibility for the killing. Frankfurt's argument is not an argument for fatalism, nor is it an argument for compatibilism. It is an argument for the possibility of being morally responsible for things one could not help but do.

8   Widerker & McKenna (2002).
9   Fischer (1994: chapter 7; 2010) offers an elaboration and defense of Frankfurt's argument.

Further Reading

Campbell, C. A. (1967). *In Defence of Free Will and Other Essays*. London: Allen & Unwin Ltd.

Clarke, Randolph (2003). *Libertarian Accounts of Free Will*. Oxford: Oxford University Press.

Clarke, Randolph (2008). "Incompatibilist (Nondeterministic) Theories of Free Will." *Stanford Encyclopedia of Philosophy*. http://plato.stanford.edu/entries/incompatibilism-theories/.

Dennett, Daniel (1984). *Elbow Room: The Varieties of Free Will Worth Having*. Cambridge, MA: MIT Press.

Fischer, John Martin (1994). *The Metaphysics of Free Will*. Oxford: Blackwell.

Fischer, John Martin (1998). *Responsibility and Control*. Cambridge: Cambridge University Press.

Fischer, John Martin (1999). "Recent Work on Moral Responsibility." *Ethics* 110, 93–139.

Fischer, John Martin (2010). "The Frankfurt Cases: The Moral of the Stories." *Philosophical Review* 119, 315–36.

Fischer, John Martin, & Mark Ravizza (1992). "When the Will is Free." In Timothy O'Connor, ed., *Agents, Causes, and Events: Essays on Indeterminism and Free Will*. New York: Oxford University Press, 239–69.

Frankfurt, Harry (1969). "Alternate Possibilities and Moral Responsibility." *Journal of Philosophy* 66, 829–39.

Frankfurt, Harry (1988). *The Importance of What We Care About*. Cambridge: Cambridge University Press.

Frankfurt, Harry (2003 [1982]). "Freedom of the Will and the Concept of a Person." In Gary Watson, ed., *Free Will*. 2nd edn. Oxford: Oxford University Press, 81–95.

Honderich, Ted (1988). *A Theory of Determinism*. Oxford: Oxford University Press.

Kane, Robert (1996). *The Significance of Free Will*. New York: Oxford University Press.

Nozick, Robert (1995). "Choice and Indeterminism." In Timothy O'Connor, ed., *Agents, Causes, and Events: Essays on Indeterminism and Free Will*. New York: Oxford University Press, 101–14.

O'Connor, Timothy, ed. (1995). *Agents, Causes, and Events: Essays on Indeterminism and Free Will*. New York: Oxford University Press.

O'Connor, Timothy (2000). *Persons and Causes: The Metaphysics of Free Will*. New York: Oxford University Press.

Pereboom, Derk (2001). *Living Without Free Will*. Cambridge: Cambridge University Press.

Pink, Thomas (2004). *Free Will: A Very Short Introduction*. Oxford: Oxford University Press.

Strawson, Galen (1986). *Freedom and Belief*. Oxford: Clarendon Press.

Van Inwagen, Peter (1983). *An Essay on Free Will*. Oxford: Oxford University Press.

Watson, Gary, ed. (2003). *Free Will*. 2nd edn. Oxford: Oxford University Press.

Wegner, Daniel (2002). *The Illusion of Conscious Will*. Cambridge, MA: MIT Press.

Widerker, David, & Michael McKenna, eds. (2002). *Moral Responsibility and Alternative Possibilities*. Aldershot: Ashgate Publishing.

8

Personal Identity: The Case of *Memento*

Introduction

Personal identity is an important and long-standing topic in philosophy and is well suited to exploration through film.[1] One of the best philosophical treatments of it in contemporary film is Christopher Nolan's *Memento* (2000).

Memento tells the story of Leonard Shelby, a man with a very severe case of amnesia. Shelby has what is called anterograde amnesia: a well-documented medical condition in which a person loses the capacity to lay down new memories in their long-term memory system.[2] Nolan's depiction of anterograde amnesia in *Memento* is pretty accurate. Shelby's case is severe, but his general cognitive abilities remain intact. His memory of experiences and facts set into long-term memory before his brain injury is unaffected. His short-term memory system is also unaffected and this allows him to concentrate on a chain of actions lasting several minutes. Nonetheless, after a few minutes of coherent conscious activity Shelby invariably loses the plot and has to reacquaint himself with his surroundings: with what he has just done, what he is trying to achieve, who he is talking to, and so on. Shelby has the power to learn some things through habituation, and so he does not have to start this process of re-acquaintance completely from scratch. As he emerges from one coherent episode of consciousness into another Shelby falls readily into the pattern of his life-plan. *Memento* illustrates this process of emerging from one coherent episode of consciousness to another quite brilliantly. Nolan runs the

Thinking Through Film: Doing Philosophy, Watching Movies, First Edition. Damian Cox, Michael P. Levine.

movie – at least a central strand of it – backwards in order to match the viewer's epistemic condition with Shelby's.

The film explores Shelby's struggle to maintain a coherent life in the midst of this debilitating amnesia. It is a thriller, so Shelby's way of doing this is a little bizarre. He is searching for revenge – or what he thinks is revenge – against the man who attacked him and his wife, causing his brain damage, sexually assaulting and murdering his wife. Since he has no capacity to create new long-term memories, the task of pursuing a plan of revenge is enormously difficult. Shelby is able to do it by using various clues or mementos. He uses clues in the form of photos: a photo of a car to identify his car (or rather what he thinks is his car); photos of people to record key facts about them and issue instructions to himself about how to treat them. He has tattooed across his body the main narrative of his plan for revenge. The tattoos represent the fundamental trusted facts at his disposal. (*Spoiler warning:* So when Shelby decides to have a license plate number tattooed onto his thigh at the very end of the film, this turns out to be an act of murder!) On emerging from one coherent episode to another, Shelby has to reacquaint himself with the basic facts of his life and his quest for revenge, but he is clearly habituated to this process. He is not surprised to find his body covered in tattoos in the way we would be surprised were we to wake up to discover our body transformed this way. He knows how to use the mementos he has collected and what they mean. He understands the significance – or rather what he takes to be the significance – of the police files he has in his possession and of the investigative notes he has made. What Shelby cannot do is forge new explicit memories – including, crucially, autobiographical or episodic memories – so he has none of the acquaintance with his immediate past which we take for granted and which gives us a sense of a coherent life.

Autobiographical or episodic memories are memories of experience rather than facts. Memory of facts is called semantic memory; memory of experiences is called episodic memory. They are very different kinds of memory. Philosophers divide up the class of episodic memories in a further way. They divide them into actual memories (which may be distorted in various ways, but which register an actual experience had by the person remembering) and quasi-memories (which appear as if they register past experience, but may not do so: they may be the experiences of another person; they may be completely false or manufactured memories; or they may be actual memories after all). Quasi-memories are experiences in which we *seem* to remember something that happened to us.[3] Actual memories are memories in which we really do remember something that happened to us. They rule out false memories (e.g. memories that have been somehow implanted) and memories that pick out the experiences of others (you remember winning the egg-and-spoon race at your sixth birthday party; in fact your sister won the race and you have adopted her winning experience and made it your own). If we say that someone has a quasi-memory we remain completely neutral as to whether it is an actual memory or only seems to be an actual memory. We will soon see why philosophers make this distinction.

What can *Memento* teach us about the philosophical issue of personal identity? To answer this, we need to set up the philosophical question at issue.

The Philosophical Puzzle of Personal Identity

In fact there are many philosophical puzzles about personal identity. Consider this set of questions. What *kind* of person am I? What *makes* me the kind of person I am? How much could I change and still be me? What makes me a person at all? Could I exist without a body? Could I continue to exist beyond my physical death? Would I survive in a persistent vegetative state, or would such a state literally spell the end for me (so that in a persistent vegetative state my body remains alive, but I no longer exist)? Among all these questions, one set of questions is particularly puzzling and has attracted the most philosophical attention. This is the general question of our persistence over time and through change.

A person is a single individual and remains that individual throughout their existence. And yet people change all the time. Our minds change as we undergo new experiences, create new memories and slowly forge or alter our character. In many traditional religious pictures of the life to come, our death represents a kind of awaking into a new existence: in death we are radically transformed and yet we somehow *survive* our death. Is this even possible? What does it mean to say that we survive in a case like this? The natural answer is to say that we survive just in case the individual who died is the very same individual who exists after death, radically transformed, singing in a choir of angels.[4] This is a question about our persistence, i.e. our identity over time and our identity in spite of change.

How can we talk about being the same person over time, even though we are clearly very different at different stages of our lives? We just have to make the right distinctions and take care with them. Philosophers distinguish between two main kinds of identity: qualitative identity and numerical identity. Qualitative identity is the identity two separate things

you died? If the criterion of your numerical identity is the continuity of your living body, then we would have to say that, in the case of your piece-by-piece transformation into a robot, you have died and been replaced by a new thing: a robotic replacement that, whatever its virtues, is not you. On the other hand, if the criterion of your numerical identity is something less specific – the continuity of your body (whether organic or not) – then we should conclude that you have become a robot. You did not cease to exist when your arm was replaced by a robotic arm. You would not cease to exist if one of your neurons were replaced by a micro-switch. So, generalizing these intuitions, you do not cease to exist when your entire body is replaced by functionally equivalent parts. On this way of interpreting the robot-replacement operation, you *become* a robot.

How can we decide which interpretation of the robot-replacement scenario is correct? It all depends upon the criterion of numerical identity we think applies to us. But how can we decide which is the correct criterion? It turns out that there are quite a few candidates, so how can we decide between them? One of the most promising ways of exploring the issue is by running thought experiments. In a personal identity thought experiment, we imagine a scenario of radical change and consult our intuitions about whether the person undergoing this change would have survived or not. Our intuitions provide us with clues about our concept of personal identity. And if our intuitions are strong, widely shared, consistent, and reliable (for example, if they are not distorted or manipulated by the way we tell the story), then they are a very good guide to our concept of personal identity. Robust and reliable intuitions should guide us to the conditions under which people retain their identity through change.

Running thought experiments is important way of performing conceptual analysis. It is a method of discovering the contours of important concepts. We presented a thought experiment – the robot-replacement experiment – a few paragraphs back. Is it obvious to you that you would survive the operation of replacing your body parts with robotic equivalents? Perhaps it isn't. Surely, it depends on just *how* successful the entire replacement operation is, and by what measure. What if your robot replacement fails to remember anything about your prior life? (Say that memory turns out to be encoded, not in the connections between your neurons – connections that can be replicated by micro-switches – but in some mysterious property of organic brain cells that is lost when they are replaced by non-organic switches.) In this case it is not at all obvious that you have survived the operation. Indeed, for many people, it just seems obvious that we would not have survived the replacement operation if we could remember *nothing* of our past life. Something vital would seem to have been lost in the translation from human brain to robot brain. What if your robot-replacement fails to have consciousness at all: it walks and talks like a conscious being, but inside the lights are out (so to speak)? (For instance, it might turn out that consciousness is not a property of the flow of information inside your brain, but is a non-physical property tied in some way to the organic nature of your central nervous system.) In this case, the operation seems clearly to have been a failure; at some stage or another, the patient died on the operating table.

Now we don't have to believe that consciousness is non-physical or that human memory is encoded in subtle organic properties of brain cells in order to learn an important lesson from the hypothetical thoughts of the last paragraph. If a failure to preserve consciousness or a failure to preserve memory would mean the end of you, this is enough to be getting on with. What the concept of personal identity is keeping track of, it seems, is our continued *conscious* existence. (Perhaps continued conscious existence is necessary, but not sufficient for your persistence. We would need to run other thought experiments to check this.)

What is perhaps the most widely held view of personal identity is based on the intuitions we have been exploring just now. It is usually called the psychological continuity theory of personal identity. In its simplest form, the psychological continuity theory says that the criterion of numerical identity for persons is continuity of consciousness. But there is a problem. Your consciousness is far from continuous: it is interrupted by periods of sleep, for example. So "continuity of consciousness" can't mean "uninterrupted flow of consciousness." To save the theory, we must come up with a different account of the continuity of consciousness. What connects one episode of the uninterrupted flow of consciousness to another episode in just the right way? The obvious, and maybe the best, answer is memory: episodic memory. You wake up from sleep and are immediately immersed in your ongoing conscious life through episodic memory. Perhaps you don't remember the very last thing you experienced before falling asleep, but you remember something of the day before. You connect that day to this new one through remembered experience. Taking up this way of thinking about the issue, we set out the following version of the psychological continuity theory. We call it Strong Psychological Continuity:

Strong Psychological Continuity
A set of person-stages (these are complete periods of the uninterrupted flow of consciousness) is a numerically distinct individual – a unique person – if and only if each person-stage is connected to the person-stage immediately prior to it through episodic memory.

There are technical problems that we have to deal with before Strong Psychological Continuity can be thought at all plausible. It has long been recognized that setting out the theory in the way we have done can be circular if we are not careful. We set out the theory in terms of episodic memory. Do we mean episodic actual memory or episodic quasi-memory? (Remember actual memories are memories of an experience that the person remembering actually had; quasi-memories are memories that seem this way, but might not be.) It can't be actual memory. If our theory says that personal identity consists of person-stages linked by actual episodic memory, this is the equivalent of saying that it consists of person-stages linked by memories of experiences had by the person in question and, in particular, not had by anyone else. In this way, we end up defining personal identity in terms of actual episodic memory and actual episodic memory in terms of personal identity. This circularity is unacceptable. To be careful, then, we should set out the psychological continuity theory in terms of quasi-memory. Our criterion of numerical identity can now be drawn in terms of the connection of person-stages through quasi-memories. A set of person-stages constitutes a unique individual if and only if every person-stage is connected to the prior person-stage through quasi-memories that were laid down in the right way. Now we need a theory of "laying down memories in the right way," one that avoids running the theory in a circle. Roughly, we might say that the right way of laying down a quasi-memory for the purposes of our theory involves telling a causal story about how the memory was created: an experience causes a memory-trace in the normal way. Laying down a memory-trace in the normal way doesn't presuppose anything about the identity of the owner of the experience or the owner of the memory-trace. If the tactic works, we will have found a way of avoiding circularity and saving the theory. Talk of quasi-memories makes things very cumbersome, so we'll ignore this complication in the rest of our discussion. But it is good to know that it can be done and the theory can be rescued from circularity. There are still plenty of questions left: the technical task of setting out Strong Psychological Continuity in a completely precise and non-circular fashion is not yet complete. But we have the rudiments of the theory to hand now.

The *Memento* Challenge

Thought experiments aren't the only way of investigating our concept of personal identity.[6] The far-fetched, science-fiction character of thought experiments might diminish their reliability. It is often hard to know what to think – to know how our concepts apply – in situations that can only be described in the most general fictional terms. For example, we had to qualify our robot-replacement thought experiment with a batch of philosophical hypotheticals in order to make headway with it. (What if memory isn't stored in the network sensitivity of neurons? What if consciousness isn't a product of information flow inside the brain?) It would be handy if we could rely on real-life cases to test our theories of personal identity, rather than bizarre thought experiments. And this brings us back to our film. *Memento* isn't a real-life case, but it is a fictional presentation of a real condition: severe anterograde amnesia. And it shows us that the version of psychological continuity theory we have just introduced is wrong.

Leonard Shelby cannot do what the theory requires of him: i.e. he cannot connect one uninterrupted flow of consciousness to the next one through episodic memory. Shelby experiences each of his person-stages as if they are set adrift from all prior stages right back to the time of his injury. The last thing he remembers (or thinks he remembers) is his wife dying. Nonetheless, as we watch the film, it seems quite clear to us that Shelby is one individual person throughout the narrative. A number of things seem to contribute to this conviction. Shelby has a settled plan and a consistent set of psychological traits and dispositions. He has one body throughout, including one voice. The film is saturated with his voiceover, and he has no trouble referring to himself as Leonard Shelby and guessing at the overarching narrative of his life – *his* life. Other people treat him as just one person. Furthermore, Shelby remembers his life before his brain injury. There appears to be little reason to doubt that Shelby is just one person throughout the film. Yet he fails to satisfy the psychological-continuity condition for personal identity we described in the previous section. So that account of personal identity is wrong. The movie proves it! (Or gives us good reason to suspect it: philosophers rarely get to the point of proving something once and for all.)

What options are we left with? Consider the features of *Memento* that bolster our conviction that Leonard Shelby is a single unique individual in spite of the endemic discontinuity of his consciousness. There are five main possibilities.

(1)   Shelby has a coherent life-plan: a single-minded pursuit of his wife's killer. (A threat to this plan is what triggers his murderous self-deception in the film; he is prepared to do almost anything to protect his plan and the fictions which support it.) Because he has this plan and

manages to pursue it with relentless focus, we tend to see Shelby as single person taking a coherent path through life; we tend not to interpret the film as witness to the disintegration of the person Shelby once was. Nonetheless, a coherent plan is neither necessary nor sufficient for personal identity. Teams, organizations, groups can have coherent long-term plans and people can drift through life aimlessly without them.

(2)   The second factor is this: Shelby has a settled set of dispositions and character traits. He is psychologically coherent in this sense even if he isn't experiencing his life as a coherent stream of consciousness. Still, psychological dispositions aren't the right sorts of things to individuate people; not by themselves. Dispositions can be shared, so they aren't sufficient for numerical identity. (Remember we are investigating Shelby's numerical identity, not his qualitative character.) One person could change psychological dispositions in all sorts of ways (as a result of a conversion experience, for example), so it seems that psychological dispositions aren't necessary for identity either.

(3)   The third aspect of *Memento* that encourages our individuating Leonard Shelby is the way Shelby and others individuate him in the film. Shelby speaks with the one voice – we hear it very often in voiceover. The voice doesn't just sound the same (clearly, having the same-sounding voice is neither necessary nor sufficient for persistence). Shelby refers to himself as Leonard Shelby, as the person he was yesterday, 10 minutes ago, or 10 years ago. Isn't Shelby's vote on this decisive? Does he have the authority to decide whether he continues to exist through all that has happened? It is tempting to think so, but in fact Shelby's vote isn't decisive. We don't have this kind of authority over our personal persistence. For example, one doesn't become continuous with Napoleon by confusing oneself with Napoleon. Shelby's consistent use of the first person only establishes that he is one individual if each use of the first person manages to pick out the same individual. And in the context of Leonard Shelby, this begs the question. In the same way, the fact that others in the film treat Shelby as one person – the memory guy – only shows that he is one person if these uses of the second and third person, and the use of the name "Lenny" and "Leonard Shelby" all manage to refer to one individual. And that is exactly what we are seeking to establish.[7]

This leaves us with two options: (4) Shelby's continuity of body and (5) Shelby's connection with his pre-injury consciousness through episodic memory. (A further option, of course, is that we give up on Shelby's personal persistence; but this should be last option given that personal persistence is such an automatic and natural way of interpreting the film.) Taking up the continuity of body angle, should we say that all it takes for Shelby to persist through this severe anterograde amnesia is that he is (or has) the same body from day to day? Is personal identity nothing more than identity of body over time? Some philosophers believe that this is the best solution.[8] However, it is difficult to be happy with it. It rules out many possibilities that look like genuine possibilities. For example, although it may not be physically possible for one consciousness to enter into and possess the body of another (or an urn, as in the case of Carl Reiner's *All of Me* (1984)) this is something which is nonetheless conceivable. And there is little doubt where, intuitively, identity follows in these scenarios: it goes with consciousness, not the body. The bodily-continuity theorist has to find a plausible way of depriving these intuitions of their force, and this is very hard.

In the absence of a good way of defending the bodily-continuity theory, we are left with one factor with which to account for Shelby's persistence. Shelby is one person in spite of the discontinuity of his consciousness because every one of his person-stages (i.e. his uninterrupted flows of consciousness) retains a shared background of memories of his pre-accident life. Shelby's memories of his dying wife, of his teasing his wife about the book she is reading (again), of his pinching her thigh (or is that an injection?), of his wife wandering through the house in contented reverie: these memories, and many, many more like them, are the things that give Shelby's life its individuation and which make his plan for revenge the plan of a single man rather than the plan of a committee of co-opted future Shelbys. Imagine the film's narrative were Shelby deprived of these pre-injury episodic memories. He would seem like a series of different conscious episodes linked by an external façade: a tattooed body; a police file; a photograph of a stolen car; nothing that could not be passed down from one distinct individual to another.

Responding to the *Memento* Challenge

Reflection on the film *Memento* leads us to critically reassess the psychological continuity theory of personal identity. Personal identity – persistence of an individual person over time and through change – may consist of a series of person-stages linked by episodic memory, but *Memento* shows us that these links can be quite indirect. Shelby remembers his life before his brain injury, but he doesn't remember what happened to him 10 minutes ago. And yet this may be enough to ensure his identity through time. Here is a form of the psychological continuity theory of personal identity, modified to accommodate the *Memento* challenge.

Weak Psychological Continuity
A person is a set of person-stages each one of which (apart from the earliest one) is linked by episodic memories to at least one earlier person-stage.

Just how plausible is Weak Psychological Continuity? Philosophers worry about another problem with psychological continuity theories of personal identity, one that Weak Psychological Continuity appears to exacerbate. This is the fission problem. Imagine a person who divides in two: becoming two streams of consciousness each linked by episodic memories to the one stream of consciousness before division.[9] Is this one person or two? It can't be both. Some philosophers say that in this situation there are two people: although it was never apparent until division, there were two separate individuals present all along.[10] Other philosophers think this is too weird. Shelby's case is an example of massive fission, of a sort. Every few minutes a stream of consciousness emerges unconnected by episodic memory to its surrounding streams of consciousness. It doesn't survive long enough to compete with other streams of consciousness, but it is unconnected to other streams in the vicinity. According to Weak Psychological Continuity, fission cases only ever produce the one person. This doesn't seem too weird in Shelby's case: no two of his streams of consciousness overlap and they each share a common ancestor in Shelby's pre-injury stream of consciousness. However, fission cases can get a lot weirder than this. What happens when a person divides into two simultaneous streams of consciousness (and two bodies along with it)? According to Weak Psychological Continuity, they remain the one person no matter what each of the streams gets up to. The streams aren't connected through episodic memory to each other, but they are connected through episodic memory to a common ancestor. One stream becomes president of the World Bank, say, and the other a bank robber. Can we really say that the president of the World Bank is a bank robber? (Maybe we can.) It seems like a further reworking of our theory might be in order. Perhaps Weak Psychological Continuity is a necessary condition for personal identity, but not a sufficient one. That is, perhaps Weak Psychological Continuity nominates something that all individuals must satisfy, but there is something else they must satisfy too. Here's a suggestion for that other thing:

Weak Agent-Restricted Psychological Continuity
A person is a set of person-stages such that: (1) each person stage (apart from the earliest one) is linked by episodic memories to at least one earlier person-stage; and (2) the set never divides into two contemporaneous subsets that (a) operate as agents independently of each other and (b) are not linked to each other through the episodic memories of their members.

Is our newly refined theory – Weak Agent-Restricted Psychological Continuity – going to work? We have to admit that it seems a little *ad hoc*. Condition (2) is merely there to rule out non-Shelby fission cases. We will need a theory of what it is to operate as an independent agent (one that doesn't rely on a difference in identity). Perhaps this can be supplied. We will also want an independent reason to accept agent restrictions like the one proposed here.

Neither Weak Psychological Continuity nor Weak Agent-Restricted Psychological Continuity is well supported among philosophers who study personal identity. (But that's not yet a reason to give up on them!) We introduce them mainly to illustrate the process of responding to a thing like the *Memento* Challenge; and how hard it is. A final resort would be to accept a version of the bodily continuity thesis (recall that Shelby's bodily continuity was one of several features of *Memento* that bolster our conviction that he is a single unique individual); perhaps the thesis that ties identity of persons to identity of a living body. (This is often called the Somatic Theory.)[11] It has its own problems, of course. In this field, it is really a matter of which problems we think we can live with best. Very often in philosophy no answer gets us everything we want.

Questions

Nolan uses a special technique to get his audience into something like the phenomenological position of *Memento's* protagonist, Leonard Shelby: he runs a crucial part of the film backwards. Does this technique succeed fully? How does the audience's experience of narrative events differ from Shelby's? Do we over-interpret Shelby's psychological coherence because of this? What difference does it make to the *Memento* Challenge?

On the psychological continuity theory of personal identity, it is important that the memories be episodic memories. Why can't semantic memory be used as the criterion instead?

On the psychological continuity theory of personal identity, episodic memory need not be accurate, but it cannot be false. What is the difference between an inaccurate memory and a false one? Why should this make a difference?

Did we interpret the robot-replacement thought experiment correctly? Does it show that continuity of a living body is not necessary for personal identity?

Is there any way of maintaining belief in Strong Psychological Continuity in the face of the Leonard Shelby example? Could we maintain that Shelby fails to act as a unique individual throughout the film? How might we explain his actions and our reaction to them without assuming his personal identity?

We argued in the chapter that, although Weak Psychological Continuity accounts for the Shelby case, it fails to account for our intuitive reactions to fission cases. This led us to propose a hybrid account of personal identity: Weak Agent-Restricted Psychological Continuity. Do fission cases really need explaining like this? Couldn't we say that, in a world in which people divide like amoeba, we would have to radically revise our concept of what a person is and our concept of personal identity? Must our concepts apply to every logically possible situation, and do so in an intuitively satisfactory way?

The theories of personal identity we have discussed in the chapter are all "four-dimensionalist" theories (sometimes called "perdurantist"). They take identity over time to be a relation between temporal parts (person-stages). The rival account of identity is called "endurantism." According to endurantists, people (and objects in general) are not collections of temporal parts, they are three-dimensional individuals that are wholly present at each moment of their existence. Can the endurantist explain Shelby cases better than the four-dimensionalist?

Notes

1   See the introduction to Martin & Barresi (2003) for a survey of this history.
2   Anterograde amnesia results from damage to the brain that is restricted to the hippocampus and surrounding tissue. The two most famous cases of anterograde amnesia are the patient known as HM and Clive Wearing. For more information about the condition, see Thompson & Madigan (2005), chapter 5.

3   Recall *Total Recall*, discussed in chapter 3. In this film, Quaid remembers his wedding to his wife Lori. His experience is a quasi-memory. It seems to him that he remembers his wedding. It is also a false memory, having been invented and implanted in him by Cohaagen and his team of villains.

4   Interestingly, some philosophers reject this answer. They argue that what matters for our survival is not identity *per se*, but something weaker: psychological connectedness. Parfit (2002) argues for this conclusion.

5   The eighteenth-century German philosopher Gottlieb Leibniz argued that no two things in the world could ever be perfectly qualitatively identical. He called this thesis *the identity of indiscernibles*. See Forrest (2010).

6   Many films run thought experiments in personal identity, including body-swap films such as *Freaky Friday* (1976 and again in 2003); narratives of possession such as *All of Me* (1984), or, even more conclusively, *Fallen* (1998); and films that play with the idea of false memory such as *Total Recall* (1990). Christopher Nolan runs another remarkable thought experiment in personal identity in *The Prestige* (2006).

7   Another, related, aspect of the film encourages our individuation of Shelby: its remarkable narrative structure. The film is divided into two narrative streams, one in color and the other in black and white. One narrative stream – the one depicted in color, and so seeming to be the more realistic stream – runs backwards: the first segment we see in the film coincides with the final stretch of Shelby's consciousness in the narrative time-frame; the second segment we see is the second-last stretch of Shelby's consciousness, and so on. This allows us to identify with Shelby to a remarkable extent because we share much of his confusion. He doesn't know why he suddenly finds himself in a motel bathroom with a bottle of whiskey in his hands. The audience doesn't know why he is there either. (The scene occurs at 0:52.) Both discover part of the solution when they see what happens next. Identifying with Shelby encourages our individuation of him. But, again, this won't stand up to philosophical scrutiny as genuine evidence of Shelby's persistence through the narrative. For that we need to turn to more basic facts about him and his situation.

8   See, for example, Williams (2002).

9   Such a division is illustrated beautifully in another film by Christopher Nolan, *The Prestige* (2006).

10   See Lewis (2003).

11   See Olsen (2002).

Further Reading

Baker, L. R. (2000). *Persons and Bodies: A Constitution View*. Cambridge: Cambridge University Press.

Forrest, Peter (2010). "The Identity of Indiscernibles." *Stanford Encyclopedia of Philosophy*. http://plato.stanford.edu/entries/identity-indiscernible/.

Lewis, David (2003). "Survival and Identity. In Raymond Martin & John Barresi, eds., *Personal Identity*. Oxford: Blackwell, 144–67.

Martin, Raymond, & John Barresi, eds. (2003). *Personal Identity*. Oxford: Blackwell.

Olsen, Eric T. (1997). *The Human Animal: Personal Identity Without Psychology*. Oxford: Oxford University Press.

Olsen, Eric T. (2002). "An Argument for Animalism." In Raymond Martin & John Barresi, eds., *Personal Identity*. Oxford: Blackwell, 318–34.

Olsen, Eric T. (2007). *What Are We? A Study in Personal Ontology*. Oxford: Oxford University Press.

Parfit, Derek (1984). *Reasons and Persons*. Oxford: Oxford University Press.

Parfit, Derek (2002). "The Unimportance of Identity." In Raymond Martin & John Barresi, eds., *Personal Identity*. Oxford: Blackwell, 292–317.

Perry, John (1972). "Can the Self Divide?" *Journal of Philosophy* 69, 463–88.

Perry, John, ed. (1975). *Personal Identity*. Los Angeles: University of California Press.

Thompson, Richard F., & Stephen A. Madigan (2005). *Memory: The Key to Consciousness*. Princeton: Princeton University Press.

Van Inwagen, Peter (1990). *Material Beings*. Ithaca: Cornell University Press.

Williams, Bernard (2002). "The Self and the Future." In Raymond Martin & John Barresi, eds., *Personal Identity*. Oxford: Blackwell, 75–91.

9

The Spectacle of Horror: *Funny Games*

Introduction

People sometimes pay good money to sit in a darkened cinema (or sit in their own room, darkened) to be frightened silly, to be horrified, to watch brutal carnage, to have their blood run cold. Why would anyone do this? Why do people watch horror films? What do they get out of horror films? Like other film genres, the borders of the horror genre are fuzzy and its rules and conventions are forever shifting. Nonetheless, the genre divides usefully into two classes: supernatural horror and realist horror.[1] Supernatural horror involves creatures that violate fundamental categories or natural laws, for example, ghosts, the living dead, the human/animal hybrid.[2] Realist horror involves no such violations and concentrates instead on horrors created by natural means.[3] What holds horror films together as a group is the priority they place in eliciting a horror response from audiences.[4] Horror films don't elicit horror responses in an incidental way, they *revel* in them.

Horror responses vary a good deal in their phenomenology, but they involve two prominent negative emotions: revulsion (or disgust) and fear. Watching a person struggle in a pit of hypodermic needles, for example, evokes an empathetic fear of injury and pain, but it also evokes a special kind of horror of bodily penetration.[5] We react with revulsion to such a scene. It gives us the creeps in the way that, for example, watching a film of a person being punched usually does not. If we are particularly sensitive (or not sufficiently desensitized) and project ourselves into the hypodermic needle scene too successfully, we will want to get our experience of

Thinking Through Film: Doing Philosophy, Watching Movies, First Edition. Damian Cox, Michael P. Levine.
© 2012 Damian Cox and Michael P. Levine. Published 2012 by Blackwell Publishing Ltd.

the scene out of our mind as quickly as possible. Horror, then, involves a very particular way of experiencing fear: one that "creeps us out." Fear and revulsion are dubbed negative emotions because they are usually deeply unpleasant and tend to trigger avoidance behavior. So the point of horror films is to generate a very particular sort of negative emotional response to the audiovisual image.

Why is horror such a successful and long-lived genre? The obvious answer may well be the best and it is the answer we are going to assume throughout the discussion to follow. People watch horror films (in big numbers) because they get considerable pleasure from them. If this is right, what *kind* of pleasure do they get? What kind of pleasure is there to be had from something that provokes negative emotion in an especially strong and intense way? This is a puzzle which is sometimes given the grandiloquent title of "the paradox of horror."[6] It isn't a paradox. There is nothing essentially paradoxical or contradictory about the notion that one may enjoy experiencing negative emotions. Negative emotions aren't *necessarily* unpleasant, they are *usually* unpleasant.[7] And yet there really is a puzzle here. What makes the revulsion and fear typically generated by horror films a reliable source of pleasure? What kind of pleasure? These are our primary questions; we will refine them as we go along. Because the horror genre is so broad and complex, we are going to narrow down our attention to realist horror films. Realist horror is inescapably violent – ghosts can get away with a haunting, vampires may simply want to feed on you, but serial killers are in the business of murder – and this raises the question of the moral standing of the genre. Although this is not our primary concern here, we will also briefly examine the moral critique of realist horror.

Scenes in which a protagonist is menaced – playing on the possibility of physical or mental violation – tend to generate the archetypal horror response of dread. Fear predominates in dread, or seems to predominate in it, but revulsion is an essential part of the mix. Compare horror films with thrillers. Thrillers typically play on the fear that something bad – even something catastrophically bad – may happen. They often depict these fears being realized, and they sometimes do this in such a way that an audience is genuinely frightened. And yet thrillers rarely count as horror films. This is because the fear evoked by thrillers is the wrong sort of fear. Horror fear is more than fear of something really bad happening. It is fear of deeply repulsive or disturbing harm: being torn apart while conscious; being haunted (driven mad) by menacing and uncanny apparitions; and so on.[8] Horror films typically work by evoking dread rather than mere fear; and they can be more or less subtle in their production of this effect.

An important kind of horror film foregrounds psychological horror rather than the display of physically repulsive harm. Depictions of monstrous cruelty or the threat of it – playing on sustained humiliation and the ever-present possibility of violation – generate feelings of being unnerved, distressed, and chilled to the bone: "one's blood runs cold" as we sometimes say. Films that concentrate on the production of this emotional response are sometimes called "chillers" and the film we discuss in the present chapter is such a film. It is *Funny Games,* by the Austrian director Michael Haneke, and it comes in two very closely matched versions: an Austrian version in 1997 (in German) and a US version in 2007 (in English). Apart from the language spoken and the actors used, the 2007 film is a scene-by-scene remake of the 1997 film. What we have to say about *Funny Games* covers either version, although our film-timings refer to the 2007 version. (The two films differ marginally in this respect.) In the final section of the chapter we address the question of why Haneke would have wanted to remake the film in English, and what he sought to achieve in making the film at all.

The Pleasures of Art-Horror

Art-horror is horror elicited by art: literature, theatre, cinema, music, painting, and other visual arts. We, of course, are concerned with the experience of art-horror in the cinema and the explanation of its attraction. We cannot canvas, nor do any kind of justice to, all possible explanatory strategies in this field. Instead, we are going to examine three strategies: physiological explanation; psychoanalytic explanation; and a cognitivist explanation advanced by Noël Carroll. First up let us consider the physiological character of the horror response. When we undergo a horror response in the cinema we get an adrenaline rush. The release of adrenaline has certain physiological effects: increased heart rate, dilatation of air passages, initiation of the flight-or-fight response of the sympathetic nervous system, and so on. Excessive adrenaline release triggers a panic attack; but art-horror responses seem to involve only moderate levels of adrenaline release and many people appear to enjoy the results. This may not be due to the effects of adrenaline *per se,* but to the simultaneous release of endorphins, a class of opioid neurotransmitters. Endorphin release may be the cause of typical pleasure responses to the experience of art-horror, but this is pure speculation. (The physiological details are not our concern here.) What we can be surer of is that the experience of art-horror differs from the experience of actual-horror in both its phenomenology and its effects. Actual-horror experience is often debilitating, distressing, traumatizing, and sometimes the cause of severe long-term symptoms. By contrast, art-horror, when it succeeds as a source of pleasure, has none of these negative effects. An audience's background recognition of the unreality of what they witness – and their detachment from it – appears to alter the physiological response to the experience of art-horror and prevent severe negative reactions to it. What is left, it seems, is a scary and disturbing ride that one can actually enjoy.

How good is this physiological-level explanation? It works best for fear responses. "Adrenaline junkies," as they are sometimes called, gain obvious pleasure from generating a fear response in themselves. Base-jumpers, for example, gain it by jumping off buildings or bridges; skydivers from jumping out of airplanes; downhill skiers from dodging other downhill skiers; and so on. The cognitive content of the thrill-seeker's experience has little or no role to play in any of this. Base-jumping, for example, isn't *about* falling in any particularly interesting way. Falling is mostly a prop; the thing that initiates the rush.[9] If this is right, then thrill-seeking is a cognitively impoverished way of generating a fear response. By contrast, art-horror is a cognitively rich way of generating a fear response. And, as we pointed out in the last section, art-horror is about much more than fear. We ordinarily go to a horror movie to get frightened, for sure; but we go to get frightened in a particular way. (Simulated skydiving or downhill skiing can be truly frightening, but not horrifying.) We go to a horror movie to be horrified, and this involves a mix of revulsion and fear, where both are cognitively and emotionally grounded in – to use a broad term – our psychological makeup or psychic economy. While the physiological basis of the pleasures of artificial fear responses may not be entirely mysterious (not that we have a full explanation of them), the pleasures of a revulsion response are harder to understand, if they exist at all. (Revulsion is unlikely to lead to the release of endorphins, for example.)

We are still being too reductive, however. Experiences of art-horror *involve* the emotions of fear and revulsion, but they don't *consist* in these emotions. (Imagine a non-horrific combination of fear and disgust: you are about to fall from a cliff, holding on to the edge for grim life, when you look to your left and see the rotting carcass of a bird. Scared and disgusted you may be, but you aren't in a horror movie.) Horror experiences are cognitively rich and cognitively specific. We find a scene horrifying or creepy because we understand something particular about it, because we are disturbed or discomforted by its content in a particular way. Having to escape a runaway truck is scary, but not creepy. Having to escape a truck whose driver is intent on running us down is scarier still, but not necessarily all that creepy. Having to escape a truck that is intent on running us down when nobody is driving it: there is at least something creepy about this.[10] So what is it that marks out some things as apt to disturb an audience in the way of horror? And why do we sometimes enjoy being disturbed in this way?

Psychoanalytic accounts of horror link the answers to these two questions. According to such accounts we enjoy being disturbed because the horror-scene means something to us, at least unconsciously or implicitly, and we respond to it in terms of its meaning. To put the point a bit vaguely, and not yet satisfactorily, its meaning interacts with our economy of desire in some way. There are numerous ways that this might happen. Psychoanalytic explanations of the appeal of horror are many and varied; and they are likely to vary from film to film and from audience member to audience member. Nonetheless, the most prominent form of psycho-analytic explanation links pleasure in being horrified with something called "the return of the repressed." According to psychoanalytic theory, people repress wishes (often, though not always, of a perverse nature) and there is pleasure to be gained when repressed wishes are satisfied in phantasy. Like a full-blown neurosis, this phantasy satisfaction of a repressed desire is a "substitutive" satisfaction – a substitute for something that never happened but that, on some level in some ways, one wished did happen. We enjoy playing out repressed wishes, or vicariously witnessing the satisfaction of repressed wishes, so long as we are saved from the full burden of acknowledging that this is what we are doing. It is just here that art-horror turns out to be particularly effective. Noël Carroll (1990: 170) describes the process in the following terms. (This is just a description: as we shall soon see Carroll has his own, non-psychoanalytic, explanation of the appeal of horror.)

> [According to typical psychoanalytic explanations[11]] the nightmare and figures of the nightmare like the vampire – i.e. the very stuff of horror fiction – attract because they manifest wishes, notably sexual wishes. However, these wishes are forbidden or repressed. They cannot be acknowledged outright. This is where the horrific, repulsive imagery comes in. It disguises or masks the unacknowledgeable wish. It functions as camouflage; the dreamer cannot be blamed for these images by her internal censor because they beset her; she finds them fearsome and repulsive, so she cannot be thought to enjoy them (though she really does savor them insofar as they express deep, psychosexual wishes, albeit in mufti).

The idea is that an audience's feelings of dread, fear, and revulsion allow them to indulge the vicarious satisfaction of repressed desires without having to admit to themselves that this is what they are doing. (*Of course I'm not enjoying this bit of the film: it's horrible.*) To achieve this, we need a way of getting around what Carroll calls our "internal censor." This somewhat crude expression – the "internal censor" – refers to many and varied operations of the mind as it rejects and disavows potential desires and wishes; operations that are themselves often quite inaccessible to us. (This process is usually called "repression," but we will stick to the more explicit formulation here.) The process of rejecting and disavowing potential desires and wishes is mostly a healthy one: a way of protecting our self-image and our self-satisfaction, perhaps, but also a way of constructing a robust moral identity.[12] Unconscious wishes are generally not our deepest or most authentic wishes (though they are real wishes); they are not the deepest wishes of our "true selves." And the rejection and disavowal of these wishes isn't (or isn't always) a way in which we lie to ourselves about "what we *really* want." On a psychoanalytic understanding of our identity as persons, we are not our identical to our unconscious wishes, we are a complex product of a conscious mind (with its values, commitments, willpower, insight, empathy, intelligence, and so on) and a largely unconscious and inaccessible way of dealing with sources of pleasure, desire, and action.

Carroll rather oversimplifies psychoanalytic accounts of the ways in which the "internal censor" must be co-opted in order for us to enjoy the horror spectacle. Quite a few things have to be in place in order for us to overcome our tendency to automatically reject the appearance of unconsciously disavowed wishes (without even noticing that this is what we are doing). The satisfaction of disavowed wishes has to be disguised in some way. It helps to be able to say to ourselves that horror images beset us, that we are not responsible for them, and that we find them disgusting and abhorrent. (As indeed we do.) This allows us to enjoy the spectacle under the cover of the belief that we are not really enjoying the horror spectacle *per se* at all. (*I enjoy a good scare at the movies, but not the really horrible bits; I enjoy a good scare at the movies, but the horrible bits are usually ridiculous and laugh-out-loud funny;* and so on.) It helps to be able to say that we are only playing, or we are only watching the movie to get a good scare, or because the story fascinates us; and that watching the occasional horror film is a normal part of contemporary life. The best way to appreciate strategies for disguising the satisfaction of repressed desire is to see what happens when they are stymied. We argue below that this is exactly what happens in *Funny Games*.

At the heart of psychoanalytic explanations of the pleasures of horror spectatorship are two claims: (1) the existence of perverse desires (these are not necessarily desires of the full person; indeed are very likely not to be); and (2) the existence of mechanisms of disavowal and rejection that we are mostly unaware of, but which can be got around nonetheless. Horror films display the satisfaction of perverse desires in ways that get around mechanisms of disavowal and rejection and consequently, in depicting the satisfaction of such perverse desires, are a source of pleasure for their audiences. Vicarious satisfaction of repressed desire is a source of pleasure, but only under the right conditions. And for many people, on many occasions, horror films satisfy these conditions. Psychoanalytic explanations of horror thus look to perverse desire in various forms, and to voyeurism, fetishism, masochism, and sadism, in order to chart the things in art-horror that yield pleasure for us, mostly in spite of ourselves. It should come as no surprise, for instance, that at times we have sadistic tendencies (say, for vengeance) that are momentarily satisfied on screen.

How promising is this approach? Critics have argued that psychoanalytic film theory is based on unscientific and implausible psychological assumptions and that it is too reductionist.[13] However, the basic framework we have described – the existence of perverse desire and of unacknowledged, largely inaccessible mechanisms of disavowal and rejection – is a very general interpretative framework compatible with a considerable amount of contemporary psychology (the more speculative reaches of which have their own problems finding plausible empirical foundations). Many of the details of psychoanalytic theory may be highly speculative and hard to empirically justify; but the basic moves made by psychoanalytic theorists studying horror film are *prima facie* plausible. Something in the horror image yields pleasure: it isn't all chance adrenaline rush; it certainly appears to have something to do with the meaning of the image and the spectator's relation to it; and that meaning is the very stuff of perverse desire.

Some critics of the psychoanalytic approach decry its appeal to "the beast within." Tudor (1997: 445), for example, describes the case like this:

> [Underlying psychoanalytic accounts of art-horror] is the belief "that human beings are rotten at the core," whether by nature or nurture, and that horror resonates with this feature of the human condition. The genre serves as a channel releasing the bestiality concealed within its users. If the model is that of catharsis, then the process is deemed to be beneficial: a safety valve. If the model is one of articulation and legitimation, then the genre is conceived to encourage consumers in their own horrific behaviour. Either way, the attraction of horror derives from its appeal to the "beast" concealed within the superficially civilized human.

In fact, however, psychoanalytic accounts do not explain the attraction of horror in terms of a "beast within." Psychoanalytic theory does not assume that human beings are rotten to the core, nor does it need such a view to claim that "horror appeals to deep-seated, psychoanalytically intelligible repressed desires" and that the genre serves as a channel for certain kinds of emotional release. If repression was incompatible with decency then we would all be indecent. But psychoanalytic theory strives to show how repression and its resulting neurotic activities are quite compatible with both "normalcy" and moral decency. There is no "beast within" because repressed desires are not the fully fledged desires of a person. They are sources of pleasure or frustration in a person, but that is a very different matter.

Tudor claims that psychoanalytic explanation is too reductionist and too *one size fits all.* If all people are supposed to have a "beast within," then explanations of why people like horror in terms of a "beast within" fail to explain why only *some* people like horror and not others (1997: 445). He rightly points out that other factors must then be employed to explain this differentiation. But those who explain the appeal of horror in psychoanalytic terms such as the return of repressed or sadistic or masochistic tendencies do not deny this.[14] Why particular individuals like horror but not others will depend upon the individual's particular psychological development – a development that depends upon nurture as well as nature.

What alternatives are there to a broadly psychoanalytic approach to horror? The most prominent alternative explanatory approach is labeled "cognitivist." Carroll offers an important example of a cognitivist explanation. Where psychoanalytic accounts direct our attention towards the vicarious satisfaction of perverse desire, Carroll directs our attention to the narrative structure of horror films.[15] An audience does not actually enjoy the horrific spectacle, according to Carroll, they enjoy the story and put up with the spectacle because this is the price they must pay to have their curiosity piqued, teased, and satisfied in a very special way. This is how Carroll sets out his account (1990: 184).

> Horror fictions are predicated on the revelation of unknown and unknowable – unbelievable and incredible – impossible beings, they often take the form of narratives of discovery and proof. For things unknown in the way of monsters obviously are natural subjects of proof. Applied to the paradox of horror, these observations suggest that the pleasure derived from the horror fiction and the source of our interest in it resides, first and foremost, in the processes of discovery, proof, and confirmation that horror fictions often employ. . . . [T]he disgust that [viewers] evince might be seen as part

of the price to be paid for the pleasure of their disclosure. That is, the narrative expectation that the horror genre puts in place is that the being whose existence is in question be something that defies standing cultural categories; thus, disgust, so to say, is itself more or less mandated by the kind of curiosity that the horror narrative puts in place.

It is easy to see the work of curiosity in supernatural horror. Supernatural monsters defy categories in an explicit and obvious way; they beg for explanation; they are mysterious in pretty much the way Carroll describes. This is not to suggest that Carroll gets supernatural horror right. However, our concern in the present chapter is with realist horror. How might Carroll's theory account for the pleasures of realist horror? The monstrosity here is psychological: the categories bent out of shape are moral ones.[16] Realist monsters are not impossible beings in the way that, for example, werewolves are impossible beings (being shape-shifters and all). Nonetheless, realist monsters are beings we wish were impossible and easily fall into thinking of as monstrous. They are moral monsters: manifestations of radical evil, whose psychopathology takes on a monstrously enlarged form. Their power – usually they are very powerful[17] – comes in large measure from their moral monstrosity. A creature capable of doing anything without scruple, bent on the destruction, violation, and humiliation of others, is powerful in part *because* of its moral monstrosity. Generally speaking, realist monsters are not villains in the ordinary sense. Villains propel a narrative forward through their evil, or at least wrongful, intentions and plans, yet audiences have little difficulty interpreting their motives and inhabiting their point of view. Realist monsters, on the other hand, tend to be largely alien to an audience: we may search for their motives and a coherent, stable, inhabitable point of view, but generally we fail to find them – which is itself a cause for consternation and upset.[18] Realist monsters are a seemingly (not actually) impossible combination of the human and the monstrous, and fascination with them might have its source in the tension generated by this hybridity.[19]

Realist horror films exploit the narrative potential of moral monsters in a variety of ways. However, they typically do not take the form Carroll identifies: that of a narrative of "discovery, proof, and confirmation." Realist monsters are primarily used to introduce vast opportunities for menace and narrative attention is rarely devoted to the revelation of their mysteriousness. The repetitiveness of slasher film franchises – *Friday the 13th, Halloween, Scream, I Know What You Did Last Summer,* and so on – both between sequels and within individual films (which mostly generate one dead teenager after another) seems to undermine any narrative appeal they may have. People did not go and see *Friday the 13th Part 8: Jason takes Manhattan* (1989) because they thought the story might take an interesting turn. (OK, people did not go and see *Friday the 13th Part 8* very much at all; but it did have a video audience.) Carroll's thesis about horror is that the pleasures of viewing horror are primarily narrative pleasures. It might seem, then, that realist horror stands as a counterexample to the thesis, or at least a limitation upon it. However, the thesis should not be dismissed too quickly. Spectatorship of realist horror may not primarily be about reveling in the strangeness of the realist monster, but the strangeness of the monster might nonetheless ground the narrative pleasures of the genre. Realist horror stories tend to be repetitive and oft repeated, but perhaps we tolerate this – and maybe even take pleasure in the repetition – because the monsters fascinate us. They are not puzzles to be solved, generally speaking, but they fascinate in their monstrosity. Imagine a wholly unmysterious version of a slasher film in which a villain with a clear and understandable motive systematically kills a group of people, one by one. This could be a film with many horror elements, but it would not entirely feel like a horror film. It would feel like a thriller.[20] As such, its power to sustain narrative interest – its capacity to keep an audience watching until the end – would depend on depth of characterization, charisma of leading players, and ingenuity of ordinary narrative elements (e.g. threat, plan, obstacle, resolution). Horror films have a strange capacity to sustain interest – narrative interest or some other interest – largely in the absence of any of these elements. (Often they sport uncharismatic leads, trite characters, uningenious plots.) The puzzle, of course, is how they manage this.[21] One possible solution, along lines Carroll sets out, is that monsters fascinate us and this suffices to sustain our narrative interest and gives us a reason to put up with the negative emotions that automatically come with a display of monstrousness.

We now have two candidate explanations of the mysterious appeal of horror films (leaving aside the physiological explanation).[22] First, we have psychoanalytic accounts, according to which the pleasure of watching horror films comes from the display of perverse desire being satisfied. We take pleasure from the horror elements of horror films because of how the horrors portrayed interact with our economy of desire. We aren't getting off like "sickos" on the evils portrayed, but we find ourselves in a position to enjoy the spectacle of the satisfaction of perverse desire. Second, we have a cognitivist account owing to Carroll, according to which the pleasures of watching horror films are primarily narrative pleasures. These are fundamentally cognitive pleasures; we are drawn to the stories because they fascinate us, not because they interact with our (sometimes hidden) desires. We enjoy the stories in spite of their general lameness and in spite of the revulsion they induce in us because at their heart they have a creature perfectly designed to pique and then sustain curiosity-driven observation. We enjoy stories of monsters because of their mysteriousness. And realist monsters are mysterious in a way that is highly significant for us: they are morally monstrous. They weird us out; but they also fascinate us.

Which is the better explanation of realist horror spectatorship? Since it is hard to deny that there are narrative pleasures to be had from horror films – they are narrative films after all – debate around the issue tends to focus on the question of whether there is any need at all for psychoanalytic explanation. Psychoanalytic theorists have no need to deny the possibility that the pleasures of spectatorship are in some measure cognitively directed narrative pleasures. They simply deny the sufficiency of this as an explanatory strategy: when narrative pleasures are exhausted there is still something that draws us perversely towards an experience of horror and this is best explained in psychoanalytic terms. Cognitive theorists, on the other hand, wish to rule out psychoanalytic explanation once and for all.[23] We are going to use the film *Funny Games* to try and work out the plausibility of the cognitivist's dismissive claim.

Funny, *Funny Games*

The first thing to point out about *Funny Games* is that it isn't much fun. In our experience, viewers rarely enjoy watching the film; they may find the film gripping, but usually they find it not at all enjoyable. Some walk out. Many more would probably walk out were they not inhibited by a desire to be seen to take the film seriously. It is a realist horror film in which the ordinary pleasures of art-horror spectatorship have been surgically removed and this makes it a fascinating test case for competing theories of the pleasures of art-horror spectatorship.

The film tells the story of the home invasion and murder of an affluent family (mother, father, young boy) at their weekend retreat in the country. Relatively little attempt is made to generate a fear response. (With the exception of a brief interlude when the young boy escapes to a neighbor's house, there is no hiding out in cupboards or creeping down darkened corridors.) Tension is nonetheless effectively maintained throughout: strange behavior from two seemingly well-mannered visitors becomes inexorably creepier until violence erupts; impossibly tormenting games are played out before a cruelly unflinching camera; hopes of escape come and go and promised murders are excruciatingly postponed. A horror response is consistently provoked, but it does not come from any visceral display of bloody carnage. It is a response of dread to bullying, intimidation, and humiliation; to murderous threats made with facetious, comedic ease; and to murders themselves, heard but unseen. Perhaps the most horrific image in the film is of the game cat-in-a-bag, in which the young boy, George, has his head covered by a cushion-slip (0:44). (That's it, but it's enough. And it demonstrates the precision of Haneke's horror imagination.) Throughout the film, we watch in mounting alarm as a family is bullied, humiliated, tormented by "funny games," and then slaughtered.

The boy is murdered first, off-screen. We witness the consequent trauma of his parents at painful length – depicted with almost unbearable intensity – while a television plays in the background. The television screens a motor race with its ceaseless noise and banal commentary (1:03–1:12). The entire scene depicts the mother, Anna/Ann, as she sits, bound hand and feet, in shock. The invaders have left (for now). She sits utterly still; then manages to rise and stumble over to the television to turn it off; she struggles out of the room, returns unbound, and helps the father to his feet and out of the room. The scene lasts over nine minutes, an extraordinary length of time for the action it depicts. It is filmed with an unflinching camera: the room is in medium shot; there is no edit; the camera pans slightly once, but is otherwise deathly still.

The two young killers – realist monsters *par excellence* – are interesting creations. They are polite, highly verbal, and usually mild of speech: one, Paul, is handsome and highly intelligent; the other, Peter, plays dumb. They are an improbable hybrid of well-brought-up young men, bullies, and sadistic tormentors and thrill-killers. In a crucial scene (0:37–0:39), Paul mocks the idea that anything might explain their psychopathology. He plays with various insincere explanations: a childhood broken by divorce; a depraved home environment; drug addiction. The killers are what they are: inexplicably cruel; delighting in their bullying; enjoying their games without scruple. They appear to enjoy the bullying more than the killing: the final killing (at 1:40) is so perfunctory they barely register it.

The killers' funny games are matched by the games that the director, Michael Haneke, plays with his audience. There are two kinds of game: playing teasingly with the expectations of the genre; and inviting complicity with the action. Consider the ways in which *Funny Games* defies genre expectations. First, denouements are either unscreened or screened perfunctorily. Murders are all off-camera save for the final one; the final murder – of Anna, drowned in the bay – is performed as if it were of no moment at all, just the ending of a game, not the point of it (1:40). Second, there are no survivors: no final girl, man, woman, boy. (This was more genre-defying in 1997 than it was 10 years later.) Third, the action is filmed in an austere "European arthouse" style, not at all the style of usual horror fare. In Haneke's hands, the style includes a complete absence of background music (apart from a blast of John Zorn's "Bonehead and Hellraiser" over the opening and closing credits). It also includes very long takes, mostly in medium shot, with minimal editing and very limited camera movement. Most horror films employ much more elaborate schemes of editing and camera movement, whose rhythms tend to lull the audience into a comfortable spectatorship. The austere style Haneke favors tends to produce a more reflective spectatorship by giving the audience plenty of occasions within scenes to register and reflect upon their response to the action. You tend not to lose yourself in a movie shot in this style and that is very much part of Haneke's artistic strategy.

Haneke's strategy becomes clear in a climactic scene near the end of the film; a fourth way in which Haneke abandons the conventions of the horror genre. The film abandons realism entirely in this scene. At 1:35, Anna manages to grab hold of a shotgun and shoot Peter. We see his body fly backwards and land, blood-soaked, against the wall. Paul rushes around in a panic, finds a television remote control and hits rewind. The film itself rewinds before our eyes and settles on a scene immediately prior to the shooting, at which point Paul hits play and the action resumes. Anna's attempt to grab the gun is easily defused the second time. (Paul knows what is coming.) What is the significance of this scene? Haneke is attempting to infuriate his audience (if he has any left) by demonstrating in unmistakable terms that the action – including all the sadistic game-playing, humiliation, and murder – has been staged for its entertainment and pleasure.

The aim is to wake up an audience to the fact that it is watching a grotesque display of violence merely for its entertainment value; that it is complicit in the violence screened because the violence is screened for it. The film is a kind of accusation directed at the audience. (We take up this theme in the next section.) Our complicity is emphasized by the other kind of game Haneke plays with us. He breaks out of the mould of realist drama by having Paul address the camera at various points. At 0:29, Paul directs Anna to the discovery of the body of the family dog, Rolfie, killed by Peter. Peter is playing the child's game "hot and cold" with her. Just as she gets "very hot," Paul turns towards the camera and winks. We aren't entirely sure at first, but he seems to be winking at us. So we are in on the game. At 0:40, Paul addresses the camera directly. He has just made a (one-sided) bet with the family: he bets they will be dead before 9:00am the next morning; they are to bet on their surviving. At this point he turns to the camera:

> PAUL: What do you think? You think they stand a chance? You're on their side, aren't you? Who are you betting on? (0:40)

Towards the end of the film Paul removes Anna's gag, addressing the audience indirectly:

> PAUL: It's boring when mutes suffer. We want to entertain our audience, right? Show them what we can do. (1:28)

These addresses break what is often called "the fourth wall," treating the audience as if it were present at the action, rather than hiding safely in a darkened cinema. It undoes the voyeuristic comfort of film spectator-ship by making us aware of our voyeurism. Haneke's use of the technique is effective because it is spare: it occurs at only four points if we include the indirect reference at 1:28. Too much of this and the audience would disconnect their experience of *Funny Games* with their experience of realist horror in general. In these conditions, *Funny Games* would likely be received as a bizarre art film with little relevance to ordinary spectator-ship. It's important that, for all its departure from conventional realist horror, Haneke's film work well enough as realist horror for its audience-spooking to encourage reflection on the genre of realist horror. And the film certainly succeeds in this respect. It comes across as a master-class in sustaining tension and evoking a chilling horror response.

How do our competing theories of the pleasures of art-horror fare in the case of *Funny Games*? We are going to make two assumptions about typical ways in which the film is experienced by audiences. First, the film is gripping and narrative interest is maintained until at least the rewind scene near the end (at which point the story is deliberately ruined). People may walk out of the film before then, but probably not because it is boring them. Second, watching the film is a deeply unpleasant experience from at least about the 44-minute mark onwards (i.e. from the game of cat-in-a-bag onwards). Even for hardened horror fans, it is hard to get any real pleasure from watching the film after this point, in spite of the fact that it is, in its nasty, sour way, utterly compelling. If these two assumptions are correct, then Carroll's narrative theory, as we have developed it, is in real trouble. Here is a film in which the narrative components of first-rate realist horror are all in place: realist monsters who exhibit a compelling and puzzling hybridity; a storyteller whose command of suspense – a strongly felt need to know what is going to happen next – is never in any doubt. The film works extraordinarily well at the level of narrative for nearly all of its length, but fails to generate the expected pleasures of art-horror spectatorship. Instead it disrupts them. The obvious conclusion to draw is that the core pleasures of art-horror don't in fact reside in the cognitive reception of narrative.

So what has the film done to deprive its audience of the pleasures of art-horror? The psychoanalytic framework furnishes a possible answer. Recall that, according to the framework, return of the repressed requires a mode of spectatorship that disguises the real nature of the audience's perverse satisfactions and thus allows it to take pleasure from them. *Funny Games* deprives its audience of the means to enjoy the spectacle of horror and it does this in two main ways. At various crucial points the film makes the audience self-consciously aware of its voyeuristic spectatorship. It treats the audience as if it were a part of the action and in doing so it removes the comfort of being lost in a series of depictions that *beset* us. The audience is made to feel complicit in the action because it is made clear to them that the action is staged for their benefit. Second, the film deprives the audience of genre comforts by exposing the consequences of violence in a numbingly precise and potent way. The scene after the boy's murder, discussed above, is the clearest example of this (1:03–1:12). An ordinary horror film would move quickly on after the depiction of such a murder. Haneke makes us watch the parents' traumatized reaction at terrible length. The scene is unbearably realistic. As a consequence, the child's murder breaks the hidden pact of movie-deaths: that they aren't soul-crushing events, but events in a fictional world, a world in which phantasies are allowed to play out without intrusion of the real. There are other ways in which Haneke deprives his audience of genre-comforts. The passivity of the family – especially of the hobbled father, George – deprives the audience of an opportunity to identify with them strongly. Masochistic identification is therefore hard to maintain; masochistic identification is one of the most reliable sources of pleasure within horror spectatorship. The passivity of the family does not signal any sort of complicity with the assault, however. They are nakedly traumatized and without the resources to take a real part in the games. This makes it hard for an audience to find pleasure in the display of the killers' sadistic mastery. Compare *Funny Games* in this respect with the *Saw* films. Throughout the *Saw* films, victims of torture are guilty of moral transgressions, sometimes quite serious transgressions, and this grants the audience a certain permission to enjoy the sadistic spectacle of their torture. (Indeed this may be a reason why the *Saw* franchise has been particularly commercially successful in spite of the generally low quality of the films.)

If our analysis is correct, then a psychoanalytic approach to the pleasures of art-horror has the resources to explain a phenomenon like *Funny Games* and the cognitive approach comes up short. Of course, cognitivists are able to explain something about our response to the film: the way in which the film fascinates and intrigues us. But if the pleasures of art-horror are wholly narrative pleasures, why doesn't this fascination translate into pleasure? After all, Haneke's film is *much* more cognitively engaging than the usual run of realist horror films. Why isn't Haneke's film *more* enjoyable than the usual realist horror fare rather than *less* enjoyable? Cognitivists might argue that the narrative pleasures of *Funny Games* are simply overwhelmed by the sadistic display on offer. A person can take pleasure in a realist horror narrative, they may insist, but that pleasure has to contend with the displeasure of viewing a repulsive and fearful spectacle. In the case of *Funny Games*, narrative pleasure has little chance competing with the displeasure occasioned by Haneke's unflinching display of sadism. However, the sadistic display of *Funny Games* is very mild compared with many other members of the species – compare it to *Hostel* (2006) and *Hostel Part 2* (2007), for example. These films are in the (often successful) business of generating pleasure from much less interesting narrative material and much stronger evocation of the horror response.

Cognitivists might respond to our argument in another way. Perhaps the narrative pleasures of horror sometimes require that we "grant ourselves permission" to enjoy the narrative, and the process of "granting ourselves permission" looks a lot like the process of disguising satisfaction of perverse desire. We are capable of enjoying a film like *Silence of the Lambs* (1991) because we have a cover-story to hand about why it is OK to witness such a disgusting spectacle: it is a terrific story (in both senses) and the figure of Hannibal Lecter is an endlessly fascinating one. Haneke's film can't be enjoyed in this way, in spite of the fact that it intrigues, because he deprives us of "permission" to enjoy the story. He makes us feel cheap and shameful in our watching and we can't take narrative pleasure from a film in these circumstances. Perhaps this is so. But the kind of narrative pleasure Carroll has in mind – pleasure taken from the piquing and teasing of our curiosity – seems to be the wrong sort of thing to need elaborate excuse-making. If we find the monstrous young men in *Funny Games* interesting, and this is, and always was going to be, the only source of our pleasure in watching the film, then why should we feel cheap and ashamed? Haneke directs our attention to what he thinks is our complicity in the depicted violence, but why should we feel especially guilty about that if all we are doing is finding something of cognitive interest in a story? Our complicity, if it exists, is not complicity in the production of violence *per se*, but in production of representations of violence. (We are not caught looking through a real peephole, at real people being hurt; we are caught watching a film, made with actors and sets, with a crew and catering and a tutor for the child.) Haneke's moral critique may or may not succeed; but as a tactic for depriving an audience of purely narrative pleasure, it seems unlikely to work very well. If Haneke's story is interesting, it is interesting. How is our finding it interesting something that requires circumvention of an "internal censor"? If this is all there is to our spectatorship, we can easily respond to Haneke's implicit critique of it: if Mr Haneke wants people to stop taking an interest in depictions of violence, he should either stop making interesting films or stop making violent ones. But clearly Haneke is onto something. The thing we would have very good reason to deny about our experience of art-horror is the extent to which we enjoy the spectacle of horror on its own terms. Haneke's surgical removal of the genre comforts that enable this kind of pleasure-taking ought to leave narrative pleasures, as Carroll understands them, largely undisturbed. But it doesn't. *Funny Games* does more than present an especially relentless and unflinching display of sadistic behavior; it systematically deprives its audience of the means of enjoying the spectacle of horror.

Haneke's Moral Critique

We conclude this chapter with an (all too) brief discussion of the moral standing of realist horror. It is a genre that has attracted a great deal of hostile criticism. Haneke's intention in *Funny Games* is to offer a moral critique of realist horror, and more broadly of the phenomenon of entertainment violence. Entertainment violence is everywhere, but reaches a peak in realist horror films.[24] This is how Haneke puts his case, speaking of those scenes in *Funny Games* in which Paul speaks to the camera:

> The killer communicates with the viewer. That means he makes him an accomplice. By making the viewer an accomplice of the killer, at the end I'm reproaching him for this position. It's a little sarcastic, but I wanted to show how you are always an accomplice of the killer if you watch this kind of film. Not in a self-reflexive film like this one, but in films that show violence in an acceptable way. We always agree that violence is happening,

it's consumable, and we don't realize that we're accomplices to this. That's what I wanted to show.[25]

This aim explains why Haneke chose to remake the film for the US market. That market produces and consumes most of the world's realist horror and, indeed, most of the world's entertainment violence. Haneke conceived of his film as an intervention in that market; a way of bringing complicity to consciousness. A subtitled German film from 1997 is hardly likely to succeed in this task. (This also might explain the strange way that the 2007 film was promoted: as a conventional realist horror/thriller.)[26]

Does Haneke's critique succeed on the basis he specifies? It is doubtful. An audience, knowingly entering a theatre to be entertained by a film that involves a blast of simulated killing, is an accomplice, in a sense, to the cultural production of simulated killing: no audience, no simulated killing and no cultural machinery to support it. But in the interview we quote, Haneke doesn't speak of a fictional killer and a simulated killing, he speaks of a killer and his violence. He appears to equivocate between violence and its representation. It may be that he thinks of the representation of violence as itself a kind of violence, but we would need an argument for such a strong claim.

What, then, might Haneke be getting at? The moral critique of entertainment violence takes two distinct forms. One is a critique on the grounds of the practical consequences of viewing entertainment violence. Perhaps cultures of entertainment violence produce more violence by setting up violent models and standards of behavior and by desensitizing people to this behavior. Perhaps. The evidence is hard to come by. A second kind of moral critique takes exception to cultures of entertainment violence on the grounds that the depiction – for no other purpose than entertainment – of terrible things happening to people, even to fictional people, is *intrinsically* wrong. It is like a form of hate speech directed at humanity and is responsible for a kind of flattening of our moral responses to others even if it doesn't increase levels of violence *per se.*[27] According to a psychoanalytic understanding of the appeal of art-horror, both moral critiques are likely to be exaggerated. Art-horror experience would be morally dangerous if it undermined those repressive psychological operations that enable decent relations between people. According to psychoanalytic theory, however, these operations are robust, so the chances of our becoming morally unhinged by the experience of art-horror are remote. Taking care not to exaggerate the danger, there may nonetheless be a depressing and unhealthy aspect to the spiraling sadism underlying much recent realist horror. Films often cited in this regard are the so-called torture porn films: *Hostel* (2006) and *Hostel Part 2* (2007); the *Saw* franchise (seven films, including one in 3D, 2004–10); *The Devil's Rejects* (2005); *Wolf Creek* (2005); and even *Passion of the Christ* (2004).[28] There is another possibility too. Cynthia Freeland (1995) has defended (some) realist horror films on the grounds that, often by their ludicrous excess, they promote reflective concern for the effects of the spectacle of violence on our moral lives. *Funny Games*, whatever else it is, is such a film.

Questions

Is *Funny Games* a horror film?

Is horror a mixture of fear and disgust? Could a horror reaction consist purely of fear? Is there a necessary cognitive element to horror experience? (In order to feel horror, is there something one must believe about the objects of one's experience? What is this?)

What is the uncanny? Can realist horror films be uncanny, or is this something reserved for supernatural horror?

In the chapter, we made the claim that negative emotions are not necessarily unpleasant; they are just usually or typically unpleasant. Is this right? When you get a shock in the cinema, do you enjoy the shock itself or the immediate aftermath of it? Might negative emotions give pleasure through their effects and consequences rather than intrinsically? What effects and consequences?

How might a psychoanalytic theorist explain the process by which we allow ourselves to gain pleasure from the vicarious satisfaction of repressed desires? Repressed desires are disavowed and rejected; how are they presented in cinema in a form that is not disavowed and rejected?

We claimed in the chapter that psychoanalytic accounts of horror don't presuppose a picture of "the beast within us." But isn't that exactly what they do? If we repress wishes that we find unacceptable (for very good reasons), then shouldn't we find ourselves unacceptable at a deep level? Is our response in the chapter – in terms of our identity and its relation to the unconscious – sufficient to disarm the claim that psychoanalysis reveals "the beast within us"?

Are people attracted to horror narratives only because of their cognitive fascination (their curiosity about) monsters? Is Carroll right to say that the pleasures of horror spectatorship are primarily narrative pleasures? Can this view really be made consistent with the narrative banality and repetitiveness of much of the horror genre?

Were we right to claim that *Funny Games* surgically removes the ordinary pleasures of horror spectatorship? Compare *Funny Games* with other realist horror films. Why are they more enjoyable (to typical horror fans) than *Funny Games*?

We used *Funny Games* to criticize Carroll's theory of the pleasures of horror spectatorship. We claimed that the film grounded narrative pleasure almost until the end, but narrative pleasure is typically not taken from the film. It's a story we should enjoy if we enjoy realist horror stories at all; but not this time. Psychoanalytic accounts explain this fact much more convincingly than Carroll's cognitivist account. Does this argument work? Is there a good reply to be made on Carroll's behalf? *Funny Games* is just one film; why place such an argumentative burden on one film?

Is there anything morally wrong with watching horror films? (Nobody is being hurt or humiliated, the actors are *acting*; people mostly enjoy making them and enjoying making money from them.)

Notes

1 See Freeland (1995).
2 Human/animal hybrids can take an obvious form (as in *The Fly* (1958;1986)) or less obvious forms (as in *The Birds* (1963), in which birds come to act with human menace and intelligence).
3 The boundary between realist and supernatural horror is fuzzy. The human killers of the *Halloween* and *Friday the 13th* franchises, for example, have a supernatural capacity to crop up again in sequels. Science fiction films, such as *Alien* (1979), *28 days later* (2002), and *Splice* (2009), are neither supernatural nor straightforwardly naturalistic.
4 Films such as *Twilight* (2008) are not horror films even though they chronicle the doings of supernatural "monsters" (in this case the seemingly young, good-looking, misunderstood undead) because their doings do not elicit a horror response.
5 The reference here is to a scene in *Saw* (2004).
6 See Carroll (1990).
7 This is, in essence, Gaut's way of dissolving the paradox of horror. See Gaut (1993).
8 Consider a typical thriller moment: the moment of impending discovery when a protagonist hides in a wardrobe that is about to be opened. (An

example is the famous scene in *Blue Velvet* (1986) when Jeffrey (Kyle MacLachlan) hides out in the wardrobe of Dorothy Vallens (Isabella Rossellini), spying on her.) The expectation of discovery generates a fear response, but not a horror response. It's the wrong sort of fear to generate a horror response. It is fear of something bad happening (discovery) rather than fear of a repulsive harm. This is the basic difference between suspense and horror.

9   Presumably, there is more that appeals about the activity of base-jumping than the adrenaline rush; but this is unlikely to be the conceptual content of what is experienced when jumping. The extra appeal of base-jumping is more likely to lie in ancillary aspects of the activity, such as planning and daring. Nevertheless, the appeal of activities that may at times be dangerous may also require further psychological explanation. The "daredevil" trait is the manifestation of a particular kind of character type.

10   Thus *Christine* (1983) (in which a car has murderous intent) is a horror film whereas *Duel* (1971) (in which a truck driver has murderous intent) is not. *Duel* is scary; it just isn't creepy.

11   Carroll is talking specifically about Ernest Jones' work on nightmares (Jones 1931) but he takes it to be typical of psychoanalytic explanations of horror.

12   Famously, according to Freudian psychoanalysis, a strong mismatch between unconscious wishes and conscious identity generates discontent and neurotic behavior. And we are all discontented and neurotic to some degree or other; a perfect match between unconscious wish and conscious avowal would be neither likely nor welcome. See Freud (1989).

13   Prince (1996); Crane (1994); Tudor (1997).

14   Masochistic identification may be more prevalent in horror experience than sadism. Masochistic identification promises to explain the prevalence of the genre convention of "the final girl" in which audiences identify or affiliate with a particularly vulnerable character, and are vicariously threatened and menaced along with her, until she turns the tables in the last reel. See Clover (1992).

15   Carroll's explanation connects closely with his general account of the power of movies. See our discussion of this in chapter 2.

16   Carroll (1995) suggests an expansion of his theory along lines like this.

17   In realist horror of the late twentieth century, realist monsters exhibited extraordinary capacities until their confrontation with "the final girl," who manages to undo them. In "final girl" confrontations, monstrous power deserts a realist monster and they become clumsy, slow, and dim-witted. In realist horror films of the early twenty-first century, the final girl (or indeed boy) is often absent. See, for example, *Wolf Creek* (2005), *The Strangers* (2008), and, in particular, *Funny Games.*

18   Not all films of serial killers are realist horror films. For example, *Monster* (2003) is a drama. Not only does it largely eschew the task of generating a horror response; it explores the non-monstrosity of the central character, Aileen.

19   *Silence of the Lambs* (1991) takes the hybridity between monstrousness and ordinary human attributes further than most realist horror films. Buffalo Bill is the classic realist monster, human in some ways, inaccessibly monstrous in most. Hannibal Lecter, by contrast, is a teasingly hybrid figure: a combination of the very human and the very monstrous. Lecter's charisma rests on his non-monstrous characteristics: his "friendship" with Clarice Starling; his "understandable" search for revenge; his wit (a sign of an understandable desire to be admired); his sophisticated love of beautiful things. Lecter's hybridity may explain the fascination he holds for audiences, and it may help to explain why *Silence of the Lambs* has been the most commercially successful realist horror film of recent decades.

20   For example, the film *Predator* (1987) is roughly along these lines (the killer is an alien hunting for sport; for all his alien-ness, he is a familiar type to us). The IMDB (Internet Movie Database) genre classification of *Predator* is Action, Adventure, Sci-Fi, Thriller; but not Horror (http://www.imdb.com/title/tt0093773/). *Frailty* (2001) has many elements of gothic horror, but the motivations of central characters are not, given their experiences, especially mysterious; they resolutely refuse to exhibit monstrosity even if they do terrible things. *Frailty* is categorized on IMDB as Crime, Drama, Thriller (http://www.imdb.com/title/tt0264616/).

21   We do not deny, of course, that horror films benefit from accomplished narrative filmmaking. We are interested in the fact that many elements of accomplished narrative filmmaking are superfluous for the genre. It can, at a pinch, get by without them.

22   Our claim isn't that the physiological account has no explanatory power at all. Our claim is that it has insufficient explanatory power and we are looking for the account which best explains the deficit.

23   See Carroll (1990), Crane (1994), Prince (1996), and Tudor (1997). Carroll (1990: 168–9) claims that although psychoanalysis is necessary for interpretation in cases where psychoanalytic themes are consciously built in (a good example of this is Lars von Trier's *Antichrist* (2009)), it is not essential to understanding and interpreting horror films generally.

24   In this book we discuss 12 films at length. Every one of them features a death; nine feature violent death. In *Total Recall*, the body count is ludicrously high. We didn't set out to write a book of death, but outside of comedies – romantic comedies in particular – death looms large in the cinema.

25   *Funny Games: Interview with Michael Haneke by Serge Toubiana* (0:06), Madman DVD release of 1997 version.

26   See the theatrical trailer on the Madman 2007 DVD release. It uses Grieg's *In the Hall of the Mountain King* to build excitement and the expectation of release; things that an audience are simply not going to get from the film itself. (The music is absent from the film, of course.)

27   The clearest comparison here is with critiques of violent heterosexual pornography as a form of hate speech directed at women. See Dworkin (1981), Langton (1990;1993), and West (2003).

28   The term "torture porn" was coined by David Edlestein, film critic for New York Magazine. It was not a friendly coinage (http://nymag.com/movies/ features/15622/). See http://www.urbandictionary.com/define.php?term =torture%20porn to find out what the fans think of the term.

Further Reading

Carroll, Noël (1990). *The Philosophy of Horror, or, Paradoxes of the Heart.* London: Routledge.

Carroll, Noël (1995). "Enjoying Horror Fictions: A Reply to Gaut." *British Journal of Aesthetics* 35, 67–72.

Clover, Carol (1992). *Men, Women and Chain Saws: Gender in the Modern Horror Film.* London: British Film Institute.

Crane, Jonathan Lake (1994). *Terror and Everyday Life: Singular Moments in the History of the Horror Film.* London: Sage.

Dworkin, Andrea (1981). *Pornography: Men Possessing Women.* London: The Women's Press.

Freeland, Cynthia A. (1995). "Realist Horror." In Cynthia A. Freeland & Thomas Wartenberg *Philosophy and Film.* New York: Routledge, 126–42.

Freeland, Cynthia A., & Thomas Wartenberg (1995). *Philosophy and Film.* New York: Routledge.

Freud, Sigmund (1989). *Civilization and Its Discontents*, trans. and ed. James Strachey. New York: *Norton.*

Gaut, Berys (1993). "The Paradox of Horror." *British Journal of Aesthetics* 33, 333–45.

Jones, Ernest (1931). *On the Nightmare.* London: Hogarth Press and Institute of Psycho-Analysis.

Langton, Rae (1990). "Whose Right? Ronald Dworkin, Women, and Pornographers." *Philosophy and Public Affairs* 19, 311–59.

Langton, Rae (1993). "Speech Acts and Unspeakable Acts." *Philosophy and Public Affairs* 22, 293–330.

Prince, Stephen (1996). "Psychoanalytic Film Theory and the Problem of the Missing Spectator." In David Bordell & Noël Carroll, eds., *Post-Theory: Reconstructing Film Studies.* Wisconsin: University of Wisconsin Press, 71–86.

Schneider, Steven J. (2004). *Horror Film and Psychoanalysis: Freud's Worst Nightmare.* Cambridge: Cambridge University Press.

Tudor, Anthony (1997). Why Horror? The Peculiar Pleasures of a Popular Genre." *Cultural Studies* 11, 443–63.

West, Caroline (2003). "The Free Speech Argument Against Pornography." *Canadian Journal of Philosophy* 33.3, 391–422.

10

Looking for Meaning in All the Wrong Places: *Ikiru* ("To Live")

> *Do not go gentle into that good night,*
> *Old age should burn and rave at close of day;*
> *Rage, rage against the dying of the light.*
>
> Dylan Thomas

Akira Kurosawa directed and co-wrote *Ikiru* in 1952. Filmed in black and white, it ostensibly tells the story of Kanji Watanabe, a bureaucrat and section chief who spends virtually his entire life working in a city office. Neither Watanabe nor anyone else in the office actually does anything much that is worthwhile or productive. They shuffle and stamp papers that simply move from useless pile to useless pile.[1] They may look as if they are actually getting something done, but it becomes clear not only that they are doing nothing but also that they are meant to be doing nothing, and that they are, on some level, aware that they do nothing. The office, with piles and piles of neatly tied and stacked folders, is itself in effect a façade – a stage set – and in some ways a quite beautiful one.

After he learns he has terminal cancer – a fact that the doctors lie to him about – Watanabe immediately becomes desolate. It is by means of this palpable despair that he becomes aware that he is faced with a problem that goes beyond his impending death. The nature of that problem is the focus of this chapter. It is, roughly, the problem of how to find meaning in life. In chapter 1 we remarked that, in the first instance, the locus of many philosophical problems is actual life, after which the issues are taken up by philosophers. *Ikiru* is a case in which a philosophical problem is

Thinking Through Film: Doing Philosophy, Watching Movies, First Edition. Damian Cox, Michael P. Levine.

presented and a solution offered *in situ*, that is, in the context of a particular life and the concrete problems encountered in it. It is, in many ways, both prior to and more powerful than treatments of the problem in professional philosophy.

Watanabe learns of his fate from a fellow patient, who tells him how to interpret the doctors' lies. The doctors tell him he has a mild stomach ulcer. In fact he has inoperable stomach cancer. Whether, as the dialogue suggests, the doctors really believe they have his best interests in mind – after all, why worry about something one can do nothing about – or whether they simply want to avoid the difficulty in telling him is ambiguous. As is often the case in Kurosawa's work, the dialogue tells one story and the visual scene another. Here narrative and dialogue are juxtaposed with filmic technique (severe and sustained close-ups) and acting to yield this specific effect. (The scene is at 0:17.) The doctors' behavior introduces the problem of paternalism, which is worth brief consideration. In most places today, the medical profession guards against the kind of paternalistic behavior shown by Watanabe's doctors. But individual autonomy is still undermined through paternalism on a daily basis in many spheres of life; medicine to be sure, but most notably in politics. A paternalistic act is one that deprives individuals of the chance to decide a course of action for themselves, either by withholding information, by making resources unavailable, or by making a potential course of action illegal. It is difficult to know when, if ever, paternalistic behavior by those in power over us – doctors, politicians, police, and so on – is justified. Typically, paternalism is justified on the grounds that it is in our best interest not to be able to decide a course of action for ourselves, or that there is some greater good that hangs in the balance. This paternalism has its counterpart in a kind of infantilism on the part of those who do not want to be informed, or what amounts to the same thing, people self-deceptively telling themselves that those in charge "know better" and have access to information that the rest of us do not. Consider just what would have happened had Watanabe believed the doctors. He would have lost his chance of finding meaning in his final months of life.

Watanabe lives with his son (Mitsuo) and daughter-in-law, or rather they live in his house with him. He is unwelcome in his own home, and seems unable or unwilling to tell them about his terminal cancer, partly because they are generally unconcerned and ignore him. When he does attempt to do so, circumstances appear to repeatedly intervene to prevent it. They remain unaware of his illness and that he knows about it until after he is dead. On the surface at least, Mitsuo and his wife are more interested in their inheritance and in getting a new house, than in

Watanabe. Although his son is distant and withdrawn, and shows neither love nor respect towards Watanabe, it is also clear that he has affection for his father – which he is perhaps not aware of until after his death.

Despite Watanabe's somewhat feeble efforts toward a rapprochement with his son, it is a mistake to think that such reconciliation would have, by itself, solved Watanabe's problem. It may have eased the isolation, the loneliness, and helped calm the fear – which are no small things. But more through visual than verbal narrative, Kurosawa intimates that in the face of death not only Watanabe, but we too, are alone. The most powerful rendering of this idea – one of the most perfectly realized scenes in all of Kurosawa's work – is the final shot of Watanabe, alone in his park – the park he constructs – on a children's swing, at night, moments before death, in the snow, alone, singing (at 2:17). Whatever resources and strengths one can muster, whatever the significance of one's own life, and no matter who is holding our hand, in facing death we do so by ourselves. Whatever good can be done by those around us, even those whom we love and who love us, it is all rendered, if not impotent, then at least relatively inconsequential, in the face of death.

The office workers are involved in an elaborate charade – a pretence in which no one says what is on their mind, or calls into question the value of what they are doing; no one, that is, except Toyo, a young girl new to the office, who soon quits because the job is "too boring." Despite her youth, indeed in part because of it, she has a natural insight into, and affinity for, that which makes life meaningful. An unlikely savior (though we seem to intuit her role immediately), she nevertheless plays a key role in Watanabe's redemption. Toyo dispenses a saving grace that is independent of supernatural power or divine connection. In the end, Watanabe acquires a sense of place and belonging – albeit briefly. In the scene we mentioned earlier (2:17), Watanabe is singing what seems to be his favorite song. This is the second time he sings it in the film, and this time he does so less with a sense of loss and more with tranquility, knowing not so much that his life has been a success, as that that he has learned "to live."

The first time he sings the song in the film is in the bar where he is led by a struggling dissolute novelist (0:49–0:52). The novelist takes Watanabe to all of the places one might expect to find life lived to the max (bars, prostitutes, etc.). He sings it just at the point where he appears to realize that, no matter how well-intentioned his worldly guide has been, the search has failed. The song is "Gondola no Uta" (The Gondola Song, 1915). It is a sentimental exhortation to find love while still young. But with Watanabe's mournful singing it becomes a powerful cinematic encapsulation of various narrative themes in the film, including the bleak loss of youthful possibilities. As Larkin (1974: 32) says, referring to the moon in his poem "Sad Steps":

> . . . the plain
> Far-reaching singleness of that wide stare
>
> Is a reminder of the strength and pain
> Of being young; that it can't come again,
> But is for others undiminished somewhere.

No doubt Watanabe's sorrow and regret is exacerbated by his illness. Nevertheless, it would be a mistake to think this was all there was to it.

We are able to identify with Watanabe because we intuitively recognize that his problem is ours as well – a reflection of the human condition. When young, he too had aspirations, desires, and goals. A flashback in the film to his wife's death intimates, with the use of sparse dialogue, that he abandoned these in order to provide for a son he loved very much (0:22–0:23). Perhaps his son was a convenient excuse. We do not know and Watanabe may not know either. But Watanabe's problem encapsulates an aspect of existence that faces us all – no matter how successful, prosperous, or full of meaningful relationships one's life has been. It is the fact that no matter what we succeed at or become, we are somehow unable to ever live up to and realize aspirations of youth, no matter how well-formed or ill-formed, realistic or fanciful and narcissistic they may have been. Stephen Spender (1986) captures it in his poem "What I Expected."

> What I expected was
> Thunder, fighting,
> Long struggles with men
> And climbing.
> After continual straining
> I should grow strong:
> Then the rocks would shake
> And I should rest long.
>
> What I had not foreseen
> Was the gradual day
> Weakening the will
> Leaking the brightness away,
> The lack of good to touch
> The fading of body and soul
> Like smoke before wind
> Corrupt, unsubstantial.

The wearing of Time,
And the watching of cripples pass
With limbs shaped like questions
In their odd twist.
The pulverous grief
Melting the bones with pity.
The sick falling from the earth
These, I could not foresee.

For I had expected always
Some brightness to hold in trust,
Some final innocence
To save from dust;
That, hanging solid,
Would dangle through all
Like the created poem
Or the dazzling crystal.

Terminal illness to one side, a realization, not always conscious, of imminent "failure" may underlie mid-life crises – some laughable and many not – that result particularly in men who otherwise cannot afford it, and who invariably are unable to see just what it is that others see, driving expensive sports cars. There is a sense in which all humans are bound to fail – and "failure" is the right word for it. It is *Ikiru*'s (Kurosawa's) ability to evoke this that binds us to Watanabe and moves us – or at least those of us it does move. (Some remain unmoved by this film.) What underlies this identification is less cognitive than affective. In particular, it may be a reflection and function of our own narcissistic tendencies, our own self-love, which we are feeling for Watanabe.

In his final meeting with Toyo, coming to grips with his illness and impending death, Watanabe asks "Why are you so incredibly alive? . . . Before I die, I want to live just one day like you do. I'll live that way before I die. Until I've done it, I can't just give up and die" (1:26–1:27). His imminent death from cancer, to be sure, is a problem for Watanabe. As this quote reveals, however, it is not his principal problem. Ikiru is often taken as an existentialist tract dealing with the meaning of life: Why should one live, and how should one live, in a meaningless, perhaps absurd world – a world capable of producing horrendous and unimaginable horror, injustice, and pain, and a world without a plausible master-narrative to explain and reconcile us to it? It is difficult to imagine what a post-war, post-Hiroshima, and post-Nagasaki Japan must have been like in 1952. (Kurosawa's film is finely tuned to the predicament of post-war Japan; it is at least as much social critique as existential tract.)

The question of the meaning of life is posed in various ways. "Does life have a meaning?" and "What is the meaning of life?" are two forms the question takes. But neither of these captures Watanabe's concern, and the form that the question takes for him rightly shows that as posed, these two questions miss the crux of the matter – or the most common form of it. Watanabe is not asking whether life has meaning, let alone "What is the meaning of life?" These particular questions are of little concern to him and may not even make much sense. He is not concerned with the question whether life as such has meaning. What matters to him is how to find meaning *in his own life*. This is different from the question of whether life, in the abstract, has meaning. It is also importantly different from the question of whether one's own life has meaning. When we ask the question in this way we seek an objective standard of significance for life: a role in a great narrative, often a religious narrative, which makes our lives important in some way. Watanabe's problem is not to find such a story, but to find a way of living "correctly" as he puts it. The problem is how to live meaningfully, not how to discover the meaning of life. The problem is how to go about finding and constructing ways of living meaningfully that are consonant with who we think we are and with the kinds of persons we would like to be – insofar as we know these things.

How to live meaningfully is the issue; not whether life is meaningful. When students, for example, are thinking about what careers to pursue, they are rightly concerned not with the meaning of life *per se* but with how best to pursue meaning in their own lives.[2] It is assumed, often rightly, that one's job is going to play an essential role, structurally, finan-cially, and in various other ways, in one's efforts to find or construct meaning. And as most students will tell you, this is no easy let alone laughing matter. Watanabe's job is of no use to him whatsoever in such a pursuit. But the sobering thought here is the Marxist one concerning people's alienation from their work, or Thoreau's confronting and insist-ent claim that "The mass of men lead lives of quiet desperation. What is called resignation is confirmed desperation" (Thoreau 2004 [1854]).[3]

Furthermore, and to complicate the matter, the problem of finding meaning in one's life is not a problem one solves once and for all – though we may pretend otherwise and put ourselves at risk in doing so. It is a reiterative task. What one takes to be satisfactory at one time in life may not be satisfactory at another time. Why suppose that it would be? It may be that no matter how full and meaningful one's life has been in terms of employment, relationships, and the like, there comes a time to don one's loincloth and head into the forest as Siddhārtha Gautama did. And some people, often through no fault of their own – not through want of trying – may have considerably more difficulty in finding and sustaining meaning than others. (See the discussion of moral luck in chapter 12.)

The claim here is that *Ikiru* illustrates that the principal question about the meaning of life is not whether life has meaning, but rather how to find meaning in one's life.

The Meaning of Life: Objective, Subjective, Other

Watanabe is not concerned with the meaning of life ("Why is there life?" or even "Why am I alive?"), but rather in finding meaning in his life, or "finding a way to make his life meaningful." Toyo points him in the right direction when she shows him the toy rabbits that she helps make (1:29). He keeps one. They are simple but they make others happy. This is the turning point in the film. Cradling the toy rabbit (a beautiful scene with Watanabe in his overcoat and hat) he suddenly realizes that his own happiness and well-being is, or can be, bound up with the lives and well-being of others. If he can make a positive difference to others he will also have succeeded in achieving a life with some meaning and purpose – no matter how transient and ephemeral his accomplishment or contribution may prove in the long run.

Susan Wolf (2007: 72) would agree. She says "living a meaningful life is a matter of at least partly successful engagement in projects of positive value." And a such a life would virtually always effect and involve others in a positive way. Even if life itself had no meaning, was purely accidental for example, this could not undermine a meaningful life in Wolf's sense. Wolf says (2007: 69) that "Living a life that is engaged with and so at least partially focussed on projects whose value has a nonsubjective source is a way of acknowledging one's non-privileged position. It harmonizes, in a way that a purely egocentric life does not, with the fact that one is not the center of the universe."

She notes (2007: 67) that a meaningful life need not be a particularly moral life nor, indeed, a moral life at all. She also claims that "Neither is a meaningful life assured of being an especially happy one."[4] It seems obvious that a meaningful life need not be a happy one since there are many people who successfully pursue projects of positive value, believe that what they do is valuable, and yet remain (on the whole) unhappy. Was the connection between Watanabe's happiness at the end and his finding meaning purely a fortuitous one, or was happiness intrinsically connected in some way to the meaning he managed to eke out just in time? Is it just that *in general* those who live meaningful lives have a better chance for a greater degree of happiness?

Aristotle claims that there is an intrinsic connection between living a meaningful life and human happiness. For Aristotle, such a life is structured by virtue. (See chapter 14 for more on this.) It is a life in which one pursues what is in fact in one's own best interest; and by that very fact a life in which one becomes what one should become given one's human nature. Aristotle has what may be called an essentialist conception of happiness. Taylor (1975: 132) says such a conception "presupposes that there is such a thing as an essential human nature." When goals are stipulated that a person *qua* person should achieve, this is indicative of an essentialist conception of human nature. What is that essential nature? Does happiness rely on it? According to an essentialist conception of happiness, one which presupposes that there is an essential human nature, "happiness" is largely a function of how well one fulfils one's nature. Taylor (1975: 132–3) says,

> According to the essentialist conception of happiness, a truly happy life is identified with the Good Life for Man . . . Happiness (*eudaimonia*, well-being) is the kind of life that is suitable or fitting for a *human* being to live, and a *human* being is one who exemplifies the essential nature (or essence) of man. Thus happiness is not to be identified with any kind of life a person might actually want to live. Instead it characterises the kind of life we all *would* want to live if we understood our true nature as human beings. Happiness, then, may be defined as that state of the "soul" or condition of life which all human beings, *insofar as they are human*, ultimately aim at.

To the extent that a human being is able to achieve "happiness" by actualizing the properties that "define the good of man as such," that is, by exemplifying the essential nature of human beings, they will be leading an intrinsically good or valuable life.

"Happiness" is then the standard by which to judge the intrinsic value of a person's life. (We discuss the concept of intrinsic value below.) Taylor develops the point (1975: 133):

> When this conception of happiness is used as the standard of intrinsic value, the standard becomes identical with the essentialist's standard of human perfection or virtue. What determines the intrinsic goodness of a person's life is the realisation of an ideal; in living a truly human life, the person is realising the good for man as man. Not everyone fulfils this standard to the same degree, but to the extent that a person does, his life takes on a worth,

a perfection, that gives it value in itself, independently of any consequences it might have in the lives of others.

The theistic conception of the essential nature of humans is different than Aristotle's. For the theist, the goal, or *telos*, of life is salvation in the form of personal immortality, and a special kind of happiness. In heaven one will have a more intimate relationship with God than is possible in this life. "Blessedness" or "happiness" (*beatitudo*) is the theist's goal, and human nature is defined in terms of this. To be human is to be a finite creature whose happiness and well-being are ultimately dependent upon a relationship with an infinite God. The pursuit of this goal involves what theists regard as a distinctive way of life.

If one rejects an essentialist conception of human happiness, then the link between meaning and happiness is broken. We can then assume what in any case we already know; that a meaningful life, even a very meaningful life, does not assure one of happiness. Nevertheless, given what we do know of human nature, it seems that the chances of being happy generally increase insofar as one pursues projects of positive value with at least a modicum of success. While Watanabe's happiness was by no means assured by his efforts to construct a park, they were (expectedly) rewarded.

We can suppose that Watanabe, like most Japanese, combines aspects of Shinto and Buddhism in his life. (Marriages and other happy and festival events like New Year's usually involve Shinto, whereas funerals are largely Buddhist. Given that Buddhism is, strictly speaking, atheist (though Buddhism in practice often contains references to various deities), the question of whether God and some divine plan are necessary for happiness isn't something that, as far as we know, Watanabe even considers. His search for a way to find meaning is also independent of the Buddhist conception of nirvana and seemingly of any other religious notions. Thus, as far as Watanabe is concerned, finding meaning in one's life is independent of whether any god or preordained plan exist. Even if God did exist, the nature, if not the substance, of Watanabe's pursuit would remain the same. Suppose God does have something in mind for us – each of us individually. Unless one appropriates the goal, recognizes and adopts it, then no such God-given purpose can help an individual establish meaning in their life. It is no use telling someone that the meaning of their life is, for example, to establish a relationship with God unless they are able to find meaning in such a project. Even if there is a God who has purposes for us all, this is logically insufficient for anyone to find meaning unless they find such a project meaningful. Even if God knew that only in doing a certain thing – let's call it x – would Lucy fulfill God's purpose, Lucy would still have to find x meaningful. And if God had made her in such a way that she could not find anything but x meaningful, then she would in effect be denied the freedom necessary to fashion her own life and its meanings. Without such freedom and choice she would also be absolved from a certain kind of responsibility for how she lived: she would not be absolved from responsibility for how she chose to respond to God's plan for her, but she would be absolved from responsibility for creating a meaningful life for herself.

Sartre (1957) claimed that if there was a God-given objective meaning to existence – a human essence, in effect – humans would not only be denied freedom and the ability to construct a meaningful life, they would also forfeit responsibility for their fundamental value choices. He therefore sees the absence of any God or human essence, as a condition of freedom and also as a burden. Freedom is a necessary condition for responsibility and establishing meaning in one's own life.

Subjective value refers to beliefs, attitudes, or other states of the agent that impute value to something. If filmmaking is subjectively valuable for Kurosawa, for example, then Kurosawa regards, believes, etc., that filmmaking is valuable. More strongly still, Kurosawa's believing filmmaking to be valuable is both necessary and sufficient for filmmaking to be subjectively valuable to Kurosawa. Filmmaking may be bad for Kurosawa in a variety of ways, or it may be good. Nevertheless, if Kurosawa thinks filmmaking is of value, if Kurosawa values filmmaking, then filmmaking has subjective value for him. No matter how good x might be for p, if p does not value x, then x cannot be subjectively valuable for p. Of course Kurosawa can be mistaken about all this. He might think he values filmmaking, but be wrong. He might be deceiving himself, for example, and sincerely affirm its value consciously while unconsciously denying it. (He is in it for the money and women.) Given that the things we generally deceive ourselves about are things that are rather important to us, one can expect that where matters of value come into play so too does self-deception.

To say that something has objective value is, generally, to say that it is valuable whether or not anyone believes it to be valuable. Believing something to be of value will generally *not* be regarded as either necessary or sufficient for that thing to be objectively valuable. Things that are subjectively valuable (e.g. my happiness that I value) may be objectively valuable as well. However, in the absence of some argument to show that there is an intrinsic connection between the two, there is little reason to assume that this is necessarily, or even frequently, the case. And if anything is objectively valuable, then again apart from an argument for an intrinsic connection, it need not be subjectively valuable to anyone.

Values differ in at least two kinds of way. They can be objective or subjective, as we have just seen. Along a different dimension, they can also be either intrinsic or extrinsic. Intrinsic value is value in and of itself, value apart from any connection with further value or states of affairs. For example, some people believe that pleasure is intrinsically valuable. This means that a particular experience of pleasure has some value no matter what comes before or after it, and no matter what its consequences are. Of course, a moment's pleasure may be outweighed by its bad consequences; but it cannot, if pleasure is intrinsically valuable, ever be entirely negated by its consequences. There is still some good in there, so to speak. Extrinsic value is the value something has in virtue of its connection with other things. The most obvious kind of extrinsic value is instrumental value. A thing's instrumental value consists in its capacity to cause or facilitate other things of value. A headache tablet has no intrinsic value, but it is instrumentally valuable. Subjective value can be either intrinsic value or extrinsic value (or both). My happiness will be subjectively valuable to me in and of itself if I so regard it. It may also be subjectively valuable to me if it enables me to achieve some further valuable end. And of course it could be both. Intrinsic and instrumental values neither entail nor exclude one another. Similarly, subjective and objective values neither necessarily entail nor exclude one another.

When we search for meaning in our lives, we are searching for positive values. But are these subjective or objective values? Are they intrinsic or extrinsic values? They have to, at least, be subjective values. They don't contribute to our finding our lives meaningful unless they are. Subjective values can be rather lonely: a person might be the only one who finds the thing valuable. Imagine a person deciding to invest value in discarded pizza boxes and busily collecting them and storing them in pride of place in a trophy room. (Is this person living meaningfully?) Subjective values don't have to be lonely like this; they can be widely held and inter-subjectively validated. It seems that a search for meaningful living is a search for ways of contributing things of shared, inter-subjectively validated, subjective value. Must they be intrinsically valuable? They must be closely connected to things of intrinsic value. Watanabe finds value in the children's park. But the park may not itself be intrinsically valuable. It may be valuable because of the joy it gives children and their families. But this joy might itself be intrinsically valuable. It looks like a good candidate for intrinsic value. Watanabe would then find deepest value in his contribution to the joys of others' childhoods. Were the park not connected quite so closely to things of intrinsic value – imagine that the only valuable thing Watanabe managed to do through his efforts was to help re-elect the deputy mayor, which is itself only valuable because the deputy mayor is a slightly less damaging political figure than his rival – then we might start questioning its role in shoring up Watanabe's sense of living meaningfully. It doesn't seem enough that one contributes as a cog in some giant machinery of instrumental value. (After all, Watanabe might have been such a cog, to a degree, even in his paper-shuffling days.) To live meaningfully, then, is to contribute in some significant way to the production of things of inter-subjective intrinsic value: to things that matter to us and matter on their own account.

But that leaves us with the question of objective value. What role might that play in meaningful living? There are those who claim that apart from God, or belief in God (or both), life lacks the possibility of achieving things of objective value and this undermines the possibility of living meaningfully. But how can such a claim be sustained? What does it even mean, given that those who do not believe in God or immortality nevertheless have meaning and significance in their lives of a certain kind? It is a kind of meaning that no one could intelligibly deny life has – the subjective meanings that we actively create for ourselves in life or find ourselves in the midst of. Jobs and relationships can contribute to a subjectively meaningful life – though they can – as in many films – also severely detract from such meaning and sense of purpose.

Bertrand Russell believed that all life in the solar system would eventually die out. He thought that acceptance of our own mortality and the eventual death of all living things in the solar system, along with accepting the lack of any divine goal or plan, was essential to any philosophically acceptable resolution to the problem of finding meaning in one's life. Russell (1981: 56) says

> That man is the product of causes which had no prevision of the end they were achieving; that his origin, his growth, his hopes and fears, his loves and his beliefs, are but the outcome of accidental collocations of atoms; that no fire, no heroism, no intensity of thought and feeling, can preserve an individual life beyond the grave; that all the labours of the ages, all the devotion, all the inspiration, all the noonday brightness of human genius, are destined to extinction in the vast death of the solar system, and that the whole temple of man's achievement must inevitably be buried beneath the debris of a universe in ruins – all these things, if not quite beyond dispute, are yet so nearly certain that no philosophy which rejects them can hope to stand.

The idea that someday "the whole temple of man's achievement" (Beethoven's sonatas, etc.) will be gone is sobering. Russell is suggesting that whatever meaning life has for us should be construed as independent of any alleged cause or purpose for life – divine or otherwise. The claim seems to be that there is no meaning of life that is independent of those for whom life has meaning – that is, independent of the subjective meaning fashioned in living.

Russell is not denying that a *belief* in God and some ordained purposes, such as a relationship with God, may make life meaningful in some ways for some people. But he is claiming that, philosophically speaking, if we are to fashion meaningful lives relatively free from delusion or illusion, then we must not only recognize our own mortality, but also acknowledge that the totality of all that humans as a species have achieved will one day vanish. Watanabe's concern, as we have seen, is not with whether life has meaning but with how to make his life meaningful. The film does suggest that recognition of one's mortality (Watanabe's imminent death) is a factor in his successfully constructing such meaning. It does not however endorse or deny Russell's further claim, that human genius is destined for extinction. In any case, the longstanding religious claim that if there is no God, divine scheme, or immortality, then life is necessarily meaningless or absurd is rejected in *Ikiru*. Why suppose that if there is no objective meaning to life – such as the meaning our lives would have if the goal to establish a relationship with God was divinely ordained – then our lives would necessarily remain meaningless? Why suppose that if all life in the universe, indeed the universe itself, is annihilated, our lives would become thereby meaningless or absurd? Why suppose that the "meaning" we construct in our lives is in any way intrinsically connected to temporality or continued existence? If the world disappeared tomorrow would Watanabe's life thereby become meaningless or absurd?

The Final Act

Ikiru has three acts: discovery, struggle, and resolution. The final act is in many ways the most interesting. With the exception of two brief scenes at the very end of the film, one in the park and one in the city offices where he worked, this last part of the film takes place just after, or as part of, Watanabe's funeral. Some viewers find the extended sequence at Watanabe's funeral, juxtaposed with a series of flashbacks, too long. Yet Kurosawa arguably used the length of sequence itself – it was intentionally long – as a cinematic technique to focus spectators' attention, present a final point of view, and offer time to reflect on the film's action. Ostensibly, the mourners are trying to figure out if Watanabe knew about his terminal illness, recognizing that this would be a likely explanation for his change of character and utter devotion to getting the park built against seemingly endless and insuperable obstacles.[5]

Of course the audience already knows that Watanabe knew he was dying, but here we witness the gradual dawning of this fact on the mourners, including his son Mitsuo. Here then is a chance to think about the role of one's death in one's own life (how "imminent" is merely a matter of degree). Given the certainty of death there is a sense in which our situation is not all that different from Watanabe's, at least when understood from a certain distant or bird's eye perspective. The final act of *Ikiru* serves as an explanation and affirmation of what at least some existentialists think about death in relation to life and its meaning for us. The fact of death makes a difference to how we live – or it should. In broad terms, this view was shared by Camus, Sartre, Russell, and many others. Wittgenstein (1961 [1921]: 147, 6.4311), though no existentialist, said "Death is not an event in life: we do not live to experience death. If we take eternity to mean not infinite temporal duration but timelessness, then eternal life belongs to those who live in the present."[6] Though "death is not an event in life," life is to be led – should be led – with the knowledge of death's certainty.

In asserting that "eternal life belongs to those who live in the present," Wittgenstein is reiterating the significance that death has for life. Eternal life – insofar as it carries a sense of salvation or redemption – must be found in the present if at all; in the way we live the only life that we have. Watanabe (Kurosawa) concurs. This admonition should not be confused with a "the world is my oyster" attitude – let alone, "we only go around once so 'anything goes.'" It does however put people on notice that living is in *some* ways a serious business and should be regarded with a certain gravitas – not moral earnestness – but seriousness. (You should still have fun, and you should still learn to cook.) As Hikmet (1975) says in his poem "On Living" (verse I)

> Living is no laughing matter:
> > you must live with great seriousness
> > like a squirrel, for example –
> I mean without looking for something beyond and above living,
> > I mean living must be your whole occupation.
> Living is no laughing matter:
> > you must take it seriously,
> > so much so and to such a degree
> > that, for example, your hands tied behind your back,
> > > your back to the wall,

or else in a laboratory
    in your white coat and safety glasses,
      you can die for people –
even for people whose faces you've never seen,
even though you know living
    is the most real, the most beautiful thing.
I mean, you must take living so seriously
    that even at seventy, for example, you'll plant olive trees –
    and not for your children, either,
    but because although you fear death you don't believe it,
    because living, I mean, weighs heavier.

There is at least one other point Kurosawa makes in the funeral scene. Having come to the conclusion that Watanabe did know of his impending death, his co-workers attribute his change and his obstinacy in getting the park built to that awareness. In those emotion-filled moments, when various deep truths about themselves and the uselessness of their work (and lives) are smack in front of them, the co-workers sincerely resolve to change their ways. However, lest one leave the cinema on that note, with that false but happy ending, Kurosawa makes sure we return to the city office. There we find what we expect to find. Nothing has changed and nothing will change. The neatly bound piles remain the same, and so do the endless and meaningless tasks the workers are involved in – with perhaps an intimation that some of them both recognize and regret the backslide.

It is the inevitability of one's own death, not merely death in the abstract, that one must become aware of in order to live authentically and wisely – or, for Watanabe, "to live" at all – though even then one may fail. This is a theme one finds at the core of Camus' *The Myth of Sisyphus* (1955 [1942]), and which is missing in Wolf (2007). One should also be aware of a kind of universal omnipresent inertia and apathy that appears to structure our very existence. (Those files remain still, neatly tied and piled in those city offices and will be added to for evermore.)

Questions

Does Watanabe have a genuine problem? What is it? To what extent can it be said that we all share Watanabe's difficulty.

In *Ikiru* the truth comes out when everyone gets to speak (at the funeral party). What truths, if any, are revealed? What difference does it make?

It has been said that knowledge can sometimes be "salvific" – it can save. Did Watanabe acquire saving knowledge? What was it? What did it save him from?

Is youth wasted on the young?

Watanabe twice sings "Gondola no Uta." How have his circumstances changed between the first and second time? Does the song mean something different each time? Try sitting on a swing and singing the song yourself.

Is it possible to live a genuine meaningless life – a life without meaning? Remember, even very bad lives can have meaning.

In his short story "Guy de Maupassant" (1932) Isaac Babel writes:

> Even in those days, when I was twenty years old, I had told myself: better starve, go to jail, or become a bum than spend ten hours every day behind a desk in an office. There was nothing particularly laudable in my resolve, but I have never broken it and I never will. The wisdom of my ancestors was firmly lodged in my head: we are born to enjoy our work, our fights, and our love; we are born for that and for nothing else.

What would Watanabe say?

Notes

1   The office is a somewhat bleaker Japanese version of the Circumlocution Office in Charles Dickens' *Little Dorrit*.
2   See Isaac Babel's short story "Guy de Maupassant" (1932):

> Even in those days, when I was twenty years old, I had told myself: better starve, go to jail, or become a bum than spend ten hours every day behind a desk in an office. There was nothing particularly laudable in my resolve, but I have never broken it and I never will. The wisdom of my ancestors was firmly lodged in my head: we are born to enjoy our work, our fights, and our love; we are born for that and for nothing else. (http://www.opus40.org/tadrichards/npaltz/Babel.htm)

3   Thoreau says "I went to the woods because I wished to live deliberately, to front only the essential facts of life, and see if I could not learn what it had to teach, and not, when I came to die, discover that I had not lived. I did not wish to live what was not life, living is so dear; nor did I wish to practice resignation." Thoreau claims ("Economy") that most men are slaves to their work and enslaved to those they work for.

4 Wolf (2007: 67) says "[M]eaning in life may not be especially moral, and . . . lives can be richly meaningful even if they are, on the whole, judged to be immoral." Still, on her account, for a life to be meaningful it would at least have to have some positive value. Can anyone, on Wolf's account, really fail to have a meaningful life? Even those she discusses, like the blob who sits in front of the television all day, are bound to have some projects of positive value and so some meaning in life.

5 This final act also portrays the gradual emergence of the truth of Watanabe's achievement after the double-dealing and hypocritical deputy mayor ties to direct credit for it away from him. In this way, *Ikiru* is an interesting companion piece to, and mirror image of, Kurosawa's earlier film *Rashamon* (1950). In *Rashamon* the truth of an incident (a sexual assault) is obscured by the inquiry into it, as a confusion of disparate, self-interested stories collide with each other.

6 Also see Wittgenstein (1961: 147, 6.4312)::

> The temporal immortality of the human soul, that is to say, its eternal survival after death, is not only in no way guaranteed, but this assumption in the first place will not do for us what we always tried to make it do. Is a riddle solved by the fact that we survive for ever? Is this eternal life not as enigmatic as our present one? The solution of the riddle of life in space and time lies outside space and time.

Further Reading

Babel, Isaac (1932). "Guy de Maupassant."

Camus, Albert (1955 [1942]). *The Myth of Sisyphus and Other Essays.* New York: Knopf.

Ecclesiastes (2011 [1973]). New International Version Bible.

Edwards, Paul (1981). "The Meaning and Value of Life." In E. D. Klemke, ed., *The Meaning of Life.* New York: Oxford University Press.

Hikmet, Nazim (1975). *Things I Didn't Know I Loved, Selected Poems.* Persea Books: New York.

Larkin, Philip (1974). "Sad Steps." In *High Windows.* New York: Farrar, Strauss and Giroux, 32.

Levine, Michael P. (1988). "Camus, Hare, and The Meaning of Life," *Sophia* 27, 13–30.

Levine, Michael P. (1988). What Does Death Have To Do With The Meaning of Life?" *Religious Studies* 24, 457–65.

Nozick, Robert (1981). "Philosophy and The Meaning of Life." In *Philosophical Explanations.* Cambridge, MA: Harvard University Press, 571–650.

Philosophical Papers (2005). 34.3. Issue on The Meaning in Life.

Russell, Bertrand (1981 [1903]). "A Free Man's Worship." In E. D. Klemke, ed., *The Meaning of Life.* Oxford: Oxford University Press, 55–62.

Sartre, Jean-Paul (1957). *Existentialism and Human Emotions.* New York: Philosophical Library. http://www.questia.com/PM.qst?a=o&d=59487415

Spender, Stephen (1986). "What I Expected." In *Collected Poems 1928–1985.* New York: Random House.

Taylor, Paul W. (1975). *Principles of Ethics.* Encino, CA: Dickenson.

Thomas, Dylan (1952 [1937]). "Do Not Go Gentle Into That Good Night." From *The Poems of Dylan Thomas.* New York: New Directions.

Thoreau, Henry David (2004 [1854]). *Walden and Other Writings,* edited with an introduction by Joseph Wood Krutch. Bantam: New York,.

Wartenberg, Thomas (2007). *Thinking on Screen: Film as Philosophy.* Basingstoke: Palgrave Macmillan.

Wittgenstein, Ludwig (1961 [1921]). *Tractatus Logico-Philosophicus.* London: Routledge & Kegan Paul.

Wolf, Susan (2007). "The Meanings of Lives." In John Perry, Michael Bratman, & John Martin Fischer, eds., *Introduction to Philosophy: Classical and Contemporary Readings.* New York: Oxford University Press, 62–73.

Part IV

Ethics and Values

Part IV examines the ethical life. We examine questions of moral motivation (what reason do we have to act rightly?) and moral luck (is our moral standing entirely up to us; you can be lucky or unlucky in love, can you also be lucky or unlucky in your moral life?). We also examine the major theories of ethics in contemporary philosophy: consequentialism, deontology, and virtue theory.

Chapter 11 is a study of moral motivation. Do we have reason to act ethically even when it is clearly in our self-interest not to? (Perhaps it is always in our self-interest to act ethically, but how could that be?) Discussions of this kind need a deeply imagined and complicated example to work with (at least one) that is also highly plausible. We have chosen to use Woody Allen's 1989 film *Crimes and Misdemeanors* to furnish the example. *Crimes and Misdemeanors* is much discussed in these terms. We add to the discussion by looking long and hard at the choice position of the film's main protagonist, Judah Rosenthal. Judah Rosenthal is a peerless example of the clash between personal interest and ethical commitment.

Chapter 12 is a study of moral luck. To what extent are we able to determine our moral fate? That is, how much has luck got to do with whether or not we are good people who act well? We employ the 2006 German film *The Lives of Others* to examine the issue. *The Lives of Others* is set in East Berlin a few years before the demise of the Democratic Republic of East Germany (which was in fact a communist state, sponsored and protected by the Soviet Union). Much of the film is about the

Thinking Through Film: Doing Philosophy, Watching Movies, First Edition. Damian Cox, Michael P. Levine.
© 2012 Damian Cox and Michael P. Levine. Published 2012 by Blackwell Publishing Ltd.

politics of personal liberty and privacy and the obligations of artists in times of repression, but vital philosophical questions are also raised about moral identity and the risks we take when we decide to transform our lives, even when we are sure that we are becoming better people in the process. The central character of Gerd Wiesler comes across a chance to make his life better. He is lucky, as it turns out. Other characters in the film are not so lucky. What has luck got to do with a moral life? It might have plenty to do with it.

Chapter 13 is about right action. What makes an action right when it is right and wrong when it is wrong? We examine the two main sorts of answers offered by philosophers. (A third kind of answer is examined in chapter 14.) The philosophical theories are consequentialism and deontology. Now we need a case study that we can use to really come to grips with what separates the two theories; one that might help us decide their relative plausibility. Christopher Nolan again supplies us with the case study. It occurs in the film *The Dark Knight* (2008) and involves two ferries and a lot of very nervous passengers. And it also involves Batman and the Joker of course. Nolan's film is a master-class in setting up ethical conundrums. We examine the way the film establishes an answer to the question of right action; and then sets about dismantling it.

Chapter 14 is about being good. Lots of films explore the goodness of characters, of course, but the film we discuss in chapter 14 is remarkable in the clear-eyed and convincing way in which it demonstrates the sheer beauty and grace of the creation of a moral identity. The film is *La Promesse*, by the Belgian filmmakers Jean-Pierre and Luc Dardenne. It is the story of a teenager who makes a promise – and keeps it. We use it to study the claims of virtue theory. Virtue theorists claim that virtues are at the core of moral goodness and can't be reduced to merely acting rightly or well. Virtues are special and fundamental. *La Promesse* shows how they are special and we use it to argue the case for virtue theory.

11

Crimes and Misdemeanors and the Fragility of Moral Motivation

Introduction

So you have been rather bad and you are in big trouble. Your life is about to come falling down around you. All you need do to prevent this happening is make a phone call. To your brother. Who will arrange a contract killing on your behalf. It will make all your troubles go away. It is a hard phone call to make, but also a hard one not to make. What should you do? The answer is simple. You ought never to make such a call. You ought to face the consequences of your behavior and allow your life to go badly, at least in some respects, as a consequence of what you have done. Of course, your future happiness is important. But it is more important that you not become a killer. And it's more important *still* that nobody be killed just so that you can be happier. From a moral point of view, all this is completely obvious. It also describes the basic setup of Woody Allen's *Crimes and Misdemeanors* (1989).

What is interesting about *Crimes and Misdemeanors* is not any moral dilemma faced by its main protagonist – Judah Rosenthal. He doesn't face a moral dilemma. A moral dilemma is a situation in which it is not at all clear, from a moral point of view, what ought to be done. Judah isn't in this kind of situation. He is in a pickle, but it's not a moral pickle. Judah has been having an affair with Delores for a few years and he wants to end it. Delores has different ideas. She thinks he has promised to leave his wife, Miriam, for her. The evidence seems to be sketchy. Judah has implied a future with Delores on at least one occasion that we witness in

Thinking Through Film: Doing Philosophy, Watching Movies, First Edition. Damian Cox, Michael P. Levine.
© 2012 Damian Cox and Michael P. Levine. Published 2012 by Blackwell Publishing Ltd.

flashback, but denies he ever promised Delores that he would leave Miriam. Delores is desperate and wants to talk things over with Miriam. If she doesn't get this, she threatens to expose both Judah's infidelity and his suspect business dealings. (Judah, it seems, has been borrowing funds from philanthropic accounts he manages. He claims to have repaid it all, but the transactions are probably illegal.)

Delores threatens to tear Judah's life apart. Judah is certain that Miriam will be unforgiving about his infidelity. His reputation for probity and philanthropy will be ruined by Delores's revelations of his business dealings. His life – as he puts it – will go down the toilet. He turns to his brother, who offers a way out: the contract killing of Delores. After a bit of (probably hypocritical) handwringing, Judah takes up the offer. When the deed is done he suffers pangs of remorse. (Or is this merely a fear of being caught and punished, either by the police or by God? Remorse is not the same thing as fear of punishment.)[1] Eventually, when he accommodates himself to what he has done and realizes that he has gotten clean away with it, the pangs subside and Judah returns to his happy, easy, and privileged life – almost as if nothing had happened.

One thing that *is* philosophically interesting about *Crimes and Misdemeanors* is the challenge it presents to our motivation to be moral. It is by no means the only interesting philosophical aspect of the film. The film is explicitly philosophical. Philosophical arguments and ruminations pervade it.[2] Its narrative is designed to demonstrate that the world is not a perfectly just place: good people (Ben and Cliff in the film) can suffer because they are good, or in spite of their being good; bad people (Judah and Lester in the film) can thrive precisely because they are prepared to be bad.[3] Allen's demonstration clearly succeeds in its own terms, but what does it show apart from the fact that the world isn't a perfectly just place? Does it show that morality is a sham, a confidence trick whose role is simply to control behavior? Does it show that, without God, there can be no objectively valid morality? The film doesn't, and indeed can't, show these things. These debates are too abstract for the story of a very particular (and unusual) set of people to contribute persuasively to them. And verbalized philosophical arguments at large in the film are too flimsy to bear much weight. We will eschew big issues of this kind and concentrate instead on one of the great strengths of the film: its examination of Judah Rosenthal's motivations and reactions. The figure of Judah Rosenthal is a remarkable one, richly imagined by Woody Allen and superbly performed by Martin Landau. We are going to examine Judah's motives philosophically. Our main task is to ask – and try to answer – the question "Why be moral?" Of course, the question might not, in the end, have a perfectly good answer; but we examine three of the most famous answers given by philosophers. Judah Rosenthal will be our guide, or at least our chief example.

Judah has good moral reasons *not to* arrange the killing of his ex-lover. But it seems, at first glance, that he also has strong personal reasons *to* arrange it. If he were to think purely about himself and what is in his own interests, and not at all about what he ought morally to do or about Delores and everyone else involved in his affairs, then it might seem that he has a very good reason to arrange the killing. There seems to be a clash here between personal reasons and moral reasons. Morality tells Judah to do one thing; personal self-interest tells him to do another. Our philosophical question is therefore going to take the following form: What motivation do we have to act morally when it is in our self-interest not to do so?

Metaethics, Normative Ethics, and Moral Psychology

Philosophical inquiry into ethics happens at a number of different levels. At the most abstract level, philosophers inquire into the nature of moral concepts. What do moral assertions – for example, "It is wrong to arrange the contract killing of a nuisance ex-lover" – express? Are moral assertions ever true? What kinds of things make them true if they are true? Could we ever know moral truths? How might we acquire this knowledge? What kind of evidence might there be that a moral claim is true? This level of inquiry – called metaethics[4] – doesn't necessarily help us work out which particular moral claims *are* true. If you want to know about the world, it's no good being told by a philosopher what truth is; you need to know which things are true and which aren't. When it comes to ethical inquiry, this is the business of working out which moral claims we ought to accept. It is called normative ethics; sometimes it is called substantive ethics. The gold standard for this level of inquiry is the discovery of an adequate moral theory: a theory that tells you how to determine correct moral claims. For example, a moral theory might say that actions are morally right if and only if they "maximize utility." (We will examine this particular theory – it is called utilitarianism – in chapter 13.) Alternatively, a moral theory might say that actions are right if and only if they satisfy a specific set of moral duties. (We also examine these kinds of theories – they are called deontological theories – in chapter 13). A different kind of moral theory eschews the task of specifying which actions are morally correct ones, at least directly, and turns instead to a characterization of moral agents. Such a theory might say that people are morally good if and only if they reliably demonstrate a specific set of moral virtues. (We will examine this particular theory – it's called virtue ethics – in chapter 14.)

Both of these forms of philosophical inquiry – metaethics and normative ethics – are very important, but they are also fairly abstract. Philosophers also think about ethics in more directly practical ways. When we investigate the moral properties of specific situations – for instance, whether voluntary assisted suicide is ever morally permissible and whether it should be made legal – we are doing what is usually called applied ethics. In this chapter, we are undertaking yet another kind of practical philosophical inquiry in ethics. The field is called moral psychology. Here philosophers investigate numerous questions about the psychology of moral agents. (In the next chapter, chapter 12, we are looking at a different, though related, aspect of our moral lives: the role that luck plays in them.)

The aim of moral psychology – as practiced by philosophers – isn't simply to describe the underlying psychology of moral agents. This is work primarily done by psychologists even though it is obviously of great interest to philosophers. The aim of *philosophical* moral psychology is to investigate philosophical questions about our nature as moral agents. One set of questions centers on the concepts of motivation and reason.[5] What kind of reasons do we have to act morally? When reasons based on self-interest clash with reasons based on the demands of morality, which counts as the stronger sort of reason? And why? This is a philosophical inquiry into the role that reason plays in a somewhat idealized version of human behavior. When people act in a self-consciously rational manner, they respond to reasons in a particular way. Roughly, they discriminate between weak reasons and strong reasons, and act on those reasons which, on balance, appear to be the strongest. The idea is that human behavior is fundamentally rational. It is an idealized picture, of course. Nonetheless, according to many philosophers, it describes the way people often behave, and also they way they tend – when they are thinking clearly – to recognize that they ought to behave. It is a rational ideal of the way people ought to behave. All this is controversial. (No surprise, surely, in philosophy.) For example, philosophers argue about what an ideal sort of moral agent would be like. Would they be someone who chooses how to act through a purely rational process of determining the relative weights of reasons? Or should they be an emotionally engaged and reactive agent: someone who acts, at least in part, on emotions: the right kinds of emotions; emotions that provide insight into what is important and valuable.[6] Without trying to sell these philosophical debates short, we can accommodate a number of different philosophical perspectives by concentrating on the most general role that moral reasons play in our ideal of a moral person. An ideal moral agent is a person who acts on the best moral reasons. Perhaps they act on these in a conscious and deliberate way. Perhaps they act on them unconsciously, but also reliably. In either case, the ideal moral agent will be someone who responds to the best and strongest moral reasons.

In the hands of many philosophers, the question of moral motivation starts out as an inquiry into people's reasons for acting. The question of why we should be moral when self-interest appears to us to clash with the demands of morality becomes a question about the nature of moral reasons. Does morality provide us with reasons to act which are strong enough to overcome conflicting prudential reasons? This is yet another refinement of our question. We are not going to canvas every possible way of answering it, including the negative answer that morality leaves us short of reasons. Instead, we are going to explore two optimistic strategies for answering it. One strategy is to argue for the normative precedence of moral reasons: moral reasons always trump other kinds of considerations because of the essential nature of moral reasons. (We explore this strategy in the final section of the chapter.) The other strategy tries to minimize the clash between morality and self-interest, perhaps even eliminate it. There are two different ways of trying to achieve this. One way is to show how moral behavior can be guided by a system of deterrence set up by society so that it is in everybody's self-interest to behave morally. The other way of minimizing the clash between morality and self-interest appeals to the value of a moral life in order to show how it is in our enlightened self-interest to be morally good.

Hobbes and the Deterrence Option

The seventeenth-century English philosopher Thomas Hobbes gives one of the clearest and most compelling cases for the public enforcement of at least some basic standards of moral behavior. Hobbes' argument starts with a thought experiment. He imagines life without any form of civil government: without laws and a justice system to enforce them. He argues that in such a condition people would be driven into conflict with each other. Such a life – a life lived, as he calls it, in the state of nature – would be terrible. Hobbes thought it would be a kind of war of all against all. Here is Hobbes' resounding description of life in the state of nature:

In such condition there is no place of industry, because the fruit thereof is uncertain, and consequently, no culture of the earth, no navigation, nor use of the commodities that may be imported by sea, no commodious building, no instruments of moving and removing such things as require much force, no knowledge of the face of the earth, no account of time, no arts, no letters, no society, and which is worst of all, continual fear and danger of violent death, and the life of man, solitary, poor, nasty, brutish, and short. (Hobbes, *Leviathan*, 89)

We have very good prudential reasons to avoid living in the state of nature, so we have very good prudential reasons to do what we can to establish or maintain a civil society in which rules of justice and fair-dealing are enforced.[7] Enforcement is essential. Just because it is in our self-interest to live within a just society, it doesn't follow that it is in our self-interest to always abide by the rules of such a society. If we can cheat and get away with it – as Judah does – then our strongest prudential reasons may well advise us to cheat. We need more than laws against murder to be on the statute books, for example. We need an effective police force and an effective justice system that backs up these laws. That is, we need an effective deterrence system. A perfectly effective deterrence system would be one that ensures that it is in everyone's self-interest to obey the law. It does this by ensuring that the risks involved in breaking the law are so great that law-breaking is always a bad gamble.[8] A perfectly effective deterrence system is very hard to achieve, of course. Is it a decent ideal? Would its existence solve the problem of the clash between prudential reasons and moral reasons? Such a system would not prevent all crime, let alone all wrongdoing. Even the precrime system of *Minority Report* failed to prevent attempted murders! (See chapter 7.) What a perfectly effective deterrence system would do is ensure that only foolish people break the law. There are plenty of foolish people about – indeed we are all foolish to one degree or another – but at least we could say, in the presence of a perfectly effective deterrence system, that law-breakers are acting against their own self-interest.

Let us return to the case of Judah to see how this might play out in practice. Judah faces a difficult choice. Assuming that he thinks only of what is in his best interests, how should he set about deciding what to do? He decides to have Delores murdered and at the end of the movie it seems like he gets away with it. (We question whether he really does get away with it in the next section.) Even if he does get away with it, it doesn't follow that he acted rationally in his self-interest. He might have been merely lucky. Even very foolish people can get lucky. So how do we make rational decisions about our self-interest? It's not enough to work out what we want out of a situation and then just go for it. We have to deal with the fact that events are uncertain and we can't be sure how our actions will turn out. Judah *might* have been caught by the police. He might have been so nervous when interviewed by the police that their suspicions were aroused. Delores might have hidden away a diary. The hired killer might have been caught for another crime, whereupon he fingers Judah's brother as part of a deal with the district attorney. (It happens on TV all the time.) Also, Judah might not have been able to deal psychologically with what he has done. In the movie, he suffers psychologically for a while and then recovers, but he didn't know that this is how things would pan out at the time he made his decision to have Delores murdered. For all he knew then, he might have faced years of severe depression. He might have been setting himself up for a life of self-loathing and guilt and remorse. He might have been setting himself up for suicide. How was Judah to really know what he is made of? How was he to know in advance that he is a hard man: someone with a shallow and flinty character; someone with large capacity for self-deception and for living happily with blood on his hands. Judah is no Lady Macbeth. But Lady Macbeth didn't know how she was going to react to her complicity in murder. How was Judah to know?

Life is so uncertain that when we seek out our own advantage, we have to work with our judgment of what might happen, how likely it is to happen, and how good or how bad it would be for us if it happened. In contemporary decision theory, the standard way of conceiving of this task is in terms of something called expected utility. Here is how it works out in Judah's case. Judah faces a choice of either confessing to Miriam or arranging the murder of Delores. (Say, for simplicity's sake, that these are his only choices.) Judah has to work out the possible consequences of confessing to Miriam. He then has to work out, for each possibility, how likely it is and how bad it would be for him. Then he has to sum up the situation to see what kind of gamble it would be to confess. This would be fairly easy if he had a way of measuring both the probability of outcomes and the goodness or badness of outcomes. (Decision theorists call the goodness or badness of outcomes their utilities.) The recipe for working out the expected utility of an action is this. For each possible outcome of the action, multiply the utility of the outcome by its probability. The sum of all these multiplications is the expected utility of the action. The expected utility of an action tells us how good or bad a gamble it is. The idea is to work out the expected utility of each action you might take and then perform the action with the highest expected utility. In other words, make the best gamble available to you. Life is a gamble, so it's natural to think that expected utilities are the stuff of rational and self-interested decision-making.

As we say, this is easy if you have a good estimate of both probabilities and utilities, but in the real world we seldom have either of these. If Judah confesses to Miriam, she might leave him. How likely is this? How bad would it be for him? Judah can only guess. Miriam might stay with him, but make his life very difficult. How likely is this? How bad would it be? Miriam might forgive him and their relationship might recover, and even deepen over the years. How likely is this? How good would it be? Somehow Judah is supposed to estimate all these things and sum them up into a judgment about just how good or bad a gamble it would be – from his own self-interested point of view – to confess to Miriam. But this is only one part of his decision-making. Judah also has to compare this possible gamble with the alternative gamble. If he orders the murder of Delores, what are his chances of getting caught by the police? How bad for him would this be? (Bad.) What are his chances of being punished by God? How bad for him would *that* be? (Really bad.) Judah is an atheist; he discounts the possibility of God's vengeance. After the deed is done, however, he begins to have doubts. What if he is wrong and God is judging him? Perhaps he shouldn't have completely discounted the God hypothesis after all. What are the chances that he is wrong about God? Quite apart from all this, it is possible that Judah will suffer such extreme remorse and self-loathing that he finds it impossible – Lady Macbeth style – to live with himself. What are the chances of this happening? Sum all these things up into the expected utility of murdering; compare the result to the expected utility of confessing his affair to Miriam. Which of the two is the better bet? How on Earth is Judah supposed to make these calculations? It is an extremely hard task, to say the least.[9] He will end up guessing most of it, not really being sure how to compare one judgment of expected utility with another. It is much, much harder to pursue your self-interest than you might think.

People can only be relied upon to make rational decisions – as judged by expected utilities – when an accurate comparison of expected utilities is completely obvious to them. This is where an effective deterrence system comes into play. If the police are effective enough and the punishment for law-breakers bad enough, then the expected utility of breaking the law can be made so low that there are hardly any circumstances at all when law-breaking is the best available gamble. It also has to be completely obvious that law-breaking is almost invariably a bad gamble. For this reason, effective deterrence systems tend to become draconian. They may offer exaggeratedly bad punishments (so that nobody in their right mind would run even a small risk of suffering them) or they may offer exaggeratedly severe police oversight (so that nobody in their right mind would be confident of getting away with law-breaking), or both.[10] Effective deterrence systems must make the expected utility of law-breaking so dramatically low that just about any alternative is to be preferred – and obviously so, without the need for finicky judgments of comparative expected utilities.

Does public enforcement of morality through effective deterrence answer our challenge? Remember the challenge is to diminish the gap between morality and self-interest. There are some problems with the appeal to deterrence. First, it doesn't help explain how morality trumps self-interest in the absence of an effective deterrence system. (Perhaps the answer here is that in the absence of such a system, morality doesn't trump self-interest, but many philosophers find this a disappointing and implausible result.) Second, an effective deterrence system won't eliminate the possibility of the genius criminal: someone clever enough and ruthless enough to skew expected utilities in favor of law-breaking. Such people may be rare – and so be unlikely to represent a major social problem – but they present a philosophical problem. The genius criminal would be someone for whom moral considerations are trumped by self-interest. We still need an answer to the question why they should be moral (assuming we are unhappy with the answer that they shouldn't be). The deterrence option doesn't provide us with one. Third, an effective deterrence system is likely to be so draconian that it does more harm than good. The price of making it completely obvious that law-breaking is a bad gamble is that everyone will suffer under excessive police surveillance or fear of terrible punishment. Fourth, it seems wrong to visit terrible punishment on people just so that a clear message can be sent to others not to follow in their footsteps. Law-breakers are people, not advertising opportunities. It seems likely that an effective deterrence system would involve an inherently unjust regime of punishment. Fifth, even if it could be made to work satisfactorily and justly, it would obviously be only a partial solution to the problem of moral motivation. Many moral imperatives are inappropriate objects of public scrutiny and control. Judah murders his ex-lover; but he also cheats on his wife. It makes sense to enforce laws against murder. But should we enforce laws against infidelity? Against lying about your fishing exploits? Against being a little impolite to your annoying neighbors? It seems that the public enforcement of morality ought to be strictly limited. This leaves moral motivation for many actions up in the air. Lastly, the deterrence option appears to give the wrong kind of motivation for moral action. It might ensure that it is in Judah's very clear self-interest not to murder, but if the only reason he refrains from having Delores murdered is that he is frightened of getting caught and punished, isn't this already a kind of moral failure? Shouldn't he refrain from killing Delores because he sees how wrong it would be? Murder is something that Judah ought to feel that he *can't* bring himself to do, not something that he just figures he can't get away with. The deterrence option shows how self-interest and moral behavior might sometimes be made to coincide, but it doesn't appear to give a *morally* satisfactory reason to be moral.

Socrates and the Pursuit of Enlightened Self-Interest

We can address some of the problems encountered in the previous section by looking more deeply at what is at stake in moral action. Judah runs a terrible risk when he decides to have Delores killed. He risks external punishments: getting caught by the police and punished; being shamed and ostracized by his community; being judged by God and punished in hellfire. He also risks internal punishments: feelings of guilt and remorse; feelings of self-loathing and depression. It is hard for Judah – for any of us – to judge these risks well, but there is a further set of considerations we haven't yet taken into account.

Judah seems to win his gamble. Delores takes her secrets with her to the grave. The murder is pinned on a serial killer. Judah takes his family on a vacation and discovers a renewed happiness with them. He retains the respect and love of his family and his friends. His career flourishes. He even has a good story to tell the hapless Cliff (Woody Allen) at the party that finishes off the film. He seems to have won, whether by luck or by good judgment. And yet . . . Judah has lost something. He may retain the love of family and friends, but he is no longer *worthy* of this love. He may retain the respect of his friends and colleagues, but he is no longer *worthy* of this respect. He retains others' love and respect only because they don't know the truth about him. Were they to learn the truth about him, love and respect would probably turn into contempt and disgust. Judah has lost love-worthiness and respect-worthiness. He has lost, we might say, his integrity. How important is this? One answer – made famous by Socrates – is that it is more important than everything else put together. According to Socrates, the most valuable part of a person is their character, or soul.[11] Keeping the moral condition of our character intact is more important – more valuable – than a thriving career or even a satisfying family life. What would you be prepared to do to avoid being in Judah's position at the end of *Crimes and Misdemeanors*? What would you be prepared to sacrifice in order not to have to live Judah's odious lie? Socrates' claim is that you should be prepared to sacrifice anything and everything, even your life. According to the Socratic view, the moral condition of our character isn't just more valuable than other things in our lives, it is of supreme value. This means that it automatically outweighs any other claims on us. It is therefore in our self-interest to maintain our integrity at all costs. It is in our *enlightened* self-interest.[12]

Just how plausible is this Socratic view? That depends upon the value claim at the heart of it: the idea that integrity is of supreme value. The view appears to presuppose that integrity has objective value. If the value of integrity is objective, it does not depend upon people happening to find it valuable. (By contrast, gold is not objectively valuable because its value depends upon the fact that people happen to value it.[13]) If Judah doesn't give a damn about his loss of integrity, he is still by far the worse for it. He is a diminished man at the end of *Crimes and Misdemeanors* even if there is nobody who both knows and cares about what he has done. (Those who know, don't care; those who would care, don't know.) What makes integrity objectively valuable? If it is objectively valuable, what makes it supremely, overridingly valuable? Perhaps it's important but other things are more important still. Perhaps happiness is objectively more important than integrity. Perhaps successful relationships are more important than it. How much genuine consolation would it be to have maintained your integrity if it means that you have lived miserably and alone? (Integrity and well-being are not ordinarily at odds like this, but imagine a case in which they are.)

The Socratic appeal to enlightened self-interest and the supreme value of integrity is a fascinating possibility; but it is far from obviously correct. It also leaves us with a problem about moral reasons familiar from our discussion of deterrence in the previous section. Just say that Judah refuses his brother's offer to have Delores murdered on the grounds that he isn't prepared to become a murderer. Judah's appeal to his enlightened self-interest seems to be an improvement on any appeal to he might have made to his unenlightened self-interest. It seems to be a morally more satisfactory reason to refuse murder than fear of punishment, for example. (To be motivated wholly by fear of punishment seems amoral, selfish, and self-centered; to be motivated wholly by fear of becoming a bad person is a self-centered motivation, to be sure, but it doesn't appear to be particularly selfish or amoral. The good person you are motivated to be isn't a selfish or amoral person.) Still, the object of the judgment – the moral protection of his character – seems misdirected. Shouldn't Judah refuse to arrange Delores's murder because of something he thinks about *her*, her rights and the respect owed to her, not because of something he wants for himself? If this is right, then enlightened self-interest doesn't count as a fully adequate moral reason.[14] Still, if the Socratic point is right, it shows that in at least some cases of immoral action – extreme, integrity-undermining cases – enlightened self-interest and moral reasons come up with the same answers. This leads us to consider our final possibility. It may be true that it is always in our enlightened self-interest to act morally, but moral reasons need not gain their authority over us because of this fact. It might be that we have stronger reasons to act morally than to act immorally irrespective of where our self-interest lies. The fact that morality trumps immorality may be a function of the nature of moral reasons.

Kant and the Authority of Moral Reasons

This last strategy is closely associated with the philosophy of Immanuel Kant and we are going to explore it in the context of Kant's practical philosophy (his philosophy of what guides actions). Kant's way of setting out the matter is only one way of seeking to establish the authority of moral reasons, but it is a famous and influential one. We won't reproduce Kant's theory of moral action here; that would take us too long. Instead, we will describe a broadly Kantian answer to the challenge we have set. Do moral reasons invariably outweigh prudential reasons? Yes – the Kantian answers – because of the nature of moral reasoning. More accurately, moral reasons invariably *trump* prudential reasons. And, as we shall see, reasons to act immorally don't in fact exist at all. But let us start nearer the beginning.

What are moral reasons? They are reasons we have to act morally. It seems like they are in competition with prudential reasons, which provide us with reasons to act in our own self-interest. If this is the right way to look at things, our problem is to show how it is that moral reasons are weightier or stronger than prudential reasons. From a Kantian perspective, however, this is a mistake. To reason morally is to seek to answer the question "What should I do?" By contrast, prudential reasoning seeks the answer to a different question: "What should I do in order to get what I want?" Moral reasons take precedence over prudential reasons because only moral reasons inform us definitively of what we should do. Prudential reasons tell us something else. They tell us what we should do *in order to get what we want*. It is an open question whether we should get what we want.[15] Judah wants his life back and he thinks that the only way he can get his life back is if Delores dies. Reasoning prudentially, he concludes that he will have to have Delores killed in order to get his life back. Perhaps. But so what? This doesn't yet tell him why he should kill Delores. He should kill Delores only if he should do whatever it takes to get his life back. And why think *that*? Morality trumps self-interest because moral reasoning, by its nature, specifies what we should do. All other considerations about what we should do must pass through the filter of morality before they are capable of informing us of what we should do.

Perhaps this sounds like a verbal trick. It seems we have merely defined moral reasoning in such a way that it always takes precedence over other considerations. But there is more to it than that. What Kant offers is a model of practical reasoning (i.e. reasoning about how to act); one that contrasts sharply with the kind of expected-utility model we examined earlier in the chapter. On the expected-utility model, practical reasoning proceeds, roughly, by working out what course of action is most likely to achieve the most valuable outcome. This kind of reasoning is called instrumental reasoning. On Kant's model, by contrast, practical reasoning proceeds by placing actions under principles. We ask ourselves: what kind of action is this? What principle does it fall under? We are then able to investigate the merits of the principle.[16] If Judah *were* following a principle (rather than acting in a selfish and unprincipled manner), what principle would this be? Perhaps it is this: *Do whatever it takes – including murder – to get what you most want*. From a Kantian perspective, the principle gives him a reason to act as he does – a genuine reason – only if it is a reasonable principle. Is the principle reasonable?

What in general makes a principle reasonable? Kantians have several answers to this question. One answer employs the following test: Would it make sense for someone acting on the principle to wish everyone else to act on it too?[17] If it does make sense, the principle is reasonable and acting on it is morally right; if it does not make sense, the principle is unreasonable and acting on it is immoral. Judah has Delores killed in order to secure his former life. But if everyone – including his enemies and including Delores herself – were to act on the principle, *Do whatever it takes – including murder – to get what you most want,* then Judah's security would be completely undermined. If everyone in his life acted on this principle, his life would surely go, in his own words, down the toilet. (For example, operating under the principle at hand, Delores would speedily arrange the murder of his wife, work rivals would speedily arrange for his own murder, and so on.) It makes no sense for Judah to wish everybody to follow his principle while using the principle as a means of getting what he wants. This is why he is being fundamentally unreasonable. He is acting on a principle that only works because he alone acts on it. Judah is treating himself like he is fundamentally different from everyone else: a special person, operating by special rules that apply to him alone. Of course, he is not a special person. The heart of his unreasonableness is that he applies one principle to himself and another to everyone else, without even a shred of justification.

From a Kantian perspective, Judah has no reason at all to order Delores's murder. A reason to do something emerges out of the application of a reasonable principle of action. And Judah's principle of action is fundamentally unreasonable. Judah's desire and self-love motivate him to order Delores's murder. But on Kant's model of moral reasoning, desire and self-love don't constitute reasons to act. They *tempt* Judah to murder and they *incline* him towards it, but they don't give him a *reason* to murder. Judah has no reason at all to kill Delores: there is no reasonable principle under which he might order her murder. On the other hand, there is a very clear reason not to kill her: the reasonable principle that tells us never to use murder as a way of getting what we want.

Remember our question is this: What reason do we have to act morally when morality and self-interest clash? On a Kantian interpretation of this question, we cannot have a reason to act immorally. When we do act immorally, we succumb to temptation and let desire and self-love substitute for reason. Of course, we are all prone to this to some degree or another, but if the Kantian model of practical reasoning is correct, our challenge has been answered. The Kantian model of practical reasoning is highly controversial, so this is hardly the final word on the matter. But in philosophy all the interesting ideas are controversial and very few words are final.

Questions

Suppose that you could – guaranteed and with no effort, simply "get away with it." Why be moral?

Does *Crimes and Misdemeanors* show that, without God, there can be no objectively valid morality? We argued in the chapter that it doesn't; indeed, that it couldn't. Were we right?

For the sake of argument, say we equate personal utility with happiness: outcomes of actions are ranked by us according to our level of happiness in them. Viewing utility even in such a narrow way as this, did Judah maximize his expected utility by arranging the murder of Delores?

We criticized implementation of a perfectly effective deterrence system in many ways. But consider a system of deterrents against seriously harmful acts (like murdering your ex-lover). If we accept that such a system will be less than perfect (and would be too extreme if we tried to perfect it), do our criticisms of the deterrence option still apply? The existence of such a system wouldn't solve our philosophical problem. Why?

In the chapter, we argued that enlightened self-interest doesn't supply us with satisfactory *moral* reasons for acting because it focuses our attention and concern on the wrong sort of thing. Is this a good argument? What reply might you make to it?

Is the Kantian argument we presented in the chapter – that, by their very nature, moral reasons automatically take precedence over personal considerations and desires – more than a verbal trick? Is this just defining the problem away? (We argued in the chapter that it wasn't, but were we right?)

Throughout the chapter, we contrasted two forms of practical reasoning: instrumental reasoning (of which maximizing expected utility is a paradigm example) and principled reasoning (of which the Kantian model of reasoning is a paradigm example). One thinks of practical reasoning as reasoning about getting what we want. The other thinks of it as reasoning under reasonable and defensible principles of action. Which is the better model of reasoning? If they both have something going for them, could they be combined or reconciled somehow? How?

Notes

1   See the discussion of remorse and regret in chapter 12.
2   Two scenes are especially noteworthy in this respect: the scene of Judah's fateful decision (0:40–0:43); and the scene of dinner-party debate, in which the philosophical star of Aunt May shines brightest (1:10–1:13).
3   In the film, Cliff isn't all that good and Lester isn't all that bad. On the other hand, Ben really is good if somewhat naïve and un-insightful. And, of course, Judah is deeply morally corrupt.
4   Although metaethics is a very important philosophical field, we are not going to explore it in the present book. Metaethics is difficult to study in the context of films. Many of the basic issues in metaethics concern the ontological status of moral properties. The fundamental theory-options are those we discussed in chapter 4: reductionism, eliminativism, and acceptance of moral properties as ontologically basic. Reductionists about moral properties think they reduce

to a non-moral category of properties, such as something's being accepted as a basic cultural norm or its contributing maximally to human welfare. Eliminativists about moral properties think they are not real; nothing literally *has* an ethical property. There are different ways of being eliminativist. One way is to say that attributions of moral properties aren't what they seem: when we insist that a person's lying is morally wrong we are not literally ascribing a moral property (wrongness) to their action, we are expressing an attitude to it (e.g. we don't approve of it). This view is called expressivism. Another way of being eliminativist about moral properties is to insist that we should take our attributions of moral properties literally: we are saying that an act of lying has the property of being wrong; it's just that we are making an ontological error. Saying that an act has the property of being wrong is like saying that somebody has the property of being a witch. There are no witches; there are no moral properties either. (This view is sometimes called "error theory" and sometimes "moral nihilism.") Those who defend the reality and fundamental ontological status of moral properties are called "moral objectivists."

5   We are landing in the middle of a complicated philosophical inquiry into the nature of reasons to act. What, in general, is a reason to act? Must a reason connect up with an agent's own perception of what they should do or what they want to do (these are called internal reasons) or might they specify more objective conditions of what they ought to do or what they ought to want to do (these are called external reasons)? We will assume that moral reasons work as external reasons that apply to people even if they do not appreciate this fact.

6   See our discussion of virtue theory in chapter 14 for an elaboration of this latter perspective on moral action.

7   Hobbes' political solution involves setting up a Sovereign with close to absolute powers over the members of society. We aren't concerned here with the merits of this proposal, but with other implications of his theory.

8   As Hobbes puts it, "there must be some coercive power to compel men equally to the performance of their covenants, by the terror of some punishment greater than the benefit they expect by the breach of the covenant" (*Leviathan*, xv, 3).

9   Don't forget that we have oversimplified Judah's choice-situation. We have restricted him to two live options; and we have ignored Delores's threat to reveal his suspect business dealings.

10   Of course, the Big Daddy of deterrence options is belief in divine retribution. Hell is as bad a place as human imagination will allow and God's powers of surveillance are peerless.

11   Socrates appears to have believed in the immortality of the soul (according to Plato in the *Phaedo*) and what is at stake in keeping our soul morally intact is the future of this immortal soul. The possibility we are presenting in this chapter involves keeping the value hierarchy of Socrates and Plato without their metaphysical assumptions. The moral condition of our character or

personality (i.e. soul) is of overriding value. Other harms we experience are always less of an evil to us than the destruction of our moral character.

12 Notice, this appeal to the supreme value of integrity appears to do away with the business of calculating expected utilities. First, Judah can know more or less with certainty that his decision to have Delores killed will undermine his integrity. Second, whatever utility we ascribe to factors such as happiness, honor, or the respect of colleagues, the value of integrity will trump it because it is supreme, i.e. overriding.

13 See our discussion of subjective and objective value in chapter 10.

14 See our discussion of virtue ethics in chapter 14 for development of a similar idea.

15 Kant draws this distinction in terms of two kinds of imperatives: hypothetical imperatives (I should do x, if I am to achieve y) and categorical imperatives (I should do x).

16 We further examine the merits of this sort of approach to moral reasoning in chapter 13, where we discuss deontological theories of right action. There is a close relationship between the Kantian approach to practical reasoning described here and deontological theories of right action discussed in chapter 13. However, Kantian scholars point out that Kant's moral theory is more complicated and more subtle than the simple deontological model we discuss in chapter 13. See Wood (2008), especially chapter 3.

17 Kant, famously, expresses the point like this: "*I ought never to act except in such a way that I could also will that my maxim should become a universal law* [italics in original]" (Kant 1999, 4.403, 57). This is the first of his formulations of the categorical imperative.

Further Reading

Allingham, Michael (2002). *Choice Theory: A Very Short Introduction*. New York: Oxford University Press.

Aune, Bruce (1979). *Kant's Theory of Morals*. Princeton: Princeton University Press.

Ewin, R. E. (1991). *Virtues and Rights: The Moral Philosophy of Thomas Hobbes*. Boulder: Westview Press.

Gauthier, D. (1969). *The Logic of "Leviathan": The Moral and Political Theory of Thomas Hobbes*. Oxford: Clarendon Press.

Herman, Barbara (1993). *The Practice of Moral Judgment*. Cambridge, MA: Harvard University Press.

Hill, Thomas E. (1992). *Dignity and Practical Reason in Kant's Moral Theory*. Ithaca: Cornell University Press.

Hobbes, Thomas (2008 [1651]). *Leviathan*. Cambridge: Cambridge University Press.

Kant, Immanuel (1999). "Groundwork of the Metaphysics of Morals." In *Practical Philosophy*, ed. and trans. Mary J. Gregor. Cambridge, Cambridge University Press.

Kavka, G. (1986). *Hobbesian Moral and Political Theory*. Princeton: Princeton University Press.

O'Neill, Onora (1975). *Acting on Principle*. New York: Columbia University Press.

Raphael, D. D. (1977). *Hobbes: Morals and Politics*. London: Routledge.

Rudebusch, George (2009). *Socrates*. Oxford: Wiley-Blackwell.

Sorell, T. (1986). *Hobbes*. London: Routledge and Kegan Paul.

Vlastos, Gregory (1991). *Socrates: Ironist and Moral Philosopher*. Cambridge: Cambridge University Press.

Wilson, Emily (2007). *The Death of Socrates*. Cambridge, MA: Harvard University Press.

Wood, Allen (2008). *Kantian Ethics*. Cambridge: Cambridge University Press.

12

The Lives of Others: Moral Luck and Regret

Introduction

What role does luck play in life? What *kind* of role does it play? If we are likeable, admirable, virtuous, or successful, how much of this is down to us and how much is down to luck? If we are miserable and unsuccessful, or even if we are despicable and guilty of terrible wrongs, how much of that is down to us and how much to luck? What kind of luck? What do we mean by luck? Or fortune? Here we are examining a question about the amount of control people exercise over their own lives, including the moral quality of their lives. We examined a related issue in chapter 7 with the help of the film *Minority Report*; we examined the metaphysics of free will and fatalism. In this chapter, we look at the issue of luck from a more practical, less metaphysical, perspective. Our guide is the 2006 film *The Lives of Others*.[1]

The Lives of Others is an example of a film that can be discussed in terms of a variety of philosophical issues, issues that are in many ways independent of one another. The film forcefully illustrates a problem that philosophers call the problem of "moral luck." It does so through a number of characters, but centrally through the transformation of Stasi agent Captain Gerd Wiesler. Margaret Walker (1991: 14) describes moral luck as consisting "in the apparent and allegedly problematic or even paradoxical fact that factors decisive for the moral standing of an agent are subject to luck." This is right, but there is much more to say about moral luck and its varieties.

Thinking Through Film: Doing Philosophy, Watching Movies, First Edition. Damian Cox, Michael P. Levine.
© 2012 Damian Cox and Michael P. Levine. Published 2012 by Blackwell Publishing Ltd.

The quality of our lives, including the moral quality of our lives, seems to depend on those things that life dishes out to us – luckily or unluckily. It depends on the way we are "constituted" with regard to things like strength of will, intelligence, and emotion. It also depends on the events and people we are accidentally subject to and that happen to influence us. The issue of moral luck came to prominence in contemporary philosophy through the work of Bernard Williams and Thomas Nagel. Williams published a famous paper "Moral Luck" in 1976 together with a response from Nagel. Both papers are important, and have come to be recognized as classics of twentieth-century moral philosophy. We are going to use *The Lives of Others* to explore both Williams' and Nagel's core ideas. The film can teach us something about moral luck, its ubiquity and variety, and the implications of both for ethics and life.

The film also raises questions about the nature and significance of liberty and privacy, along with and in the context of, corruption, unchecked political power, deprivation, fear, and torture – and the human condition. It is a film whose aesthetics are worth closely examining; for example, in terms of the way the architecture we see in the film – the cityscape, the interrogation rooms, the prison cells – plays a philosophically significant role. It is neither possible nor desirable to discuss all of the philosophical issues involved in *The Lives of Others* at once. However, the strength of the film is in no small measure due to its not isolating the important questions, but bringing them together cinematically in ways that mutually contextualize and entail, or dramatically segue into, one another – thereby leading a willing audience along. The narrative and accompanying drama, aided by the music, are constructed in such a way that problems implicate and connect with one another in numerous ways. Here then is a way that film seems closer to life than philosophy, since life inconveniently refuses to isolate philosophical conundrums and allow them to be treated one at a time. In much the same way, good films drop us in the thick of it and this contrasts with more formal philosophical writing, say in professional journal articles. In formal philosophical writing, no matter how thoroughly or eloquently a philosophical matter is discussed, one may be left feeling that justice has not been done to the philosophical complexity of life.

One important question *The Lives of Others* raises is about the nature of integrity. Each of the characters in *The Lives of Others* exemplifies a different way of possessing or failing to possess integrity. But what is integrity? In Cox, La Caze, and Levine (2003: 14, 41–2) we say:

> Integrity resists easy definition. Integrity is not the same as authentic-
> ity. . . . And it is a great deal more than the virtue of the incorrupt and

honest. Integrity is a virtue located at the means of various excesses. On the one side we find conditions of capriciousness, wantonness, weakness of will, disintegration, hypocrisy, dishonesty, and an incapacity for self-reflection or self-understanding. On the other side we find conditions of fanaticism, dogmatism, monomania, sanctimoniousness, hyperreflexivity and the narrowness and hollowed out character of a life closed off from the multiplicity of human experience. . . . The person of integrity lives in a fragile balance between every one of these all-too-human traits. . . . Attributions of integrity presuppose fundamental moral decency. . . . Integrity is not a kind of wholeness, solidity of character or moral purity. It involves a capacity to respond to change in one's values or circumstances, a kind of continual remaking of the self, to take responsibility for one's work and thought. Understanding integrity involves taking the self to be always in process, rather than static and unchanging or containing some inner "core" around which reasonably superficial changes are made. . . . Striving for . . . integrity involves determining what one's desires, values and commitments are. This is very close to, if not the same as, striving for self-understanding [and] meaning.[2]

Integrity, we go on to say, is not an all or nothing thing and not only allows for, but at times requires, a degree of ambivalence. Everyone has integrity and also lacks it to a degree. With these admittedly imprecise criteria for "integrity" in hand, each of the film's characters can be examined so as to determine the extent to which they exhibit integrity; where and how they distinctively succeed, and where and why they fail – each in their own way. This can be done consciously, as a kind of moral exercise; or the viewer may find that ruminations of this sort about integrity naturally accompany one's engagement with the film.

Before turning to an examination of some of the philosophical questions that are integral to *The Lives of Others* and contribute to its success and power, we need reminding of the fairly complicated plot of the film. Our discussion of the film will be more interpretative and more detailed than other plot summaries given in the book. It also helps to have a little background information, and we will furnish some of this. (As usual, make sure you have seen the film before reading on!) Setting out a film's plot may seem like a relatively straightforward exercise. However, it is worth noting that in a philosophically complex film, such a synopsis, whether detailed or not, may significantly presuppose just what the core philosophical issues in the film are, and even prejudge the characters. It can do this either explicitly, for example by describing an act as a "betrayal," or by omission, for instance by failing to mention morally relevant features about some situation. Some such question-begging is probably unavoidable. Issues relating to freedom, privacy, and power saturate the film and its characters.[3] Viewing the film with these issues in mind, along with questions about the characters' integrity, is a way of approaching it by means of ethical and political issues it raises. The role that moral luck plays in the lives of some characters presents us with an additional approach, one that we focus upon.

The Lives of Others

It is 1984, East Germany, five years before the fall of the Berlin Wall. The minister of culture (Bruno Hempf) develops an "interest" in an actress (Sieland) and begins to sexually blackmail her: *Sleep with me or I will end your career*. As a result of this unlucky attraction, and because he wants her playwright partner (Dreyman) out of the way, an agent of the East German secret police (Stasi)[4] is told to conduct surveillance on the playwright and his longstanding actress lover. This is Captain Gerd Wiesler, codenamed HGWXX/7, who is to become the central figure of the film. Wiesler takes up his eavesdropping post in the attic of the couple's apartment building and becomes increasingly interested in and later drawn into their personal lives.

Minister Hempf's world is one in which he can ignore moral decency, ride roughshod over individuals' rights with impunity, and refer loosely and hypocritically to issues of state security and socialist ideals by way of justifying his actions.[5] On the face of it, Hempf seems like an arch hypocrite, espousing socialist ideals as cover for venal desires and demands, but there is another reading of his character in which he is not so much a hypocrite as a powerful, indecent, bullying, creep. He isn't a hypocrite because he has the power to enforce his will without dissembling. So what exactly is hypocrisy? McKinnon (1991: 322) says

> We think of the hypocrite as one who dissembles or shams regarding her motives or intentions in regions where we take such things seriously, namely religion and morality, and probably also politics. . . . Her real intentions must be known to herself, and the decision to conceal them must be deliberate. . . . [S]he must wish for different, more favorable, judgments and must imagine and implement a course of action that is designed to bring about these other assessments.

Hempf's situation is rather different, however. There is no real need for him to dissemble or sham his real motives. No one doubts them and no one is taken in – except perhaps Wiesler who soon sees Hempf for what he is. It is doubtful, therefore, that Hempf is a hypocrite in the strict sense articulated by McKinnon. Here is the façade of hypocrisy rather than the genuine thing, and it is a pervasive feature of totalitarian regimes. The mere façade of hypocrisy, in which displays of allegiance to political ideals are mandatory, but fool nobody, is something that democratic institutions, are meant to guard against. One – perhaps rather cynical – way of putting the point is to say that democratic institutions are designed to at least ensure there is a need for hypocrisy when government officials lie, sham, and dissemble.

There is no reason for the surveillance of Dreyman and Sieland other than the minister's sordid interest in Sieland and his wish to eliminate her lover. Though virtually anyone could be investigated and watched in East Germany at the time, and any high-profile person with a degree of influence was a likely candidate for secret surveillance, artists were particularly targeted. As Philippa Hawker (2007) says in a review of the film, "The Stasi are particularly interested in creative figures and their capacity to shape, undermine and subvert. A character talks about writers as 'engineers of the human soul', a beguiling phrase that turns out to have been used by Stalin." Artists may have a particular role to play in the promulgation of ideas, even if they cannot know for sure just what the impact of their art will be.

Part of the *modus operandi* of the Stasi was to know all they could about citizens, including their private lives, just *in case* it became "necessary" in the eyes of the authorities, for whatever reason, to undermine, manage, or destroy them on the pretext of state security. The film makes it clear that "pretext" is the right word here – that few believed state security was at risk no matter what they said publicly or privately. The minister's attraction to Sieland tragically ends more than her career. It also starts a chain of events that dramatically alters Wiesler's life. It is this difficult and profound change that Wiesler goes through as he watches and listens to what happens to Dreyman and Sieland that the film primarily focuses upon.

The most important and effective part of how the Stasi operated was through fear. Since the Stasi could not be in all places at all times, they used a very wide circle of informants so that no one was ever certain of who was and who was not a spy. In effect, the population became self-policing since everyone suspected almost everyone else of spying on them – and not without reason. The film cinematically evokes this blanket of suspicion and fear. The brutal architecture, gray skies, cold weather, and empty streets add to the effect. They might be perceived as a natural and gloomy extension of the state, as well as a kind of cosmic endorsement of the political, social, and personal status quo. By means of a subtitle at the start of the film, the audience knows that it is five years before a radical change takes place: the fall of the Berlin Wall and the unification of East Germany (the "German Democratic Republic") and West Germany (the "Federal Republic of Germany"). In 1990, former East Germany was finally integrated into the Federal Republic of Germany. But the time in which the film is set, 1984, is one in which there is very little hope of radical change. The totalitarian government and its way of life seemed to be here to stay. The characters' actions are intelligible only in this context and against this background. And it is against such a background that Wiesler makes his choice, "risks" his life and is morally lucky. His risk was very real. He was a respected member of the Stasi, but the Stasi themselves were, to a large extent, controlled by fear. Their doors too could be knocked on in the middle of the night and they too could be presumptively arrested. There is no reliable and legitimate legal recourse in a totalitarian regime and this is a key to their repressive character. Who would know better what to fear than the Stasi themselves?

While eavesdropping on the private conversations and activities of Dreyman and Sieland, Wiesler's interest, perhaps to his surprise, appears increasingly accompanied by thoughtful or reflective envy – not an envy grounded primarily in a desire to simply have what someone else has or be what someone else is, but a kind of regret at the lack of the kinds of things that make Dreyman's and Sieland's lives rich. Through this comparison, Wiesler appears to become aware of the kind of life he leads and the kind of person he is. His life is juxtaposed with theirs and he appears to see them as they are; with meaningful work they enjoy, and a loving and intimate relationship. The difference between their cozy and welcoming apartment and his stark, empty, impersonal one is striking. The difference between their passionate sex and Wiesler's own desultory encounter with a prostitute, who charges him by the half hour and refuses to linger after sex because she has another client waiting, is stark and depressing. As an *apparatchik*, Wiesler has internalized the cold, dispassionate, lifeless cynicism of the state as compared with the vitality, passion, and modicum of hope that Dreyman and Sieland have found.

One thing Wiesler is not, however, is a full-blown hypocrite. Early on in the film, he is presented as someone who believes in the goal of defending socialism from corruption by western self-indulgence and liberal ideals. He seems on the face of it to be a true believer; someone committed to doing a dirty and deeply unpleasant job because it is necessary in order to defend the great socialist experiment of the German Democratic Republic. In this he contrasts strongly with his boss in the Stasi – Anton

Grubitz – a self-serving and cynical opportunist. It is hard to imagine Grubitz being much affected by voyeuristically inspecting the lives of others. In part because he is not a self-serving opportunist, Wiesler is open to the influence of others in a deep way. We are reminded what a difference others can unknowingly make in our life. The film's principal theme is Wiesler's transformation by means of recognizing, in the nick of time, important facts about himself and others: what he values; what he takes to be right; the price he is willing to pay.

Wiesler realizes early on that Dreyman has, up to that point, been a loyal citizen. (Dreyman's loyalty also changes in the course of the film.) Wiesler comes to see, as an awakening of sorts, that the surveillance he is in charge of has to do with the minister's sexual blackmailing of Sieland, rather than with state security. Against all odds and in a bleakness, interior and exterior, that envelops an entire state (their world) – one which the film manages to a degree to recreate; where those who repress, confine, and brutalize others are themselves repressed and confined – Wiesler struggles for a modicum of integrity and freedom. He moves from the cold-hearted professional agent of the state depicted at the start to something remarkably different and better. First, he must find what he values, what he desires and thinks right. Then, in the face of fierce opposition, justified fear, and the eerie absence of others he might turn to in order to validate his views, he must somehow try to live as he thinks he should, or at least would like to. He finds himself in a situation that offers him redemption of sorts, and to his credit he recognizes it as such and takes it up.[6]

Each of the principal characters has a devil to face. The playwright Dreyman lives with Sieland in a nice apartment. He thus far has managed to satisfy government officials by writing inspiring plays about the proletariat while also maintaining the friendship and perhaps respect of at least some of his fellow writers. Dreyman is increasingly disillusioned with the state as he sees its effect on his fellow writers. The regime, in the form of Hempf, the same minister of culture sexually blackmailing Sieland, drives his friend Albert Jerska to suicide by preventing him working and impoverishing him. This is the key event in Dreyman's transformation from artist working in what has been called "the velvet prison" (a very comfortable and supportive situation for artists, provided they play by the regime's ideological rules) into a critic of the regime.[7]

Dreyman agrees to defy the authorities and help smuggle his article about the extent of suicides in the German Democratic Republic, something the government had been covering up, to the West German paper *Der Spiegel*. Wiesler systematically covers up Dreyman's activities. He has his surveillance partner reassigned; he produces a series of (often rather funny) false reports about Dreyman's activity. (Dreyman is supposedly writing a play about Lenin.)

The situation unravels because of the minister's infatuation with Sieland. Since her rejection of him, the minister is out to destroy her. Sieland has a drug addiction that the minister becomes aware of: she has been purchasing banned pharmaceuticals. At the minister's behest, Grubitz arrests Sieland on this pretext and uses it to pressure her into revealing the author of the *Der Spiegel* article. She is threatened with imprisonment and the loss of her career. Sieland offers to spy for the Stasi, she even offers sexual favors to Grubitz. Grubitz, ever the career man, is interested only in her knowledge of the author of the *Der Spiegel* article. Although we don't witness the scene, Sieland eventually names Dreyman, but withholds crucial information about him. She does not reveal where the typewriter Dreyman used to write the article is hidden. This is crucial evidence needed for Dreyman's arrest and imprisonment. The Stasi search of Dreyman's apartment comes up empty. But now even more pressure is applied to Sieland. Grubitz brings in Wiesler (who he now suspects has been playing a double game) to interrogate her. This is Wiesler's last chance to clear his name with Grubitz, his boss: he must extract the whereabouts of the typewriter from Sieland. In one of the saddest scenes of the film (1:40–1:44), we follow the interrogation as Wiesler tries to extract the information from Sieland, all the while trying – and failing – to send subtle reassuring signals her way that all will be well. (Wiesler's plan, it turns out, is to remove the typewriter before any search can produce it.) Sieland does not pick up on any of this. Wiesler expertly traps her throughout the interrogation and makes it seem like there is no choice for her but to inform on Dreyman. Wiesler lies to her, claiming that Dreyman is to be imprisoned on evidence already discovered. He tells her she must complete her betrayal or face imprisonment on perjury charges. He appeals to her deep need of her art; he begs her to "remember her audience." The confiscation of her drugs and her terrified, lonely ordeal in a Stasi prison cell has ramped up the pressure. Sieland succumbs quickly and quietly.

The Stasi search for the typewriter but are unable to locate it where she told them it was. Wiesler has removed it. In what is, for some viewers, a slightly contrived moment, Sieland rushes from the apartment before the search's failure becomes apparent and walks deliberately in front of a van. Her suicide (a careful inspection of the scene reveals that she knowingly walks in front of the van) means that Wiesler's plan fails in one very significant respect. He has saved Dreyman, but he has been instrumental in the death of Sieland. Having failed to find the typewriter, and in the face of a death even the Stasi had not expected, the surveillance of Dreyman is ended and Grubitz demotes Wiesler.

The remainder of the film portrays Dreyman's discovery, six and a half years later, of what really happened throughout these terrible events. He had assumed that Sieland had removed the typewriter and saved him. However, an encounter with Hempf – still at large in the new Germany – alters Dreyman's perceptions. Hempf reveals the surveillance operation, the traces of which are still installed in his apartment. Dreyman now reviews his Stasi file and discovers that Wiesler had been his silent protector. He discovers that Sieland could not have removed the typewriter; that Wiesler had. He also learns of Wiesler's subsequent demotion. As a result of these revelations, Dreyman dedicates his new book, *Sonata for a Good Man*, to Wiesler, under his Stasi codename. The final scene of the movie has Wiesler discovering this dedication: *Dedicated to HGW/XX7, with gratitude*. As he purchases the book he is asked whether it should be gift-wrapped. "No," he says, "it's for me." (2:07). A concluding freeze-frame of Wiesler's face (less grim, more open, clearly moved, he is almost smiling!) and the lightly sentimental music (subtly distinct from other music in the film) portray this moment as a kind of delayed redemption. Wiesler's struggle to protect the dissident artist has at last been acknowledged: quietly, almost secretly, by the artist himself.

Kinds of Luck

So what part does luck play in this story? Obviously, it plays many roles; but to look deeper into this question, we will examine some influential philosophical discussions of luck and its role in life, particularly in the moral quality of life. Anything is a matter of luck – good luck or bad luck – if it affects something important to us and is out of our control. Thomas Nagel (1979) distinguishes four relevant kinds of luck. First, one can be lucky or unlucky in one's circumstances. Sieland had the terrible bad luck of attracting the salacious attention of Minister Hempf. Nagel calls this kind of luck circumstantial luck. Second, one can be lucky or unlucky in one's looks, personality, character, talents, and so on. Crucially for our judgment of others, we ought to recognize that people are not wholly in control of every aspect of the kind of person they are; in particular, they are not in complete control of the personality or character traits they possess. (Though, as we argue in chapter 14, a person's possession of virtues and vices is not wholly out of their control either.) Nagel calls this kind of luck constitutive luck. Both circumstantial and constitutive luck are utterly pervasive features of our lives; and they influence the extent to which we lead good or worthwhile or admirable lives to an extraordinary degree. Few of us have our loyalty to others tested in the way Sieland's loyalty to Dreyman was tested. Many people lead what seem to be perfectly good lives only because they have not been put in similarly invidious positions.

Although these two kinds of luck are pervasive and significant, they do not trouble philosophers in the way that a third kind of luck does. Nagel calls this kind of luck resultant luck.[8] We can be lucky or unlucky in the results of our actions. We make plans and judge ourselves on whether our plans are wise and good; but nothing succeeds like success and many a plan that would be condemned were it to fail is praised because it succeeds. Bernard Williams (1981) gives the example of the painter Paul Gauguin – who abandoned his family to go painting in the South Pacific. (Williams plays fast and loose with the details and so admits his example is a fictionalized version of Gauguin's life.) Had Gauguin not turned out to be a painter of genius, his decision to abandon his family would have been cast in a very negative light. Because he succeeds, we are, perhaps rightly, much more forgiving of the decision. We have reason to be grateful that he made it. Or so Williams thinks. In Nagel's terms, Gauguin had good resultant luck. And if we think that this positively affects moral judgment of his action, his good luck is called good moral luck.

The reason philosophers have been puzzled by the possibility of moral luck is that it seems, on the face of it, that we ought to be held responsible only for things we can control. Morality ought not to be a matter of luck. But, intuitively, in many instances, it seems to be exactly a matter of luck. Consider the case of a gardener working next to a tall garden wall. The gardener is cleaning up a yard by hurling large stones over the wall onto a path that runs the other side of it. The gardener can't tell where the stones are landing; they could land on someone walking down the path. The gardener's action is reckless. With good resultant luck, the stones will miss everyone and nobody will be harmed. The wrong done by the gardener will consist in reckless behavior. But then imagine somebody being struck and killed by an especially large stone hurled over the wall. The wrong now takes on an altogether more serious dimension. The gardener is a killer (not a murderer). Bad luck makes him a killer; good luck makes him merely a fool. Luck seems to play an enormous role in our moral standing because it affects the extent and nature of the wrong we do.[9]

In *The Lives of Others* we see this kind of resultant moral luck in events surrounding Sieland. Under intense pressure, she betrays her lover. The results of this betrayal could have been disastrous for Dreyman, leading to his arrest and imprisonment. From Sieland's point of view, this is what surely *must* happen as a result of her betrayal. As we know, Wiesler intervenes and removes the crucial evidence (the guilty typewriter) preventing such an outcome. This is lucky for Dreyman of course. But it is also lucky for Sieland. She is spared the full moral consequences of her betrayal.[10] Her betrayal is bad, but it is an ineffectual betrayal rather than a life-wrecking betrayal. And an ineffectual betrayal is unlikely to be judged as harshly as a life-wrecking betrayal. If moral luck is a real phenomenon, then our propensity to judge an ineffectual betrayal less harshly than a life-wrecking betrayal is correct. The ineffectual betrayal *is* less wrongful than the life-wrecking betrayal.[11] Sieland has a great deal of bad circumstantial luck; but at the very end she also has a modicum of good moral luck. Alas, she does not live long enough to know of this.

Luck and Regret

So far we have observed the possible effect of luck on third-person moral judgment and we have concentrated on the simplest cases of moral luck. Bernard Williams' original paper, "Moral Luck," investigated more subtle cases in search of a rather different point. Williams was concerned with the nature of a person's retrospective judgment of their own profound life-decisions. His example of Gauguin is crucial here. The key question for Williams was not whether Gauguin's decision to abandon his family in order to paint in the South Pacific was morally vindicated by his success as an artist. Williams was interested in whether or not we are able, in retrospect, to justify a significant decision to ourselves, if not to others, and the way this is often linked to whether the project or goal it forms part of succeeds or fails. The success or failure of the project is something we may have little if any control over. Nevertheless, it will determine the way we assess the decision – and, importantly, whether or not we come to deeply regret it.

Williams (1981: 35–6) puts it this way in the following (quite difficult) passage:

> There are certain . . . decisions [about significant projects affecting the course of one's life where] the project in the interest of which the decisions is made is one with which the agent is identified in such a way that if it succeeds, his stand-point of assessment will be from a life which then derives an important part of its significance for him from that very fact; if he fails, it can, necessarily have no such significance in his life. If he succeeds, it

cannot be that while welcoming the outcome he more basically regrets the
decision. If he fails, his standpoint will be of one for whom the ground
project of the decisions has proved worthless, and this . . . must leave him
with the most basic regrets. . . . That is the sense in which his decision can
be justified, for him, [not necessarily for others] by success.

When we make profound life choices – as Gauguin did and as, eventually, Wiesler does – we start out on something like a project, something
that can succeed or fail in various ways and to various degrees. Whether
the project succeeds or fails is not entirely up to us. Profound life choices
also determine the sort of person we become; and this future person
will be the one making retrospective judgment of the choice. This can
be a something of a trap: if a person chooses to join a religious cult,
for example, the cult may well – probably will – affect the terms in which
they come to judge their decision to join. It will distort this judgment
until they eventually extract themselves from the cult. Williams is not
concerned with traps like this in the passage we have just quoted, but
he is concerned with the conditions under which a person will, in the
future, judge their basic life choices and whether they ought to regret
them or not.

In order to avoid occasions for deep regret, we have to be lucky in at
least two ways. First, we nearly always need some luck (or at least the
absence of bad luck) to secure the success of our most important projects.
Second, we have to be in a position, in the future, to value that success
in approximately the way we first conceived of it. And this is not something that we can necessarily control. Gauguin could not have been
completely sure that his project to become a great artist would succeed.
He also could not have been completely sure that he would continue to
love painting passionately and devotedly. What if he had got bored with
painting and came to think of it as a trivial pastime, one for self-indulgent
dilettantes running from the demands of a decent, hardworking life? Basic
choices are risky. They can – and do – go badly wrong. (Williams' example
of a choice going badly wrong is from Tolstoy's novel *Anna Karenina*,
and involves Anna's choice to leave her husband and try to build a life
with her lover, Vronksy.)

Not all failures are alike. Williams contrasts Gauguin's potential failure
of artistic talent or temperament with the possibility of his taking ill on
the way to the South Pacific. The former is what Williams calls an intrinsic
failure of the project. The latter is an extrinsic failure. This is how Williams
sets up the contrast (1981: 36). Fundamental life choices are not

merely very risky ones . . . with a substantial outcome. The outcome has to be substantial in a special way – in a way which importantly conditions the agent's sense of what is significant in his life, and hence his standpoint of retrospective assessment. It follows from this that they are, indeed, risky, and in a way which helps to explain the importance for such projects of the difference between extrinsic and intrinsic failure. With an intrinsic failure, the project which generated the decision is revealed as an empty thing, incapable of grounding the agent's life. With extrinsic failure, it is not so revealed, and while he must acknowledge that it has failed, nevertheless it has not been discredited, and may, perhaps in the form of some new aspiration, contribute to making sense of what is left. [In the case of extrinsic failure] in his retrospective thought, and its allocation of basic regret, he cannot in the fullest sense identify with his decision, and so does not find himself justified; but he is not totally alienated from it either, cannot just see it as a disastrous error, and so does not finally find himself unjustified.

With the intrinsic failure of our fundamental projects, the rug is pulled out from under a central aspect of our life. We are entirely without justification for the harm we may have done others in our pursuit of them. With extrinsic failure of a fundamental project, the project still makes sense to us and we cannot see it as a "disastrous error." Williams does not think that Gauguin can justify his behavior to his abandoned family; they are under no obligation to think "well, the man is a creative genius after all; it was just as well that he abandoned us to our fate and took off for the islands." But if his trip to the South Pacific had turned out to be a delusional and worthless adventure, Gauguin would have *nothing at all* to say to himself or to others in his own defense. Gauguin's moral luck consists in the fact that he dodged that particular bullet.

Wiesler's Luck

In many ways, the character of Wiesler in *The Lives of Others* is even more interesting than Gauguin. Wiesler takes great risks, but unlike Gauguin he isn't triumphantly successful. Nonetheless he is successful, and also lucky, both in obvious ways and in more subtle and interesting ways. In the course of the film Wiesler makes a fundamental life choice. He abandons the story that held his rather desultory life together. He abandons his faith in the worth and genuineness of his role in the Stasi. The behavior of Hempf and Grubitz provides the opportunity for him to do that. He comes to respect and admire Dreyman and Sieland. He does not become a dissident himself, and after his demotion continues working in the Stasi (steaming open envelopes in the basement) right up until the collapse of the Berlin Wall. Wiesler's life after the wall comes down is surely going to be difficult; his former role as a Stasi agent likely ensures this. He is now a postman and we see him delivering letters along Berlin streets that are grey, graffiti-marred, and ugly. He cuts a lonely and reduced figure. (Compare his life now to his life when we first encounter him in the film. Then he was at the zenith of his career: a brilliantly skilled interrogator teaching an admiring class of students.) So why is he lucky?

Wiesler decided to protect a dissident writer. In this he was successful. However, he also sought to protect Sieland and in this he failed. He must be burdened with regret over her fate given his role in it. Williams' term for this kind of regret is "agent-regret." It isn't the same thing as remorse. Remorse involves a lively sense of one's own profound moral failure and perhaps Wiesler needn't feel deep remorse for his behavior in this particular affair. He interrogated Sieland and this led, unexpectedly, to her suicide; but Wiesler had no easy choice in the matter. And he did his very best, and risked a great deal, to undo as much of the damage caused by his actions as he could. Still, he was the proximate cause of Sieland's downfall and we would think very little of him were he to react to this fact as if it were merely a piece of bad luck; or if he could slough it off by saying, "If I hadn't interrogated her, somebody else, much less sympathetic, would have." Wiesler ought to feel agent-regret about his role in Sieland's interrogation (and real remorse over his role in the interrogation of others).

Wiesler did more than merely decide to protect someone. He chose to protect things he had hitherto seen no real value in: the right of political dissent; the right of privacy; the right to live how one pleases without the controlling attention of the state. Wiesler appears from his actions (we are never privy to his thoughts) to move to a liberal conception of a just society and to abandon the ambitions of the socialist experiment that was East Germany. This is a fundamental reorientation of outlook, and probably reflects his growing appreciation of the riches available in life lived in liberal conditions. Wiesler's recasting of fundamental values might have gone deeper than this. Inspired both by his new experience of art and by the intimate, passionate, and caring relationship he witnessed in Dreyman and Sieland's life together, he might have determined to live a richer, more connected and engaged life himself. The film doesn't settle this question one way or another. (Wiesler remains an enigmatic figure; ironically, a very private man who never articulates his motives or reveals his basic thoughts and attitudes except through action.)

In any case, Wiesler changes sides. In doing so he risks failure, both extrinsic and intrinsic. Extrinsic failure would be, for example, a failure to protect Dreyman. (Imagine a scenario in which his clumsily falsified reports put Dreyman in harm's way rather than protect him.) Extrinsic failure would have led to real regret, but not to the kind of regret generated by intrinsic failure. The possibility of intrinsic failure means that Wiesler risked his future sense of a justified life when he changed sides. Imagine that the values he adopted in this transformation later proved hollow to him: he might have come to think of the dissident writer as banging on self-indulgently and self-importantly about very little; as being genuinely disloyal. Imagine that he came to regard the liberal ascension in Germany as itself a failure: an abandonment of the role of government in caring for the people, and for equality and fraternity among them; a thoughtless substitution of neoliberal brutality in place of a deeply flawed, but fixable, system of socialist ideals. Wiesler risks intrinsic failure, but luckily for him it does not happen. The final scene of the film has seemed contrived and sentimental to some. In fact, however, it signals in an unambiguous and unsentimental way that Wiesler has succeeded in his self-transformative project. He has become someone who can gladly accept the thanks of a man he once saved at considerable cost to himself. Wiesler earned that moment. (And it is important to notice that the moment does not stand for the redemption of the East German state, or of the Stasi who poisoned it. It is about the possibility of someone like Wiesler.)

It is clear that Wiesler does not regret his decision from the perspective of the person he has become. This was never a certainty. Nobody knows themselves well enough – and certainly Wiesler did not know himself well enough – to be sure of such an outcome. And Wiesler had some contingent help along the way. He is helped by the transformation of society after the wall came down. His choice is the sort of choice that is now validated by many others. His newfound liberal conception of justice is shared by his new community; his reneging of his professional past is the sort of thing that would be almost universally welcomed in the new Germany. He is no longer ground down by an organization – the Stasi – that holds him in obvious contempt. Most importantly, Wiesler got himself right. He succeeded in becoming a person who can reflectively endorse his fundamental revaluation and dismiss any concern that he acted disloyally and unprofessionally. He lost a great deal, but he gained a much more robust self-respect than he had previously enjoyed. Still, he might have failed to gain even that.[12]

If we are right about the transformative character of Wiesler's decision to protect Dreyman, then the film nicely illustrates Williams' contrast between extrinsic and intrinsic failure and the consequent extent to which the moral success of our lives depends deeply on things we cannot control. Some writers have questioned the plausibility of Wiesler's change of character in the course of the film. The assumption is "Once a Stasi, always a Stasi." Others have even gone so far as to suggest that Wiesler's redemption is meant to somehow exculpate or at least mitigate Stasi responsibility; for example, that the Stasi too were caught in a bind and were just following orders. Hawker (2007) says

> there are . . . occasions in which von Donnersmarck [the film's director] appears to be more interested in . . . presenting – with a combination of irony and melancholy – the figure of Wiesler as a kind of romantic idealist, a true believer who has the power to redeem himself and others. There's something disconcerting about this tendency, something that lets the context of the story, the world of the Stasi, slip away and dissolve.

However, given that Wiesler is the only one who undergoes such change – Hempf, the disgusting minister certainly does not, nor does Grubitz – it could be argued that the film's creators agree that such change is implausible. This does not mean, however, that it is impossible, and if such a radical change were *prima facie* plausible, then there would hardly be a story worth telling. The success and power of *The Lives of Others* depends upon the implausibility of Wiesler changing as he does. But implausibility is not impossibility. Successful self-transformation requires luck, but sometimes people get lucky. Wiesler didn't *just* get lucky, of course, but luck was involved. He might never have encountered the writer and the actress. He might have not liked them. He might have got himself all wrong; thinking that he had discovered something deep and significant when in fact he was merely infatuated with a couple of glamorous arty-types. But none of these things happened. Fortune eventually favored the dour and lonely Stasi agent who changed into someone better.

Questions

Is the question "What would I do in such a situation?" an important philosophical question? Is it a philosophical question at all?

What is "constitutive luck?" How important is it in assessing moral responsibility?

How does regret relate to the problem of moral luck?

Is Wiesler a man of integrity?

Does Sieland love Dreyman? Does she betray him?

What are some of the implications regarding issues of privacy, surveillance, and exceptional state power in *The Lives of Others* for the behavior of liberal democratic governments, particularly in their prosecution of the "war on terror?"

Notes

1 *Das Leben der Anderen* (2006), directed by Florian Henckel von Donnersmarck.

2 The quotation is from pages 14, and 41–42 but some of the sentences have been rearranged here. For an account of integrity in relation to the "fragile self" see Cox, La Caze & Levine (2003).

3 See Havel (1985 [1978]) for a paper relevant to *The Lives of Others*. Havel gives both a theoretical and practical account of the nature and workings of what he terms the "post-totalitarian" state and something of how people lived and functioned in it. He distinguishes states like the German Democratic Republic and his own Czech state at the time from previous dictatorships and totalitarian states.

4 The Ministry for State Security, (German: Ministerium für Staatssicherheit) known as the Stasi. The Stasi had one spy for every 66 citizens and, according to one report, an additional 189,000 informers. That is about one in 100 informers, including about 12,000 West German informers, in a country of 16 million. "[P]olitical ideals served as the primary motivation for people to turn in their neighbors, friends and acquaintances to the secret police. Financial incentives played only a minor role and blackmail was rare" (http://www.dw-world.de/dw/article/0,,3184486,00.html, March 11, 2008, retrieved July 13, 2010).

5 See Feder (1982); Martin (1986); McKinnon (1991).

6 One aspect of Wiesler's transformation, which we have not emphasized here, is his growing experience of art. The first really notable alteration in him is observed (at 0:52) when he listens in on Dreyman playing a piano piece, "Sonata for a Good Man," in honor of his friend Albert Jerska, who had just committed suicide. Earlier, Wiesler steals a book of Brecht's poetry from Dreyman and (at 0:50) we listen in as he reads a poem about aesthetic attentiveness. The role of art in political and ethical transformation is an important theme of the film, though not one developed with philosophical depth.

7 See Haraszti (1987).

8 The fourth kind of luck Nagel calls causal luck. It is the kind of luck we examined when we discussed free will in chapter 7.

9 This example was used by Adam Smith in his *Theory of Moral Sentiments* (1759). Smith thinks that the gardener who kills negligently ought to be hanged; the lucky gardener ought to be chastised or fined.

10   Of course, the mitigating circumstances surrounding Sieland's betrayal of Dreyman are profound. Throughout the course of the movie's action, she has been abused, raped, threatened, and lied to by agents of the state.

11   We are merely illustrating the phenomenon here. There is considerable controversy about how to respond to cases like this. Moral theorists inspired by Kant tend to reject the possibility of moral luck (see chapter 13 for a discussion of these kinds of theories). Virtue theorists may respond to the cases in various ways, accepting that exhibitions of virtue and vice are not properly subject to resultant luck; but saying that such luck has significant effects on a person's assessment of their lives anyway. (See chapter 14 for a discussion of these kinds of theories.)

12   Contrast Wiesler's success with morally unlucky Briony Tallis in the movie *Atonement* (2007). As a 13-year-old she changes the course of several lives including her own when she accuses her older sister's lover of a crime she knows he did not commit – though at the time she is unable to fully acknowledge she knows he did not commit it. From that point on her life is focused on and absorbed by an irrevocable, basic, and consuming regret. She has made a horribly risky significant decision with which she cannot possibly identify, and so endorse, in the future. Her failure is an intrinsic failure. She cannot possibly justify those harmful actions to herself from the perspective of the person she becomes. Briony suffers what many unconsciously fear; a life consumed by and given over to regret. She has done something that can never be made right. *The Lives of Others* focuses on Wiesler's transformation, but, considering how many lives he must have wrecked in his Stasi career, is he not more like Briony than the audience is encouraged to believe? The difference seems to be that Wiesler's atonement is real, Briony's is imaginary.

Further Reading

Berlin, Isaiah (1967). "Two Concepts of Liberty." In Anthony Quinton, ed., *Political Philosophy*. Oxford: Oxford University Press, 141–52.

Calhoun, Cheshire (1995). "Standing for Something." *Journal of Philosophy* 92, 235–60.

Cox, Damian, Marguerite La Caze, & Michael Levine (2003). *Integrity and the Fragile Self*. London: Ashgate.

Cox, Damian, Michael Levine, & Saul Newman (2009). *Politics Most Unusual: Violence, Sovereignty and Democracy in the War on Terror."* London: Palgrave Macmillan.

Dillon, Robin S. (1997). "Self-Respect: Moral, Emotional, Political." *Ethics* 107, 226–49.

Haraszti, Miklos (1987). *The Velvet Prison: Artists Under State Socialism*. New York: Basic Books.

Havel, Václav (1985 [1978]). "The Power of the Powerless: To the Memory of Jan Patocka." Reprinted in John Keane, ed., *The Power of the Powerless: Citizens Against the State in Central-Eastern Europe*, trans. Paul Wilson. London: Hutchinson. http://www.vaclavhavel.cz/Index.php?sec=6&id=2&kat=&from=6&setln=2.

Hawker, Philippa (2007). Review of *The Lives of Others*. *The Age* (Melbourne, Australia), March 29. http://www.theage.com.au/news/film-reviews/the-lives-of-others/2007/03/29/1174761613403.html.

Kittay, Eva Feder (1982). "On Hypocrisy." *Metaphilosophy* 13, 277–89.

Martin, Mike (1986). *Self-Deception and Morality*. Lawrence, KS: University Press of Kansas.

McKinnon, Christine (1991). "Hypocrisy, With a Note on Integrity." *American Philosophical Quarterly* 28, 321–30.

Nagel, Thomas (1979). *Mortal Questions*. Cambridge: Cambridge University Press.

Nussbaum, Martha (1986). *The Fragility of Goodness*. Cambridge: Cambridge University Press.

Richards, Norvin (1986). "Luck and Desert." *Mind* 95, 198–209.

Thomson, Judith Jarvis (1986). *Rights, Restitution, and Risk*. Cambridge, MA: Harvard University Press.

Walker, Margaret Urban (1991). "Moral Luck and the Virtues of Impure Agency." *Metaphilosophy* 22, 14–26.

Williams, Bernard (1981). "Moral Luck." In *Moral Luck: Philosophical Papers 1973–1980*. Cambridge: Cambridge University Press, 20–39.

Zimmerman, Michael (1987). "Luck and Moral Responsibility." *Ethics* 97, 374–86.

13

The Dark Knight: Batman on Deontology and Consequentialism

Introduction

When an action is morally right, what makes it right? Say you find a wallet lost on a lonely stretch of beach. Nobody has seen you approach the wallet. Nobody knows that you are even on the beach. Inside is $1000 in used bills. And the address of the owner: Mrs Agatha Wallace. What's the right thing to do? (Not what is right-for-you, but what is right, period?) Obviously, the right thing is to return the wallet intact to Mrs Wallace. It's not that it would simply be very nice of you to return the wallet, like it would be very nice of you to give a $1000 of your own money to charity. From a moral point of view, you *must* return the wallet and all the money inside it. Returning the wallet is morally obligatory. But what makes it obligatory? That is, what is it about the act of returning the wallet that, in the circumstances, *makes* it obligatory? If you are religious, you might answer that God commands us not to steal, and keeping the wallet would be stealing. A prohibition against stealing is one of the Ten Commandments after all. But this is not much of an answer. What is it about stealing that qualifies it to be included amongst the Ten Commandments? God must have based her judgment on something about stealing, unless we think that God just makes up arbitrary rules for us[1] So whether we are religious or not we face a difficult philosophical question. What makes certain actions right? What makes other actions wrong? What is it about the *actions* themselves that determines these moral properties? As philosophers sometimes put the question, what are the right-making features of actions? What are the wrong-making features of them?

Thinking Through Film: Doing Philosophy, Watching Movies, First Edition. Damian Cox, Michael P. Levine.
© 2012 Damian Cox and Michael P. Levine. Published 2012 by Blackwell Publishing Ltd.

As usual, philosophers have come up with numerous answers to these questions. (Often the difficulty of philosophy is not that philosophers pose questions that can't be answered; it's that philosophers pose questions that have many incompatible answers, each one of which looks pretty good from some angles.) In contemporary philosophy there are three dominant approaches to answering the questions we pose. The approaches are called consequentialism, deontology, and virtue ethics. In this chapter we are going to explore the confrontation between consequentialism and deontology using a Batman movie: *The Dark Knight* (2008). We examine virtue ethics in chapter 14. *The Dark Knight* depicts some brilliant moral conundrums that allow us to get to the heart of the clash between consequentialist and deontological moral thinking. *The Dark Knight* also has an agenda. It is firmly on the side of deontology (until the end, when it seems to change its mind; but more of this a little later in the chapter). Let's start with the major set-piece of the film, at the very climax of the action.

The Joker's Experiment

Batman has his hands full. Two ferries float stranded in a river. One carries prisoners; the other carries ordinary civilians. Both are rigged to blow. The Joker has an experiment in mind. As he tells the passengers on the ferries (1:57),

> Tonight you're all going to be part of a social experiment. I'm ready right now to blow you all sky high. Anyone attempts to get off their boat, you all die. Each of you has a remote to blow up the other boat. At midnight, I blow you all up. If however, one of you presses the button, I'll let that boat live. So, who's it going to be? Harvey Dent's most wanted scumbag collection or the sweet and innocent civilians? You choose. Oh, and you might want to decide quickly because the people on the other boat might not be so noble.

Eventually Batman is going to save the day and stop the Joker blowing up both ferries. But the people on the ferries don't even know that he is on the case. What should they do? What should they do from a moral point of view?

Here's a thought. In order to work out what should be done, work out the best outcome – not just for one person involved, but for everybody – and then recommend the thing most likely to bring about this outcome. This is, roughly, the consequentialist's way of thinking about the matter. At first sight, it looks like common sense. But is it? First, note that we have oversimplified things drastically. You may recall from chapter 11 that decision-making is more complicated than deciding what would be best and trying to get it. In that chapter we introduced the idea of maximizing expected utility. Expected utility is a function of the rankings of outcomes from best to worst (this gives us the "utility" of the outcome) and the probabilities of outcomes. To work out expected utility of an action we need to know the utilities of potential outcomes of the action and the probability or likelihood of these outcomes. As we pointed out in chapter 11, this is a very hard thing to determine in practice.

If we stick with the maximization of expected utility, the passengers on our ferries should frame their decision – not in terms of what would maximize the chance of their getting the best available outcome – but in terms of which action has the maximum expected utility. (These look similar, but they are different. Maximizing the chance of getting the best outcome leads one to ignore the chances of getting the second- or third-best outcome; expected-utility calculations take all potential outcomes into account.) In chapter 11, we discussed expected utility in the context of Judah Rosenthal's problem with his ex-lover (*Crimes and Misdemeanors*, 1989). Rosenthal's thinking was entirely self-centered; it was an example of what we called prudential reasoning. The difference between prudential reasoning and the sort of consequentialist reasoning we are now considering rests on how we describe utilities. In prudential reasoning, an individual decision-maker works out utilities based on her own self-interest. In the sort of ethical decision-making we are exploring here, a decision-maker works out utilities based on a summation of everybody's interest, where no person's interest counts for more than anyone else's interest. It is important to keep all these complications in the back of your mind as we continue our discussion of the Joker's social experiment, however, the choice-situation of all the ferry passengers doesn't require them to ponder the probability or utility of second- or third-best outcomes. (There is nothing they can do to factor in such outcomes; going for the best available outcome and maximizing expected utility turn out to be the same thing in this scenario.)

How does consequentialist thinking fare in the Joker's social experiment? What is the best outcome, taking the interests of everybody who might be affected equally into account? That everybody survives. The Joker, it seems, has ensured that this won't happen. Or so everybody on the boats ought to believe. All ferry passengers ought to believe the Joker's threats – he has been true to his word for the entire movie. He said he would blow up a hospital if a certain lawyer wasn't murdered. The lawyer wasn't murdered (not for want of trying) and the hospital was blown up. He said he would assassinate the mayor, and was only prevented by some last-second heroics by Commissioner Gordon. Batman hasn't been able to stop the Joker so far; why think he could stop him this time? (As you know, he does stop him; but not till the ferry passengers had made their decision.) So if the Batman solution rightly appears unavailable, what should the passengers think is the best available option? That the folks on the civilian boat survive. Why? Because they have so much more to contribute to society than the prisoners; they have more to offer others, they have careers and families and taxes to pay. If we take everybody's interests into account, including everybody *off* the ferries as well as everybody on them, the best available outcome will have the civilians saved rather than the prisoners. (There is a complication here arising from the decision-makers' limitation of knowledge – for all we know, one of the prisoners (unjustly convicted by the way) is going to discover a cure for stupidity; blowing him up would be by far and away the worst available outcome. Judgments of best outcomes are always made relative to imperfect knowledge.) Let us stick with the, somewhat unpalatable, conclusion that all passengers (including the prisoners themselves) ought to accept that the best available outcome is that the civilian ferry survives intact. So what must be done to achieve this outcome? Passengers on the civilian ferry must detonate the bomb on the prisoner's ferry. (And quickly: the longer they delay, the greater the probability that the prisoners will press their button first.)

As you know – having watched the film – neither group detonates a bomb. The civilians take a vote and decide by a wide margin (396 to 140) to blow up the prisoner's ferry. When it comes to the crunch, however, they lose their nerve. One civilian seems convinced that pressing the button is the right thing. He tries to step up (2:06):

> No one wants to get their hands dirty. Fine. I'll do it. Those men in that boat, they made their choices. They choose to murder and steal. It doesn't make sense for us to have to die too.

But this man loses his nerve and sits down again, bomb undetonated. He just couldn't bring himself to blow up a boatload of people. It's hard to work out exactly what the man is thinking. He says of the prisoners that they made their choices. Certainly they made choices, and they weren't all good choices. They chose to murder and steal (or sell narcotics, or evade their taxes, or not to pay their parking fines; we can't be sure exactly what they chose). What they didn't choose, however, is to be on a ferry packed with explosives. And that seems to be the relevant choice here.

Perhaps the man thinks that the prisoners deserve to survive less than the innocent civilians do, and if anyone is going to survive the Joker's experiment, it ought to be the group whose members most deserve to survive. That is not a consequentialist way of thinking; at least not in any obvious way. Desert is a backward-looking property: what one deserves depends on what one has already done. Consequentialists look forward: what we should do depends on future consequences, not on what has already happened.

On the prisoners' ferry, an exceptionally tough-looking prisoner convinces the guards to let him push the button. As he tells the chief guard (2:06):

> You don't want to die, but you don't know how to take a life. Give it to me. . . . You can tell them I took it by force. Give it to me and I'll do what you should have did ten minutes ago.

He takes the detonator and promptly throws it overboard. The prisoner's action can be interpreted in at least three ways: as a refusal to cooperate with evil; as a refusal to do evil (kill other passengers); and as an attempt to secure the best outcome (that the civilians, not the prisoners, survive). On every interpretation his action seems to be heroically good.

Here is how Batman sums up both groups' moral performance, including the civilians. Chatting with the Joker, he asks:

> What were you trying to prove? That deep down everyone is exactly as you? You're alone [2:07]. . . . This city just showed you that it's full of people ready to believe in good. (2:08)

Is Batman right? Is he thinking clearly? (The Joker is throttling him as they chat, so perhaps we can't blame him if he's not thinking *very* clearly.) The citizens of Gotham City trapped on the civilian ferry have shown that they are unprepared to do what it takes to achieve the best available outcome, taking everybody's interests into equal account. (They were prepared to vote to do it, but they weren't prepared to do it.) How is this a moral triumph? If the passengers on one ferry blew up those on the other, how would this show that they are just like the Joker? The Joker is pure agent provocateur – someone who just wants to see the world burn. The passengers on the ferries would have been trying to save their own lives. In the case of the civilians, they might have been doing this with a sense of justification. How would they be like the Joker? Perhaps they would be like him in this respect: by blowing up a ferry full of passengers, they would have shown that they were prepared to break moral principles in order to get what they want. Our moral principles tell us that we shouldn't kill. The Joker wants to show just how superficial our commitment to this principle is. Under sufficient pressure, just about anybody can be made to kill. He wants to show that the grip of morality is weak, but the citizens of Gotham show him just how wrong he is. Morality grips more strongly than the Joker realized. Even though they wanted to blow up the prisoner's boat, the civilians just couldn't bring themselves to do it. Just when fear and temptation were about to overwhelm the guards on the prisoners' boat, a man of exceptional moral courage stands up and does the right thing. Moral principle wins out. Whether this is a realistic account of what would happen in the Joker's social experiment is a good question. The key philosophical question for us, however, is not about what people *would* do in these circumstances; it is about what they *should* do. If the civilians had pressed the button, would they have acted wrongly? Why?

Batman's thinking seems like a typical example of deontological thinking. The alternative take on the situation – that the passengers should do what it takes to secure the best available outcome or that they should maximize expected utility – is an example of consequentialist thinking. Let's get this into perspective by examining the relevant philosophies.

Utilitarianism and the Joker's Experiment

According to consequentialists, moral properties are a function of consequences, or likely consequences. There are many varieties of consequentialism because there are many ways of setting up the function in question. Which consequences count? Consequences of what: actions, institutions, rules, habits? How do we factor consequences in? The best-known example of a consequentialist theory is utilitarianism, and the best-known champion of utilitarianism is the British philosopher John Stuart Mill. According to utilitarians, we measure the utility of consequences by working out how well everybody's life goes. Many actions have consequences for how well peoples' lives go. They might make some people's lives go well (if, say, one person suddenly finds herself $1000 richer, with no strings attached) and others' go badly (if, say, another person suddenly finds himself $1000 poorer and can't pay the rent). According to utilitarians, how well people's lives go is the only thing that really matters, and the aim of morality is to maximize how well they go.

How do we measure how well or badly people's lives go? Mill thought that we could measure this psychologically, in terms of happiness. A person's life goes well if they are happy and they are happy if they enjoy life – that is, they are happy if they experience the pleasures of life. Mill also thought that pleasure is a complicated affair and that some kinds of pleasure are intrinsically more desirable than others. He called more desirable pleasures "higher pleasures." Contemporary utilitarians tend to be unconvinced by Mill's hedonism, and to favor a different account of what it is for a life to go well. A common move among contemporary utilitarians is to measure how well lives go in terms of the satisfaction of preferences.[2] A's life goes better than B's life if A has more of her preferences satisfied than B. Since a person might form preferences without knowing relevant facts – someone might have a preference eating fried chicken every night without realizing that it dramatically increases the likelihood of their getting diabetes – utilitarians often talk about fully informed preferences rather than actual preferences: A's life goes better than B's if A has more of her fully informed preferences satisfied than B does. A gets her fully informed preferences satisfied if she gets what she would have preferred if she were fully informed of all facts relevant to her potential preferences. Of course, we can't really measure these things, so utilitarians often opt for an indirect strategy. In order to advance the life prospects of A, A needs to be furnished with the resources, including knowledge and education, required for her to satisfy a goodly proportion of her informed preferences. The indirect strategy works some of the time, but we still face many situations in which we have to make a moral choice about whose preferences are to be satisfied. Assuming nearly everyone has an informed preference for being alive rather than being dead, we sometimes have to decide whose lives should be saved. This is the decision that the ferry passengers faced.

Utilitarianism is an impartial theory about what is right. Everybody's well-being counts, and counts for the same as everybody else's. The utilitarian treats everybody's informed preferences on a par and tries to ensure that as many preferences are satisfied as possible. It's like a form of democracy in which everybody's preference gets exactly one vote. Of course there are problems. What if some people have especially fussy or expensive preferences? (People with very selfish and expensive preferences are sometimes called "utility pigs.") What if some people have been conditioned by an oppressive society to have very limited and inexpensive preferences? Should those with expensive preferences get more resources than those with inexpensive preferences? Would that be fair? Wouldn't it be especially unfair if those with inexpensive preferences only had them because they were socialized to expect very little from life? Now consider preferences directed towards others. What if somebody, C, doesn't want to be rich *per se*, but only richer than his neighbor, D? Should this preference count? Utilitarians often want to exclude such external preferences on the grounds that they don't properly reflect quality of life. If C gets what he wants, so that D is poorer than him, how would this mere fact make C's life genuinely better? C might feel a bit better about his life if his external preferences were satisfied, but this doesn't necessarily make his life actually better. Perhaps utilitarians are right to exclude external preferences from their calculations and count only internal preferences: preferences people have about how their own life goes. This still leaves us with the problem of whether or not to count selfish, oppressed, and perhaps other kinds of illegitimate preferences in utilitarian calculations. Utilitarians will have to sort out these problems: perhaps by refining their account of utility to exclude problematic preferences; perhaps by defending the presence of problematic preferences in utilitarian calculation. We aren't going to follow them down that track. Instead we are going to concentrate on another aspect of utilitarianism: its focus on consequences to the exclusion of all else.

According to utilitarians, how well people's lives go is the only thing that really matters, and the aim of morality is to maximize how well they go. Numerous things are subject to moral judgment: actions, habits, laws, rules, policies, institutions, and so on. Concentrate on actions for the moment. An action is right if and only if it maximizes utility. No action can change past utilities. For example, there is nothing you can do to make your childhood happier (assuming you aren't still in the middle of it). If something somebody does makes your childhood seem happier than it used to seem (say by reminding you of good times), this can still only affect your future appreciation of your childhood. You can't change your childhood itself. (You can't change it even if you had a time machine, as we discovered in chapter 6.) So utilitarianism is all about the future. The right-making features of actions reside wholly in the future consequences of them. This is so no matter what thing we make the subject of moral judgment. A law is morally right only if it has the best kind of consequences. A social policy is right only if it yields the best kind of results. While there is nothing wrong with taking future effects into account, the question is whether good consequences are the only relevant right-making features of things.

Deontology and the Joker's Experiment

Deontology is a moral theory that focuses on principles rather than consequences. Kant is often cited as the paradigm deontologist, although some Kant scholars regard this as an oversimplification of his view.[3] An action is right, according to deontologists, if it falls under an appropriate moral principle. Returning the wallet you find on a beach is right because it falls under the principle: *respect others' property*. Refusing to blow up a ferry loaded with passengers falls under the principle: *respect others' lives*. And so on. How do we decide which principles are genuinely moral ones and which principles aren't?[4] Imagine that the prisoners on the ferry decided to blow up the civilians; imagine that they overwhelm the guards and press the button. They justify doing this by appealing to a principle: *if you can prevent someone killing you, do so*. Is this a moral principle? It's a principle that seems intuitively to give the right answer a lot of the time, but could we use it to justify the prisoners blowing up the civilians in the Joker's experiment? Deontologists need to tell us, not only what principles are moral principles, but also when they apply and how we resolve potential conflicts between them.

How might a deontologist deal with the moral dilemma posed by the Joker's experiment? We might generally agree with the principle of self-protection – that we shouldn't just stand by and allow others to take our life – but also think that it can be overridden. Other principles can take precedence over it. What happens when our only chance of preventing another taking our life requires us to kill innocent strangers? Doesn't the principle *respect others' lives* take precedence over any principle of self-protection? What we need is a principle that sets out the conditions in which killing in self-defense is morally permissible. Here is a suggestion. In lethal self-defense, A kills B in order to prevent B killing A. If killing B is the only defense available to A, and if B is intentionally and wrongly attempting to kill A (and is not, say, being used as a pawn in someone else's plan to kill A), then lethal self-defense is morally permissible. That sounds OK in theory. How does it work in concrete situations?

Our Batman example doesn't fall under the principle of justifiable self-defense, as we have specified it. If the civilians, for example, were to kill the prison inmates, they would not necessarily be killing people who are intentionally and wrongly trying to kill them. They would not be killing in justifiable self-defense. They would be killing people who, for all they know, mean them no harm at all. And they would be doing this in order to prevent someone else (the Joker) killing them. This is a terrible situation, but it doesn't license killing in self-defense. We ought not to kill people who mean us no harm simply in order to prevent our own death at the hands of another. And nor ought we to kill people simply because there is a chance that they will soon try to kill us. We have to be sure that they are intentionally and wrongly attempting to kill us, or at least confident beyond any real doubt that they are. Imagine that the Joker had sent a video feed of each ferry to the other ferry. The passengers in one ferry see those in the other making for the button with the clear intention of pressing it. Is this enough to justify them getting in first and pushing the button before their rivals? Perhaps. They could reason as follows. We are sure that our rivals in the Joker's experiment are intentionally and wrongly attempting to kill us, right now. Our only hope of stopping them is to kill them first. So we can push the button in justified self-defense. In the Joker's game, those who move first become justifiable targets for their rivals. On the other hand, those who move first have by far the better chance of surviving (Batman notwithstanding). And neither the civilians nor the prisoners can be confident of this.

How do contemporary deontologists derive moral principles? Our procedure was to think up a principle that seemed intuitively right and then apply it to a concrete situation to see if its intuitive plausibility held up. Obviously we ought to examine a wide variety of cases. If we encounter a problem, we should return to our principle and see if we can modify it to deal with the problem case. We seek a balance between the theoretical merits of the general principle and the intuitive support it gains when it is applied to particular cases. Is the principle sufficiently general? Is it consistent with other principles? Is there an effective and intuitively compelling way of ordering conflicting principles? Does the principle yield intuitively compelling results in the clear cases? Are these intuitions reliable or are they open to manipulation and distortion? Does it help make sense of unclear cases? And so on. This methodology is described by philosophers as a search for "reflective equilibrium."[5] Deontologists have alternative methodologies. Kantians, for example, derive moral principles from presuppositions about practical reason. When we reason in a principled way, we implicitly commit ourselves to a certain logical rigor. We ought not, for example, to apply one principle to ourselves and a different principle to others. We ought to follow principles that could be used by everybody, not principles specially designed to serve our individual purposes. As Kant puts it, we ought to apply principles that we could will to become universal laws of nature (i.e. principles that everybody abides by all the time). This yields an attempt to derive moral principles from the conditions of rational agency itself. A lively and inconclusive debate is happening amongst deontologists about which methodology is best; just as a lively and inconclusive debate rages amongst consequentialists about what is the best form of consequentialism.

Utilitarianism vs Deontology: Technical Knockout or Split Decision?

If our deontological analysis of the Joker's experiment is correct, then it comes up with exactly the opposite conclusion to our earlier utilitarian analysis. The Joker's experiment doesn't just test the mettle of Gotham City ferry passengers. It tests the *bona fides* of utilitarian and deontological reasoning. It tests this reasoning against intuition. It's a reasonably simple social experiment that the Joker concocts for us. Our intuitions are probably a good guide to the right response to it. Batman, we know, takes the deontologist's path, or at least he concurs with the conclusion of our deontological analysis of the situation. Intuition seems to be on his side. We don't baulk at his response. It seems overwhelmingly to be the natural and proper response. The people of Gotham *have* just shown the Joker what they are made of; they have shown him that they have greater moral courage and greater moral sensitivity than he supposed; they are people prepared to believe in good, as Batman puts it. Admittedly, a more cynical reading is available – at least in the case of the civilians. After all, they were willing to vote to blow up the prisoners. How should we interpret their failure to follow through on the vote? Is this moral sense breaking through or is it a kind of moral cowardice? Perhaps it reflects no more than an unwillingness to get one's hands dirty. (That is, perhaps, it reflects no more than an unwillingness to do something that *seems* bad and will be condemned as bad, even though it is the right thing to do in the circumstances. This is the essence of what philosophers call "dirty hands scenarios." We have more to say on this below.) Notwithstanding the cynical interpretation of their motives, our reaction to the civilian decision not to blow up the prisoners' ferry is positive. Imagine our response if they had done the opposite. If the civilians had blown up the prisoners, it would have seemed like a bad decision: understandable, but wrong; and a bit creepy.

So does this prove that consequentialism is an inadequate framework for moral theory? Not necessarily. Consequentialists still have a lot of responses up their sleeve. They might dispute our reading of intuitive judgments of the case. They might reject the evidential value of our appeal to intuitions. They might argue that our intuitions are unreliable in cases like this. They might argue that in this particular case our intuitions are being manipulated by the filmmakers. (The Joker is a freak; of course it seems bad to play along with his game.) Or they might argue that our intuitions are unreliable in general.

The Rule-Utilitarian Compromise

Another way for consequentialists to respond is to opt for a different version of consequentialism with the hope of getting the right result in cases like the Joker's social experiment. In our utilitarian analysis of the case, we employed a version of utilitarianism that specifies the morality of individual actions in terms of the consequences of actions judged one at a time. This version is called act-utilitarianism. But this is one very specific form of consequentialism and we can't condemn consequentialist ways of framing moral theories on the basis of the unintuitive nature of act-utilitarianism alone. Perhaps the right conclusion to draw from the Joker's experiment is that utilitarian reasoning should not be applied on a case-by-case basis. It's true that in the experiment – assuming Batman doesn't wreck it – the best available impartial outcome has the civilians blowing up the prisoners. But what if we framed utilitarianism, not in terms of the consequences of individual actions, but in terms of the consequences of our adopting particular rules or principles? This is a kind of compromise between consequentialism and deontology. It is called rule-utilitarianism. It judges actions in terms of principles or rules, just like deontology, but it derives these rules from consequences, as you would expect a consequentialist to do. The rule-utilitarian might agree that neither the prisoners nor the civilians should push the button. But which principle or rule makes it wrong to push the button? What makes one potential moral rule a better rule than another? Our principle of justifiable lethal self-defense was based on an appeal to intuition, and eventually, we might hope, on an appeal to reflective equilibrium. Rule-utilitarians are dismissive of this methodology. A much better way to arrive at an acceptable moral principle, they argue, is to work through the consequences of adopting the principle.

What principle of self-defense would maximize utility over the long haul if it were generally observed? If we followed too lenient a principle, it would be too easy to kill someone in presumed self-defense: too many people would end up dead and the rest of us would start to feel rather unsafe. If we followed too strict a principle, potential killers would be encouraged: again, too many people would end up dead, with the rest of us feeling helpless in the face of potential attacks upon our persons. We want a principle that will minimize the killing, maximize our security and maximize our control over our lives. Our principle of justifiable self-defense might be just the ticket. Or it might not be. For the rule-utilitarian, the devil is in the detail. The fact that a principle appeals to us intuitively means very little. What matters is how effective the principle would be if it were it generally observed.

Is rule-utilitarianism a satisfactory moral theory? Much work needs to be done to refine and defend it. The main task is to defend the idea that we should follow utility-maximizing rules even if other people aren't following them; i.e. even if our following them is a poor effort from a utilitarian point of view. One of the most attractive features of utilitarianism is its emphasis on getting results. We can see the point of being utilitarians. Utilitarians make the world better; and making a better world is a sensible project. Acting on rules that would only make the world better if everybody else were to follow them (which, for many rules, they won't) is hard to motivate. From a consequentialist perspective, rule-utilitarianism begins to look like a kind of rule worship. Deontologists appeal to intuitions to support their principles, or they appeal to normative commitments implicit in rational agency, or some other such thing. What do rule-utilitarians appeal to? There isn't any obvious intuitive support for their rule-following proclivities. This is the outstanding problem for rule-utilitarianism: how to motivate the position. Rule-utilitarianism might generate intuitively satisfactory answers to moral conundrums, such as the one played out for us in *The Dark Knight*, but it is in danger of coming up with the right results in the wrong way, or at least in an unconvincing way. As is often the case in philosophy, matters are still up in the air.

Conclusion: From Integrity to the Noble Lie

For much of the film, *The Dark Knight* appears to illustrate, and generate in the viewer, intuitions that are firmly on the side of the deontologists. Unwillingness to compromise with evil, even if there are significant goods to be got from compromising, is a sign of moral goodness and integrity. But at the very end of the film matters take a turn. The Joker manages to corrupt Harvey Dent, the all-shining hero, legal crusader against crime, someone who, unlike Batman, wears his underpants under his pants. After the Joker is finished with him, Dent becomes a vengeful murderer, Harvey Two-Face. Commissioner Gordon is devastated: there goes his hope for Gotham's future; the Joker wins after all; the people of Gotham City will lose hope in legal and constitutionally legitimate forms of social power when they see how easily the Joker undermined the personification of these things in Harvey Dent. Once more Batman comes to the rescue. But this time he does so by originating a lie: he colludes with Gordon to pretend that it is Batman who has been turned by the Joker into a rampaging, murdering force of vengeance, not Dent. Batman already operates outside the law. To lose faith in Batman is not to lose faith in the law and the legitimate exercise of power. Batman becomes the Dark Knight. Social order and social hope are preserved by means of a lie: a noble lie.[6]

This is not a matter of cooperating with evil. The Joker had already done his work. It is more a matter of mopping up after evil. Nonetheless, moral principle is sacrificed for political purposes. Being honest with the citizens of Gotham City suddenly takes a back seat to the urgent need to keep their spirits up; to keep up their faith in the power of ordinary legal processes. Interestingly, the film frames the moral issue in broadly deontological terms. Instead of being unheroically pragmatic – doing what it takes to get the best outcome – Batman frames his choice is in terms of desert. He puts it like this:

> Sometimes truth isn't good enough. Sometimes people deserve more. Sometimes people deserve to have their faith rewarded. (2:17)

And then a bit later, Gordon sums it all up in downright creepy terms. His young son asks why the police are chasing Batman since he hasn't done anything wrong:

> Because he is not our hero. He is a silent guardian. A watchful protector. The Dark Knight. (2:18)

How did the principle-driven moral perspective of the movie morph into this lazy appeal to totalitarian thinking? Is it a change from a fundamentally deontological perspective to a fundamentally consequentialist one? Or is it a shift from one kind of deontological perspective – one based on the primacy of moral integrity – to another, one based on a duty of care owed a citizenry in whom one has very little faith? Is the moral strangeness of the change softened by the heroic self-sacrifice made by Batman? These are hard questions to answer, and the film probably doesn't furnish enough information to answer them. However, at least one obvious justification of the lie is consequentialist. The lie must be told because the truth would wreak too much harm.

Just when is it OK to lie in order to advance a social purpose? How do we answer this question: with appeal to consequentialist reasons or to deontological ones? That puzzle lingers. Our initial question – what makes actions right when they are right and what makes them wrong when they are wrong – is with us still. As you might expect.

Questions

Early on in the chapter, we quickly dismissed the view that actions are made right by the commands of God. Is the Euthyphro problem (note 1) an insurmountable difficulty for this view?

Say that the passengers on one ferry decide to push their button, reasoning as follows:

> If we don't push our button, we leave the choice up to the passengers on the other ferry. Either they will push their button or they won't. If they push their button, they blow us up. And if that's what they plan to do we don't do anything wrong by getting in first. If they aren't going to push their button, they are going to die anyway (according to the Joker), so we don't make them worse off by pushing our button. In either case, we don't significantly and wrongly harm the other ferry passengers by pushing our button. How can it be wrong to save our lives by doing something that doesn't wrongly harm anybody else?

Just how good is this argument? Is it mere rationalization or it is on to something? Does it demonstrate a consequentialist or deontological style of reasoning?

Does it make sense to say that pushing the button was the right thing to do in the circumstances for the civilians, but not for the prisoners? Should there be equality of button-pushing opportunity in the case?

Does it make sense to say that pushing the button was the right thing to do in the circumstances for the civilians, but if any of the civilians had actually pushed the button we would rightly regard them as quite a vicious individual? (That is, can judgments of right action and judgments of virtuous behavior come apart like this? We take up related issues in chapter 14.)

Was the civilian who couldn't bring himself to push the button a coward? (Can you be a coward by doing the right thing?)

Is preference satisfaction a philosophically adequate measure of welfare? Is it the thing that utilitarians ought to be trying to maximize?

According to deontology, an action is morally justified if it falls under an appropriate moral principle. What principle might a decision to blow up a ferry fall under? We suggested one in the chapter, but had a fairly easy time showing that it didn't stack up as a reasonable or intuitively plausible principle. Is there a better principle ferry passengers might have employed to justify blowing up the other ferry?

Batman comes down on the side of principle over consequences; and equates this with moral goodness. Viewers of the film tend to agree; the setup makes it seem intuitively compelling as a response. But has the film set this up in a philosophically illegitimate way? Are our intuitions misled by the heroics of Batman or the raving (if charismatic) spite of the Joker? Is there any other way in which the film's director, Christopher Nolan, has contrived matters to lead our intuitions in a particular direction?

Rule-utilitarianism seems like it might agree with the sort of deontological principle we deemed relevant to the Joker's social experiment. Would it?

What sort of constraints would apply to the consequentially-best rules? Must they be rules that only angels could obey? Or should they be rules that can feasibly be followed?

Is the best rule, from a utilitarian point of view, the rule that says maximize utility in your every action? Why not?

Was Batman right to take on as his own the sins of Harvey Dent? Was Commissioner Gordon right to perpetrate the lie that Batman is a killer?

Notes

1   The claim that actions are made right by God's commands is known as divine command theory. The core issue was raised in Plato's *Euthyphro*, 9e. Are actions morally obligatory or forbidden because God commands or forbids them; or does God command or forbid them because they are morally obligatory or forbidden? Does God's commanding them make them obligatory or forbidden; or are some actions obligatory or forbidden apart from God's commanding them? Divine command theory states either that ethical wrongness *consists in* being contrary to God's commands or that the word "wrong" in ethical contexts *means* "contrary to God's commands." See Nielsen (1990).

2   Other options, apart from hedonism as championed by Mill, include experientialism (one life is better than another if it contains more valuable experiences (including pleasure, but not only pleasure), and objective lists (one life is better than another if it achieves or contains more good things, as specified on a (probably open-ended) list of good things. Good experiences are on the list, but they are not enough. It is not enough (at least not on most accounts) to experience the feeling that another loves you, for example; it is better that they actually *do* love you.

3   See Wood (2008). Also see our discussion of Kant in chapter 11.

4   We briefly examined Kant's answer to this question in chapter 11. Here we concentrate on contemporary, non-Kantian ways of coming to grips with it.

5   The methodology we describe here is called "narrow reflective equilibrium." The contrasting term is "wide reflective equilibrium." Narrow reflective equilibrium represents a balance between intuitions about cases and theoretical merit. Wide reflective equilibrium incorporates supporting and contextual information; for example, information about sociology, psychology, or economics. If a moral theory achieves a wide reflective equilibrium, it furnishes a set of moral principles that cohere with our best understanding of how the world works, not just our intuitions about cases.

6   The idea of a noble lie has a long history in philosophy, beginning with Plato's advocacy of a noble lie in *The Republic*. At the other end of the philosophical spectrum lies Kant, who argued that one never, under any circumstances, has a moral right to lie to another.

Further Reading

Hooker, Brad (2000). *Ideal Code, Real World: A Rule-Consequentialist Theory of Morality*. Oxford: Oxford University Press.

Kagan, Shelly (1998). *Normative Ethics*. Boulder: Westview.

Kamm, F. M. (2007). *Intricate Ethics: Rights, Responsibilities, and Permissible Harms*. Oxford: Oxford University Press.

Kant, Immanuel (1996). "On a Supposed Right to Tell Lies from Benevolent Motives." In *Practical Philosophy*, ed. and trans. Mary J. Gregor. Cambridge: Cambridge University Press.

Korsgaard, Christine (1986). "The Right to Lie: Kant on Dealing with Evil." *Philosophy and Public Affairs* 15, 325–49.

Mill, John Stuart (1987). *Utilitarianism and Other Essays*. New York: Penguin.

Nielsen, Kai (1990). *Ethics Without God*. Buffalo, NY: Prometheus Books.

Plato (2006). *The Republic*, translated and with an introduction by R. E. Allen. New Haven: Yale University Press.

Rawls, John (1971). *A Theory of Justice*, Cambridge: Belknap Press of Harvard University Press.

Scarre, Geoffrey (1996). *Utilitarianism*. London: Routledge.

Singer, Peter (1993). *Practical Ethics*. Cambridge: Cambridge University Press.

Skorupski, John (2006). *Why Read Mill Today?* London: Routledge.

Unger, Peter (1996). *Living High and Letting Die*. Oxford: Oxford University Press.

Wood, Allen (2008). *Kantian Ethics*. Cambridge: Cambridge University Press.

14

Dangerous Childhood: *La Promesse* and the Possibility of Virtue

Introduction

In the previous two chapters we examined morality in two different ways. First, we asked the question "Why be moral?" Then we asked the question "What makes actions right or wrong?" In particular, we asked whether actions are made right or wrong by their satisfying moral principles or by their bringing about the impartially best consequences. In this chapter, we look at morality from yet another angle. Instead of focusing on types of actions and their right-making properties, we focus on people and ask what features of people make them morally good or bad. In doing so, we will be examining something that contemporary philosophers call virtue theory.

Our guide through this will be a 1996 film by the Belgian filmmakers Jean-Pierre and Luc Dardenne, *La Promesse* (in English, *The Promise*). As usual, make sure you watch the film before reading further (there are spoilers galore in what follows). The Dardenne brothers (Jean-Pierre and Luc are brothers) first came to international attention with *La Promesse* and have since made a series of extraordinary films: *Rossetta* (1999), *Le Fils* (2002), *L'Enfant* (2005), and *Le Silence de Lorna* (2008) focusing on the moral lives of people facing extreme moral challenges. What is most remarkable about the Dardenne brothers' work, from our point of view, is that they explore the possibility and the beauty of moral goodness and moral redemption with considerable rigor and an absence of sentimentality. *La Promesse* may seem a little austere and slow-moving when

Thinking Through Film: Doing Philosophy, Watching Movies, First Edition. Damian Cox, Michael P. Levine.
© 2012 Damian Cox and Michael P. Levine. Published 2012 by Blackwell Publishing Ltd.

you first watch it, but in fact the film is as tightly scripted as just about any film you will see. (For example, it is *much* more tightly and carefully scripted than *The Dark Knight*). A great deal happens in the film and tension mounts inexorably. Watching the film is a deeply involving experience once you accustom yourself to its austere style. Strong currents of feeling are revealed, but only through the most direct means: by watching characters do things and say things, observing the expression on their faces and in their bodies as they do things and say things. A complete absence of background music and tightly framed, mostly hand-held camera work gives the superficial impression of a documentary style, but on closer inspection you will notice that every scene is carefully organized. The power of the Dardenne brothers' technique lies in its capacity to focus the viewer's attention on the way the characters live in their environment; not how they operate in a fictional setting, but how they live in a (seemingly) real environment. The settings are messy, unlovely, inconvenient, and (apparently) unstaged. We follow characters up stairs and through doorways, into cars, along the street; sometimes from behind, or the side, or the front. It's like observing action as an accidental bystander rather than having a scene staged for us. Unlike conventional filmic setups (mise-en-scènes), where the aim is to optimize the communication of narrative information – What is happening? Who is talking to whom? Who is in charge? What are these people feeling? What are their motives? What kind of people are they? – the Dardenne brothers' technique aims to show characters' action as if nothing is staged; as if the filmmakers have happened upon it. Narrative information seems to emerge non-deliberately.[1] This film style resembles a style called *cinéma vérité*, which has a long and distinguished history in the cinema. The Dardenne brothers use of it is particularly elegant because the artifice behind it is so well disguised. *La Promesse*'s narrative progression seems almost accidental; as if one scene could easily be substituted for endlessly many other scenes, so little precise information seems at first glance to be conveyed in them. In fact, however, every scene is designed to make a special point about the life and troubles of the main character, Igor, and could not easily be substituted with other scenes.[2]

And Igor's troubles are very real. He is a 15-year-old apprentice motor mechanic whose real job appears to be to aid his father, Roger, in various odious criminal activities. (Indeed Igor is soon fired from his job as apprentice mechanic.) We first see Igor steal a purse from a customer, but much worse is soon to follow. He helps his father run a kind of hostel for undocumented arrivals to Belgium (people who face deportation if discovered by Belgian immigration officials). These people come from various places – including Yugoslavia, Korea, and, crucially, the West African nation of Burkina Faso. Roger extorts cash and cheap labor from them. He also seems to run, or at least profit from, the people-smuggling operation that brings the undocumented migrants into Belgium in the first place. To get immigration officials off his back, Roger also sets up some of his hostel residents for arrest and deportation, and enlists Igor's help in the operation. Roger is building a house – for his son, he tells us at the very end of the film – and the worksite is a disorganized and unsafe mess. The work is dangerous and safety precautions are ignored. During a sweep by labor inspectors, while everybody else rushes to hide, one worker falls from scaffolding (he has no safety harness). This is Hamidu, a man from Burkina Faso, whose wife (Assita) and child have just joined him in Belgium. As he lies seriously injured, Hamidu gets Igor to promise to look after Assita and the child. Igor's immediate actions, however, are to hide the injured man and then help his father lie to the inspectors. After the inspectors leave, Igor tries to get Hamidu taken to hospital but his father will not hear of it. Under orders, Igor helps his father hide Hamidu under a plastic tarpaulin and a slab of wood (a detached, wooden door); they cover traces of his blood with sand. At some point in the day Hamidu dies. That night, Roger and Igor bury his body in the building site. Igor runs off in the middle of the burial. He hasn't the stomach for it.

This is the basic setup. The film focuses on Igor's gradual response to the moral calamity of Hamidu's death and the culpability he shares with his father (though, of course, it is mostly owned by his father). In one way, Igor's response is quite simple. He makes good on his promise to Hamidu. But this way of putting things does little service to the subtlety of the film's portrayal of Igor's moral awakening. This awakening is the philosophical heart of the film.[3] Igor responds to a promise: the promise to a dying man. In the end, he does the right thing. But what is the best way to understand this whole affair from a moral point of view? Is Igor's moral awakening simply a matter of his repaying an obligation? Does Igor become a morally decent person by becoming a promise-keeper (rather than a thief and a liar)? Or is there a better way of describing what happens to Igor throughout the film? Igor establishes a clear moral identity in the film, but how should we describe this identity? What sort of person has he become? Virtue theorists hold that the most crucial feature of our moral identities is our possession of virtues (and vices). Virtue theorists tend to think of virtues in complicated ways. To be a virtuous person is not the same thing as being a person who is predisposed to do the right thing. Virtues are more complicated than this. Virtues (specifically moral virtues) are morally excellent ways of being. *La Promesse* furnishes a powerful case for virtue theory. Or so we are going to argue. First, however, let us give some philosophical background about virtues and virtue theory.

What is a Virtue?

The most influential virtue theorist in the history of philosophy is Aristotle (384–322 BC). Aristotle takes virtues to be especially admirable states of character. They are character states that ennoble us and constitute the core of a good and worthwhile life. Virtues involve dispositions to behave in certain appropriate ways, but they are more than this. They also involve dispositions to experience appropriate emotions, perceive situations in insightful ways, and think matters through wisely. Virtues are more than behavioral habits and more than skills: they are complicated ways of responding to situations that involve many aspects of our personality, our emotional temperament, and our intelligence. Aristotle divides virtues into two classes: virtues of character (sometimes called the "moral virtues") and virtues of reason (sometimes called the "intellectual virtues"). Virtues of character crucially involve mastering our emotions. Virtues of reason involve excellences of reason. Being good at science, for example, requires intellectual virtues. Being good at living requires virtues of character. In this chapter, we are specifically concerned with virtues of character (though, as we shall see, virtues of character crucially involve a particular intellectual virtue: a virtue Aristotle calls *phronesis*, often translated as practical wisdom).

On Aristotle's view, virtues of character include such things as courage, temperance (this involves our wisely responding to pleasure and pain), generosity, even-temperedness, magnanimity, and justice. His primary account of them is given in terms of something called the doctrine of the golden mean. According to the doctrine of the golden mean, virtues lie between excess and deficiency. Here is how Aristotle sets it up:

> First, then, let us consider this – the fact that states like this are naturally corrupted by deficiency and excess, as we see in the cases of strength and health (we must use clear examples to illustrate the unclear); for both too much exercise and too little ruin one's strength, and likewise too much food and drink and too little ruin one's health, while the right amount produces, increases and preserves it. The same goes, then, for temperance, courage and the other virtues: the person who avoids and fears everything, never standing his ground, becomes cowardly, while he who fears nothing, but confronts every danger, becomes rash. In the same way, the person who

enjoys every pleasure and never restrains himself becomes intemperate, while he who avoids all pleasure – as boors do – becomes, as it were, insensible. Temperance and courage, then, are ruined by excess and deficiency, and preserved by the mean.[4]

It is important to note that Aristotle's doctrine of the golden mean is not recommending moderation in all things. Virtue may require great feeling: anger or generosity, for instance. The mean is not an arithmetical measure, but varies from circumstance to circumstance. Here is how Aristotle describes the relationship between virtues and emotions:

> I am talking here about virtue of character, since it is this that is concerned with feelings and actions, and it is in these that we find excess, deficiency and the mean. For example, fear, confidence, appetite, anger, pity, and in general pleasure and pain can be experienced too much or too little, and in both ways not well. But to have them at the right time, about the right things, towards the right people, for the right end, and in the right way, is the mean and the best; and this is the business of virtue.[5]

Aristotle also thought that to truly possess a virtue, a person must take pleasure in performing virtuous actions. This is important for Aristotle because he thinks that possessing virtues enables us to lead a good life, which he thinks of as an admirable, successful, and enjoyable life. Aristotle's term for this quality of life is *eudaimonia*. Aristotle thinks it is the highest good for all people; it is the thing that all our rational or sensible efforts are ultimately aimed at. What do we ultimately want out of life? Aristotle's answer is to live well: to achieve excellence in the art and business of life; to be happy and successful; to achieve eudaimonia.[6] A person truly acts from virtue when they do so willingly, taking pleasure in their action. Thus a person does not genuinely exemplify the virtue of courage if they act bravely and yet hate doing so. And a person does not exemplify generosity if they give their money away resentfully.

How are virtues of character acquired? Aristotle's answer is that we begin to acquire them in childhood, through habituation. For example, children are not automatically generous, but by getting them to act as if they are generous, even when they don't like doing so, children become accustomed to generous action. Eventually a child may acquire key psychological aspects of virtue: responding to situations with appropriate emotions, taking pleasure in acting well. If a child is to develop into a genuinely virtuous adult, they must also acquire the kind of practical wisdom or intelligence that enables them to respond to situations appropriately. As we noted above, Aristotle calls this particular intellectual virtue, phronesis, and it's possession is necessary for anyone to fully acquire a virtue of character. A generous adult, for example, not only gives of her time and money willingly and happily, she gives of it wisely, when it really matters.

This is Aristotle's view of the virtues of character, or the moral virtues. It is highly influential, but also controversial.[7] Aristotle's core list of virtues included courage, temperance, even-temperedness, justice, and magnanimity (being big-hearted, generous, and proud; being a big man around town – this is the ultimate virtue of status). To modern eyes the list seems to be a rather poor one: limited and biased. Aristotle's virtue of magnanimity evens seems rather repulsive to many eyes. Aristotle's views on women were irredeemably sexist and his views of non-Greeks and slaves, racist. However, many contemporary virtue theorists hope to take the basic structure of Aristotle's account of the virtues and adapt it to contemporary moral perspectives, leaving Aristotle's parochial, archaic, and sexist prejudices behind.

Another controversial aspect of Aristotle's theory is his speculative account of the acquisition of virtue. Virtues depend upon personality traits (although it is important to remember that they involve more than personality traits: being outgoing and optimistic are typical personality traits; being courageous and generous are typical virtue-traits). For example, an impulsive person, someone who lacks inhibition and foresight, is unlikely to acquire Aristotelian virtues such as temperance and even-temperedness. Do we acquire personality traits like impulsiveness through habituation in childhood? There is evidence to suggest that a good part of our personality is inherited, rather than acquired.[8] Aristotle may have been too optimistic about the extent to which parents and others can forge the characters of children in their care. (Just ask any parent.) And yet Aristotle may have been too pessimistic on another front. Although it is unlikely that we can alter fundamental personality traits in adulthood, it seems that we are capable of growing in moral stature, even in adulthood. In part we do this by consciously trying to become better people, by practice, and by adapting our habits and self-understandings to the strengths of our personalities. If we are outgoing and gregarious, for example, we might exploit this personality trait to become a domineering sort of person, using our easy sociability to acquire status and to enlist the support of others in achieving our personal goals. On the other hand, we are capable of adapting to the same personality trait in very different ways; for example, by becoming a successful and wise leader of others. A deeply introverted person is unlikely to adopt the role of leader; and it is doubtful that they could turn themselves into an extrovert by willpower or training. But virtues depend upon what we do with our personality traits, not only upon which personality traits we happen to possess. The possibility that we can sometimes construct a moral identity for ourselves, even in adulthood, even in the face of a disastrous upbringing, appears to remain open in spite of Aristotle's emphasis on early-childhood training.

Recall our discussion of the character Wiesler in *The Lives of Others* (chapter 12). This is a picture of someone in full adulthood changing their fundamental moral approach to life. It is a remarkable, even unlikely, story; but it is far from an impossible one. Again, we encounter a figure of this sort in the shape of Watanabe from *Ikiru* (chapter 10). In *La Promesse* Igor is a teenager; no longer a child, not yet solidly set in his ways. All three characters begin a process of moral self-transformation because of a striking and challenging happenstance: Wiesler's vicariously intimate encounter with Dreyman and Sieland; Ikiru's diagnosis of terminal cancer; Igor's promise to a dying man. The sobering thought for each of them is just how contingent their transformations are. What if Wiesler had not been asked to spy on the artist couple? What if Watanabe had not learned of his prognosis (after all, the doctors did their best to hide it from him)? What if Hamidu had not extracted a last promise from Igor? Perhaps each of these characters would have continued travelling along the dismal paths their lives were taking.

Virtue Theory and Right Action

In the last chapter we puzzled over the case of the ferry passengers in *The Dark Knight*. We asked what makes an action right or wrong. We focused on actions and their properties, and we examined two kinds of properties: consequences and principles. According to consequentialist theories, an action is right, roughly, if it brings about the best available consequences when these are considered from an impartial perspective. According to deontological theories (and also rule-consequentialist theories) an action is right if it falls under an appropriate moral principle or rule. What is the relationship between the last chapter's discussion of acting rightly and our present discussion of virtue? There are four basic philosophical stances we might adopt here.

First, we might seek to reduce talk of virtues to talk of right action. The simplest way to do this is to identify virtues with stable dispositions to perform right actions across a wide range of situations. For example, say we think that it is always morally wrong to lie to others. We might then define the virtue of honesty as the disposition not to lie. In this way, talk of the virtue is defined in terms of right action. Right action is the basic moral notion here. Of course, you might not agree with the analysis of honesty as a disposition to never lie. We could try to be a bit more subtle, or at least more flexible, in our characterization of honesty. We might say that it is morally wrong to lie unless we are obligated to do so. (And now we owe an account of obligations to lie that is framed in terms of other moral principles or rules; for example, rules that tell us when we have a higher duty to protect others.) We could jazz it up a bit more, allowing for cases in which we are released from an obligation to tell the truth because of the malfeasance of others. Perhaps people sometimes forfeit their right to be told the truth (say, if they are lying to us themselves or are going to use the truth unjustly against us). In light of this, we could define the virtue of honesty as a stable disposition not to tell unjustified lies (where the justification of lies is determined by higher obligations or forfeitures of rights to the truth).

Now if we could do this sort thing for all virtue terms, we would have constructed a theoretical reduction of virtue talk. We would still be able to talk about virtues, but only as shorthand for talk of dispositions to do the right thing. Deontologists and consequentialists can both talk about virtues, but they are sorely tempted to adopt the reductive strategy we have just described and therefore to think of virtue-talk as shorthand for talk about dispositions to do the right thing. (This doesn't mean that they are forced into this reductive position; only that it is a position many consequentialists and deontologists have found congenial.)[9]

Virtue theorists reject the reductive proposal. Virtue theorists are philosophers who take the virtues seriously, and this means, at a minimum, thinking that virtues play a valuable, independent role in our moral lives, one that is conceptually independent of the category of right action. This leads us to the second way of relating virtues and right action: virtues supplement accounts of right action by adding an extra dimension to discussions of morality. Nearly all virtue theorists agree that virtues are more than mere dispositions to do the right thing. Recall from our discussion of Aristotle that, on his way of thinking about virtues, possessing a virtue also involves a disposition to respond well to situations: to feel the appropriate emotions, to the appropriate extent, at the appropriate time, about the appropriate things or people; and to think about situations in insightful and wise ways. That we possess a particular virtue – says the virtue theorist – indicates much more about our moral identity than would a mere disposition to obey moral principles or pursue best consequences.[10] Virtues make an independent and vital contribution to our moral identity.[11]

The third way of thinking about the relationship between right action and virtue is more ambitious. On this view, virtues don't just supplement conceptions of right action, they are conceptually fundamental. The relation between virtue and right action is turned around. Instead of defining virtues in terms of dispositions to act rightly, acting rightly is defined in terms of acting virtuously. Here is the most direct and straightforward way of spelling out such a theory: to act rightly is to act virtuously. We use the concept of virtuous action to explain the concept of right action. It is right to help a stranger in trouble because in doing so you are being kind and generous. It isn't a kind and generous thing to do because it is right; it is right because it is kind and generous. Virtue terms are basic and are used to define right action. Here is another way of defining right action in terms of virtues: to act rightly is to do what a fully virtuous person would characteristically do in the circumstances. Such an equation allows us to distinguish between doing the right thing and doing it virtuously. A person might help a stranger in trouble (which is the right sort of thing to do in the circumstances) without having virtuous motives. They might be doing it to impress their friends, in which case they aren't acting virtuously (they are pretending to act virtuously, which obviously isn't the same thing). Nonetheless, it seems they are still doing the right thing. They are doing what a virtuous person would do in the circumstances, even though they aren't virtuous themselves.[12]

This third option is the mirror image of the first option. It is an attempt to run the reduction in a reverse direction: from virtues to right actions. It requires us to have a way of characterizing virtues independently of the right-making properties of actions. We have to be able to specify what it is to be generous or honest without talking about moral principles or a duty to pursue the best consequences. On such a proposal, a generous act wouldn't be defined as one that obeys a moral rule like this one: *Always help others when you can do so without sacrificing anything of comparable importance to yourself.*[13] And nor would it be defined as an act that produces the best impartial consequences when this requires that the agent sacrifice something of significant value to them. Generosity must be defined in a different way. As a virtue, generosity is a complex affair and hard to define. It isn't simply a disposition to help others or to be free with one's time, money, and possessions. It involves a way of thinking about and responding to situations we confront so that the cares and concerns of others involved in the situation are apt to be salient to us; and it involves a way of responding to this perception by thinking of things we might do to help; and in light of this, happily providing resources and time to help; and so on. This is not the place to develop a theory of the virtue of generosity. The point is that it will be a complicated affair. Most virtues are going to be complex and hard to define; and yet, according to those who defend this third option, they are philosophically basic. The third option is sometimes distinguished from the second option by calling it virtue ethics (as opposed to an exercise in virtue theory). As such, it is a competitor to the consequentialist and deontological theories of right action we encountered in the last chapter.

The fourth way of framing the relationship between virtues and right action involves the idea that virtue theory should *replace* right-action theory.[14] Of course, we tend to discuss moral quandaries in terms of what the right thing to do is; but we are better off, says the defender of this kind of virtue theory, if we concentrate instead on discussing moral quandaries in terms of what it would be for people to act well (i.e. virtuously) in the situations they encounter. For example, in the ferry situation in *The Dark Knight*, instead of trying to work out whether it is morally permissible to press the button (and thus blow the other ferry out of the water), we might try to work out whether the people in each of the ferries acted well. How might they have acted better? Did the prisoner who threw the detonator out of his ferry act well? Did he act courageously? Did he act wisely? Did he act dishonestly? Was his action heroic or was it stubborn and arrogant? (He acted as if the decision was, in the end, his alone to make and he condemned everyone on his ferry to – what at the time seemed to be – almost certain death.) We can always ask: Which action was likely to bring about the best outcome? However, our moral judgment of the people on the ferries needn't consist in our answering this question. We might think that (impartially speaking and assuming that Batman is not coming to the rescue) the likely best outcome is to be had by the civilians blowing up the prisoners. It's hardly ideal, but it's better than everyone dying and its better (if only by a small margin) than the prisoners surviving at the expense of the civilians. Nonetheless, we might also think that no person on the civilian ferry could bring about this outcome without acting viciously, acting in a way we would strongly disapprove of. According to the virtue theorist, morality is not in the business of ensuring that we get what we most want, it is in the business of ensuring that we live well. And sometimes it is better to die virtuously than to live (horribly) viciously.

The quandary now is to work out what happens when, in a particular situation, we deliberate over what we should do. Had we adopted a theory of right action, we could, it seems, merely inspect the appropriate right-making properties of potential actions to determine which of them we should do. But this only makes sense as a procedure if we have ready-to-hand formulas or procedures for determining right action. According to the version of virtue theory we are currently examining, there are no such formulas or procedures. What happens if we reject the characterization of situations in terms of right and wrong (i.e. in terms of morally permissible, morally obligatory, and morally forbidden actions)? How are we supposed to deliberate morally? Are we supposed to deliberate about what would be the most virtuous thing for us to do in the circumstances? This seems like a plausible tactic at first glance, but it doesn't work. Often, deliberating about our own virtue is exactly the wrong way to respond to a situation; it is a vicious way to respond. It would be morally narcissistic of us to deliberate in these terms; as if what really matters in the situation is that we come out of the business looking good (or, rather, being good). Imagine that in *La Promesse* Igor decides to help Assita, not because he is responding to her and her child, but because he is concerned to be a good boy. There is something depressing and empty about this moral motivation. Its narcissistic self-concern undermines the possibility of real virtue. It isn't good to be narcissistic, so we can't be good by aiming single-mindedly at being good. You might also have noticed that if we deliberate in these terms, we are coming very close to accepting the third, reductionist, option described above. On this proposal, we discover the right thing to do by searching out what would be the virtuous thing to do. And the best way of making sense of this is to simply equate acting rightly with acting virtuously. If anyone wishes to defend this fourth non-reductive form of virtue theory, they owe us an account of virtuous moral deliberation which is more than deliberating about what would be a virtuous thing to do, but doesn't reduce to the application of other formulas for right action either. As we might expect from a virtue theorist, any such account is likely to be a complicated affair.

To sum up: there are four ways of characterizing the relationship between doing the right thing and acting virtuously. (1) Acting virtuously just is doing the right thing. (2) Acting virtuously is more than doing the right thing. (3) Acting rightly just is acting virtuously (or acting as the virtuous would characteristically act in the circumstances). (4) Acting virtuously is something other than acting rightly (and there is no satisfactory philosophical theory of what it is to act rightly; we are better off not relying on the concept of right action to do important philosophical work). To be a virtue theorist you must defend (2), (3), or (4) and reject (1). All three forms of virtue theory have their defenders. All three have something going for them; (3) is the most commonsensical – it merely requires us to reserve a special place in our moral theories for the role of the virtues – and (4) is the most radical – it requires us to jettison our reflex appeal to theories of right action such as those described in chapter 13. We won't take a stand on the matter here. The film doesn't help us discriminate between these options either. What it does do, however, is offer strong evidence that one of (2), (3), and (4) is correct; and that (1) is wrong.

The Promise and its Effect

Let's return to the movie. Igor promises Hamidu that he will take care of Assita and her child. At first he doesn't do much. He helps her hammer in a peg (big deal) and brings her a wood stove. This isn't the first time Igor has paid attention to Assita. Since her arrival at the hostel Igor has been spying on her. He is fascinated by her. She has brilliantly white teeth and we see Igor trying out his own teeth-whitening methods (which involve applying white-out to his upper incisors – he looks like a goose, of course). The film portrays a growing involvement between the boy and Assita after the promise. He attends her sacrifice of a chicken in an oracle ceremony (she wants to know the whereabouts of her husband). He gives her money and earns a vicious beating from his father for his trouble. The bond between Igor and Assita grows gradually, mostly on his part: she welcomes his help, but is also distant and discouraging; she has little warmth for this peculiar white boy who takes an inexplicable interest in her well-being. At the same time, the bond between father and son weakens. Roger has dominated the boy: issuing sharp commands and brooking no discussion or dissent, punishing Igor viciously when he acts against his father's interests. Roger rewards Igor when he cooperates in various ways and he also tries to compensate for violent outbursts against the boy in various ways: with the gift of a ring, a homemade tattoo, a driving lesson, a karaoke session (of all things). But something in the link between father and son seems broken after the father allows Hamidu to die.

This is signaled in Igor's expression as much as his actions. Early in the film, Igor responds to Roger's commands with a facial expression that signals satisfaction and self-importance. When Igor is ordered home from his job in the garage (to help deal with the labor inspectors) he shows no sign of regret. When his boss lays down an ultimatum – defy his father or lose his apprenticeship – Igor sides with his father with no sign of hesitancy or anxiety. He is needed for more important things than fixing cars and pumping petrol. (This occurs at 0:22 in the film.) Earlier, when Roger enlists Igor's help to betray four hostel residents and lead them to the immigration police, Igor carries an expression of cold indifference (0:16). As the film progresses, Igor's expression softens. He frowns more often; he *looks* more concerned, more vulnerable, and more troubled. For example, contrast Igor's expression in the betrayal scene (0:16) with his reaction to an attack on Assita (0:45). In the later scene, Roger organizes a staged sexual assault of Assita in an attempt to convince her to travel home. We follow Igor as he hears the attack on Assita take place. From his reaction we deduce that he is aware of the setup. (He doesn't run to help; he continues loading paving stones.) Nonetheless, Igor's face tells a very different story here than it did in the earlier betrayal scene. The boy looks distressed and dissatisfied, as if he is worried and tired of his father's games. (The effect is not emphatic; the range of expression Jérémie Renier uses to play Igor is narrow; the alterations are small and nuanced, but still obvious to an audience. Since it is a natural reaction, the actor need do little to signal this attitudinal change; but signal it he does.)

Igor's movement from thoughtless exploitation of others and blind obedience to his father towards a robust moral identity is portrayed as an evolution in his emotional response to others. And this seems exactly right. There are three main candidates for the thing that motivates Igor as he cares for Assita. First, there is Igor's promise to the dying Hamidu and the sense of obligation that might have spawned in him. Second, there is the remorse – a sense of culpability combined with feelings of guilt and regret – that Igor probably feels about his role in the death of Hamidu. Third, there is the deepening emotional responsiveness to Assita we have described above. Very likely, all three play a role in motivating his actions, but the best evidence elicited from the film is for the last of these factors. The promise in *La Promesse* is primarily an initiator of Igor's deepening concern for Assita and his emotional responsiveness to her and her needs. As Igor attempts to save Assita from Roger, the promise does not appear to be the immediate object of his concern; Assita and her child are.

Igor's guilt over the death of Hamidu doesn't appear to be the primary thing that eventually brings him to defy his father and save Assita (and nor should we expect it to be). What primarily motivates him seems to be his alarm at the prospect his father has in store for Assita. Why think this? After all, this is a film in which the interior states of characters are only revealed by their actions and emotive expressions. Roger and Igor are both very inarticulate. They rarely, if ever, say what's on their mind. They both use language as a tool to get things done; rarely as a means of expression and communication.

So how does an audience decide what motivates Igor most strongly and most immediately? First, and most importantly, there is consistent evidence of Igor's growing emotional capacity and his growing responsiveness to Assita. We outlined some of this evidence earlier. Second, there is a lack of self-regarding emotional expression from Igor. Igor does not wring his hands; he is no Lady Macbeth. He manifests none of the expected expressive behavior of a guilt-ridden person – a person driven by concern for their own troubles and their own moral standing. Third, the Dardenne brothers have helped this interpretation by providing an alarming occasion for Igor's decisive break with his father. Roger has forged a telegram from Hamidu, calling Assita to Cologne. He plans to sell her into sex slavery. In this context, Igor has little opportunity to dwell on himself and his guilt. He must focus on Assita and her rescue. And this is exactly what he does (0:57). We might imagine a self-obsessed person responding to this situation in fundamentally self-regarding ways – displaying horror at what he has allowed to happen, as well as self-pity and self-disgust – but Igor is not this person.[15] We might imagine a person determined to keep the promise, doing what Igor does, but doing it with little evidence of growing emotional responsiveness and deepening concern. Igor is not this person either.

If our interpretation is correct, then Igor becomes much more than a promise-keeper throughout the film. He keeps his promise, but not simply because he made it; not simply because he sees promise-keeping as the right thing to do. He acquires robust virtues and these virtues consist in a great deal more than a propensity to act appropriately. Virtue lies as much within as it does without. The film makes this obvious and so it offers robust support to one or another of the three versions of virtue theory we identified in the previous section. Recall, that the one anti-virtue-theory option we discussion (1) equated virtues with a disposition to act rightly. Igor's moral transformation does not *merely* consist in such a thing. And if it did, we would not respond to it in the same positive way. In this way, the film makes it obvious that (1) is false and that virtue is intimately connected to capacities for emotional responsiveness. Recall from our discussion of Aristotle on virtue, that virtues are especially admirable states of character; they are states that ennoble us and constitute the core of what it is to live a good and worthwhile life. In *La Promesse* we witness Igor's transformation from a child living a mostly worthless and despicable life into a person – no longer a child – who we can admire quite deeply. The transformation of his character is beautiful, and moves us. But it is also obvious that this transformation is intimately connected to the way he feels about things, the way he perceives things, the way he thinks about things, the way he judges things, and the way he acts in light of all this. Imagine somebody fulfilling the equivalent of Igor's promise without a concomitant transformation of character: it is unlikely that we would be much moved by the portrait. This tells us something of philosophical significance. It tells us that moral identity is a complex affair and is not reducible to the performance of moral duty. Virtues are essential components of our moral lives and transcend the performance of moral duty. The film is not in the business of discriminating between the three variants of virtue theory we examined in the previous section – (2), (3), and (4) – but it decisively refutes option (1).

The film's philosophical persuasiveness lies in the unforced and unsentimental way in which Igor's small moral triumph is portrayed. Perhaps the best way to think of it is this. The film works as philosophical testimony about what is possible from a virtue-theoretical point of view. It is possible to forge a strong moral character even in very difficult circumstances: domination by a despicable and tyrannical father; culpability and guilt; social vulnerability and fear of the law. Fifteen-year-olds may not often respond to the kinds of challenges Igor faces in the way Igor does. But they *can* do so. And when they do, it is obvious that they have achieved something deeply valuable. The film thus elicits intuitions about the value of acquiring moral virtues; these are both very powerful intuitions (they affect us strongly) and very robust intuitions (it is hard to imagine a clear-headed person not being affected in much the same way). The film does this without employing unduly manipulative narrative or filmic devices. Our sympathies are clear, but aren't contrived by making Igor an especially attractive or appealing figure or Assita an especially warm and lovable character. The film doesn't boost the appearance of Igor's transformation with visual or musical cues. It works because it shows in a clear and largely unadorned way the transformation of a person. Merely describing moral virtues and their positive effects in a philosophical treatise cannot do the work that *La Promesse* does; it cannot make a case for the value and the beauty of acting well with the intuitive force achieved by this clear-eyed and unsentimental film.

Which Virtues?

Igor grows in moral stature throughout the film, but in what ways? He becomes more virtuous, but which specific virtues does he appear to acquire? There are three main virtues: courage, generosity, and integrity. It's important to notice that Igor's path is a difficult one. First, he has to

defy his bullying father. He has to deal with his father's threats and plead-
ing on the phone (1:06). He is forced to confront his father physically,
and would have been badly beaten if it weren't for Assita's timely intervention. This requires remarkable courage from a slight 15-year-old who
knows just how desperate his father has become and what he is capable
of. Igor's second difficulty is his negotiation of his relationship with Assita.
Assita does not make it easy for him. She does not react warmly to his
attempts to help her. When he takes off with her in his father's van, she
threatens him with a blade (0:57). Assita rebuffs him decisively when he
later embraces her in a flood of tears (1:04). (She is surely wondering
what is motivating this odd child.) Her own child becomes dangerously
ill and she consequently attacks Igor, throwing stones at him (small
stones: gravel really) and accusing him of intentionally infecting the child
(1:08). (The audience's sympathy for Assita is never endangered because
it is based on an understanding of the extremity of her situation and her
vulnerability within it, as well as admiration of her resourcefulness, deter-
mination, and resilience (which are simply astonishing). Earlier in the day
the audience witnesses (and Igor does not witness) a Belgium thug urinat-
ing on her from a bridge (1:01). She must surely be near her wits' end.)
Igor doesn't allow Assita's attack to deter his focus on the need to help
her and her child. A generous person is someone who focuses their attention on the needs of another wisely. The other's need is their focus, and
they are able to keep this focus in spite of distractions. A generous person
isn't a person who helps others only when it's easy and rewarding; they
are someone who helps when it's hard to do so and easy to get distracted,
take umbrage, and flee with excuse.

  The third difficulty Igor faces has to do with the truth. This is where
the virtue of integrity comes into play. Igor has lied to Assita about her
husband's fate. He has told her repeatedly that Hamidu has simply run
away, he knows not where. Until the very last scene of the film, Igor has
been helping Assita under the cover of this lie. It has enabled him to help
her. Had he told her the truth, she may well have rejected his help. But
this is unlikely to be the only motive for his lie. He is probably lying – at
least in part – to hide from her reaction: her likely anger, scorn, and contempt. Igor's physical confrontation with his father turns on this question
of their telling Assita the truth. At the first he tells his father (translating)
"We have to tell her the truth. Come with me; we'll tell her" (1: 21).
Roger's reaction is to chase the boy, force him to the ground, and start
to beat him; at which point Assita intervenes and strikes Roger over the
head. Igor shackles an unconscious Roger and when he comes to, the
father tempts the son, offering to give Assita money and the freedom to
go anywhere she wishes (as long – it is implied – as she is not told the

truth about Hamidu). Here is the ensuing dialogue between father and son (in translation):

ROGER: Why do you want to tell her? What'll it serve? She leaves. We never talk about it again. (Give me my glasses at least.) The home – it's for you. I did everything for you. Only you. You're my son.

IGOR: Shut up! Shut up! Shut up!

OK, so Igor has not become an articulate defender of honesty; but he has become a defender of it. It has become fundamentally important to him that they not continue the lie.[16] Only in the very last scene – as Assita is about to board a train for Italy and depart from Igor's life forever – does he tell her the truth about the death of her husband. He does so in a few, succinct, precise, unadorned sentences (1: 27). Assita reacts by removing her headscarf, slowly turning from the station platform, looking at Igor long and hard: sadly, severely. She walks out of the station; Igor accompanies her. We watch them walking away together until they disappear from view. We have no idea what happens next; but Igor's moral victory has been won.

Questions

Watanabe (chapter 10), Wiesler (chapter 12), and Igor (chapter 14) all undergo a profound moral transformation. How do they differ? Whose task was the most difficult? Whose victory the most remarkable? (Is there any sensible way of answering such questions?)

Is the austere style of *La Promesse* an advantage for the sorts of use we make of it in this chapter?

We suggested in the chapter that Aristotle's list of virtues is sadly lacking. What is a better list? Why are the members of your list central or fundamental virtues? Why are they important?

In the chapter, we identify four different ways in which virtue theory and theories of right action might interact. We only set out to refute one of them, the first. Of the other three, which is the most plausible? Which is the least plausible?

Does the reduction of right action to virtuous action lead to an unacceptable moral narcissism? Is there anything fundamentally wrong with thinking that an action is right just because it would be a virtuous thing to do?

Are we right to argue that the film shows decisively that there is more to being virtuous than doing the right thing (and doing it because you see that it is right)? How can a film show this? It is just one film; should we generalize from the example of Igor?

Should Igor have kept lying to Assita about her husband until the very last moment (just before she boards the train for Italy)? Would the reason why Igor lied (we can't be sure what it is) matter to our judgment of the case?

Notes

1   For example, consider an important scene in the first half of the film: the scene of Hamidu's accident (0:24). We follow Igor as he warns Hamidu of the imminent arrival of labor inspectors; Hamidu is working on scaffolding outside the house; Igor rushes in and up the stairs – we follow him, as we do throughout almost the entire film – and he hears a noise. It is just a dull thud. This is all the "action" associated with Hamidu's accident. The audience sees what Igor sees and hears what he hears. It's as if the filmmakers have had the bad luck to be in the wrong spot to witness the spectacle of the fall. It makes perfect sense, of course. The accident is something that happens. It isn't staged for Igor and it isn't staged for an audience either.

2   Compare this with horror films using the basic techniques of *cinéma vérité* to establish a pretended authenticity. Films such as *The Blair Witch Project* (1999), *Paranormal Activity* (2007), *Rec* (2007) and its remake *Quarantine* (2008), and *Cloverfield* (2008) rely on the pretence that they consist of recovered footage to sustain the illusion that what you are seeing on screen really happened and isn't just another staged spectacle. The early periods of the films are full of trite, uninformative, and redundant scenes, the dullness of which is meant to lull audiences into a receptive state for the horrors to come.

3   Igor's moral awakening makes for an interesting comparison with that of Wiesler in *The Lives of Others* (see chapter 12). Igor is still a child and has few of Wiesler's resources at hand. Like Wiesler, however, he has luck on his side.

4   Aristotle, *Nicomachean Ethics*, 1104a.

5   Aristotle, *Nicomachean Ethics*, 1106b.

6   See our discussion of the character of Watanabe in the film *Ikiru* (chapter 10). Watanabe struggles with the idea of what it is to live well, what it is to *really* be alive. His answer has the key features of Aristotle's conception of eudaimonia; in particular, it is important that Watanabe enjoy his struggle to build a children's playground and that he succeed in it.

7   One challenge to virtue theory, worth mentioning even if we haven't the space to discuss it in detail, comes from philosophers responding to the results of experimental work in social psychology. Gilbert Harman and John Doris are the most prominent figures prosecuting this case against virtue theory. Harman and Doris argue that experimentation reveals that people lack stable dispositions to perform ethical actions. According to a wide range of experiments, whether or not a person acts ethically in experimental setups is better predicted by a host of situational variables, rather than their personality or character dispositions. There are no such things as virtues, Harman and Doris argue, because there are no stable dispositions to act ethically independently of situational variables. The argument has attracted considerable critical attention from virtue theorists and moral psychologists. See Doris (2002) and Harman (1999).

8   See Pinker (2002, chapter 19) for a summary of this evidence.

9   One of the best-known examples of a thinker taking this attitude to the virtues is Benjamin Franklin (1986 [1791]), whose 13 virtues (with the exception of his thirteenth rule: *Imitate Jesus and Socrates*) are dispositions to follow particular rules of behavior. These are dispositions Franklin purposely set about acquiring in adulthood.

10 Julia Driver (2001) disagrees with this position. Driver develops a consequentialist theory of virtues, according to which virtues do not essentially involve admirable inner psychological states but involve dispositions to efficiently produce good outcomes.

11 Adams (2006) defends the idea that virtues are independent of, and supplementary to, other aspects of morality.

12 Slote (2001) develops the first way of effecting the reduction; Hursthouse (1999), the second.

13 Singer (1972) advances this very moral principle.

14 Anscombe (1958) and MacIntyre (2007) both defend a replacement view of this sort. (You might (*might*) recall from chapter 4 that this is an eliminativist strategy.)

15 Two contrasts are worth pointing out here. First, contrast Igor's emotional transformation to Judah's displays of fear and self-pity in *Crimes and Misdemeanors* (chapter 11). A closer comparison is afforded by Gus van Sant's film *Paranoid Park* (2007). In this film, a boy about Igor's age is involved in the accidental though blameworthy death of a security guard. The boy, Alex, responds to the trauma by withdrawing into himself. The film displays the turmoil of his inner life by a variety of means: a vertiginous, heterogeneous soundtrack, a temporally disordered narrative sequence, and a highly aestheticized visual display corresponding to the intensity of the boy's experience in the aftermath of the killing. Alex's response is the mirror opposite of Igor's; and Gus van Sant's technique is the mirror opposite of the Dardenne brothers' technique.

16 This isn't just about retrieving his integrity, of course. Igor has come to learn of the cultural significance of Hamidu's whereabouts; about the importance

to Assita of recovering his body if he is dead. (He learns this primarily at the faith-healing ceremony (1:12–1:14).) Acting well is rarely a matter of exemplifying a virtue in isolation from others. Courage, integrity, and generosity are each involved in Igor's confession scene.

Further Reading

Adams, Robert Merihew (2006). *A Theory of Virtue*. New York: Oxford University Press.

Anscombe, G. E. M. (1958). "Modern Moral Philosophy." *Philosophy* 33, No. 124. http://www.philosophy.uncc.edu/mleldrid/cmt/mmp.html.

Aristotle (2000). *Nicomachean Ethics*, trans. Roger Crisp. Cambridge: Cambridge University Press.

Doris, John (2002). *Lack of Character: Personality and Moral Behaviour*. Cambridge: Cambridge University Press.

Driver, Julia (2001). *Uneasy Virtue*. New York: Cambridge University Press.

Franklin, Benjamin (1986 [1791]). *The Autobiography and Other Writings*. London: Penguin Classics.

Harman, Gilbert (1999). "Moral Philosophy Meets Moral Psychology: Virtue Ethics and the Fundamental Attribution Error." *Proceedings of the Aristotelian Society* 99, part 3.

Hursthouse, Rosalind (1999). *On Virtue Ethics*. Oxford: Oxford University Press.

MacIntyre, Alasdair (2007). *After Virtue*. 3rd edn. Notre Dame: University of Notre Dame Press.

Pinker, Steven (2002). *The Blank State: The Modern Denial of Human Nature*. London: Penguin Books.

Singer, Peter (1972). "Famine, Affluence and Morality." *Philosophy and Public Affairs* 1, 229–43.

Slote, Michael (2001). *Morals from Motives*. Oxford: Oxford University Press.

Tessman, Lisa (2005). *Burdened Virtues*. New York: Oxford University Press.

Index

Thinking Through Film: Doing Philosophy, Watching Movies, First Edition. Damian Cox,
Michael P. Levine.
© 2012 Damian Cox and Michael P. Levine. Published 2012 by Blackwell Publishing Ltd.